THE PARENTING HANDBOOK

THE

PARENTING HANDBOOK

YOUR GUIDE TO RAISING RESILIENT CHILDREN

TANIA JOHNSON, R. PSYCH and **TAMMY SCHAMUHN, R. PSYCH**

BARLOW BOOKS

Library and Archives Canada Cataloguing in Publication data available upon request.

978-1-998841-10-3 (hardcover)

Printed in Canada

Publisher: Sarah Scott
Cover design: Ruth Dwight
Interior design and layout: Ruth Dwight
Illustrator: Mirjana Miljkovic

For more information, visit www.barlowbooks.com

Barlow Book Publishing Inc.
96 Elm Avenue, Toronto, ON
M4W 1P2 Canada

BARLOW
BOOKS

For our beautiful children:
Ayden, Dixie, Maya, Oona, and Rosie

This book would not have been possible without the support of our village. With thanks to Mary-Anne Wright, Mirjana Miljkovic, Chelsea Pakulak, the Digital Media and IT Department at NAIT, and the ICP team!

CONTENTS

INTRODUCTION

Who You Are as a Parent

We encounter the journey of parenthood with a picture of how things are "going to be" and how things are "supposed to be." We dream of children who follow our lead, of family holidays spent smiling and connecting, of cuddles and books before bed, and of children who excel in dance, soccer, or academics. We reflect on our childhoods and we say, "I'm going to be different than my crazy mother" or "I'm going to give my children all the things I never had." But life is never so simple.

If there is one thing I, Tammy Schamuhn, and my coauthor, Tania Johnson, learned as parents—and as child psychologists and "supposed" experts in child-rearing—parenting a child is the most challenging job in the world. None of us has it all figured out.

When you hold that newborn baby in your arms—with love bursting from every pore of your body—you don't think of the struggles you will endure in the not-so-distant future. You don't think about the exhaustion, the worrying, the yelling you will shame yourself for when they become a reckless toddler, the grief from the loss of your freedom, or the disillusionment about the true toll raising a family takes. Parenting a child is exhilarating, demanding, soul-crushing, and soul-fulfilling. As you traverse the emotional landscape of parenting; there may be brief "aha" moments, but there is no "figuring it out."

I recall holding my son for the first time after hours of labor and thinking: Is this doctor really going to trust me to just take him home? Shouldn't there be some test I need to pass to ensure I can handle this? Soon after, I realized that there was a test of sorts, and that test occurred every single day—a test accented by love and joy but also full of bewilderment, exhaustion, anxiety, and frustration. I would soon learn that even after twenty years of formal education and hundreds of teachers and professors, my son and my future stepdaughters would prove to be my most influential teachers in terms of what it means to truly understand child development.

In reality, we don't come into this role as a parent with a clean slate. We all carry our childhood baggage, world views, social scripts we inherited from our upbringing and, often, society's crippling expectations of what it means to be a parent. Our mission in writing this book, as both parents and clinicians who live and breathe child psychology, is to normalize your struggles. We will piece together the psychology of your child in an accessible way, providing pointers on parenting that have a foundation in neuroscience and attachment research, to help you understand your journey as a parent.

While each one of us has a different path as a parent, we all share a collective love for our children and a desire for our children to find happiness and well-being. Similarly, we also share a yearning to be better versions of ourselves so we can do right by our children and find our own path to joy. These two desires unite us as parents, and the world we currently live in could use a little more unity and a little less division these days.

But how do you ensure your children will live fulfilling, beautiful lives? The short answer: you don't. You can't control how your child's life will unfold. This is probably the most difficult truth to accept about parenting. You aren't in control, and the more you live from a place of fear, the worse the outcome for your children and for your own emotional health.

We will expand on this in the upcoming chapters, but know this—while you can't control your child or how their lives will unfold, you can have a profound influence on them. You can guide them. You can provide the conditions in which your child has the opportunity to blossom into the truest version of themselves. You can control your actions and your words. You can work on yourself. This is what you have control over—your behavior and evolution not only as a parent, but as a human being. This is true empowerment.

Many of you may be hoping for a single set of strategies to ensure your child will be "okay." Unfortunately, we can't provide this. Your child is unique, and there is no child on this earth who is the same as yours. They have their own distinctive set of personality traits and a genetic blueprint unlike any other.

This book will provide you with the latest parenting research, tools, and strategies so that you are empowered to create the best path forward with your child. In doing so, we hope that you approach parenting with a different lens, because when you see your children differently, you respond differently. You end up parenting from a place of compassion.

When you come from a place of being informed about your child's development and individual psychology, you parent from a place of intention. When you know better, you do better.

Our children do not experience our good intentions; they experience our words and actions. If our actions are attuned, and our children experience unconditional safety, belonging and love, then our job as caregivers is complete. We have cultivated safety, belonging, and love. We hope to guide you to this place of intentionality.

CHAPTER ONE

THE NEUROBIOLOGY OF PARENTING

THE BRAIN MATTERS

Tania and I both knew we wanted to be parents, and we waited longer than most to have children. I think we both knew from working with children the kind of commitment it would be, but nothing truly prepares you for this job: the late-night feedings, the constant demand for attention and connection, an endless number of messes to clean, grieving the social life and freedom you once had, and being able to shower every day without interruption.

At the end of the day, we are raising tiny humans with the hope that they will turn out to be happy, resilient, kind adults. There is no road map, no perfect toolbox—every step of the parenting journey has its own triumphs and tribulations. Parenting elicits deep-seated feelings of love, affection, and joy; parenting also elicits impatience, anger, and frustration. In this chapter, we will delve into some basic science of what we call compassionate parenting, as well as times where we veer off course and enter a state of reactive parenting.

The neurological changes our children undergo as they advance through the variety of ages and stages of development are nothing short of remarkable. Healthy neurological growth requires parents to set the stage for our children to reach their full potential, and this demands an immense amount of effort from our own brains to sustain this process.

Many years ago, it was believed that we arrived in this world as a blank slate, and that is far from true. Children are born with approximately 100 billion neurons, and by adulthood this will have decreased to 85 billion neurons. This is because of a process called synaptic pruning in adolescence, which we will cover later on. But even with that many neurons, the process of developing the brain is far from over. Human brains take longer than any other mammals' to mature, and it is both an individual's experiences and the quality of their relationships that will determine the process of maturation. This is where parenting could not be more important.

GROWTH OF THE BRAIN: STAGES

Based on the work of heroes in neurobiology and child development—such as Dr. Daniel Siegal, Dr. Tina Bryson, Dr. Bruce Perry, Dr. David Eagleman, Dr. Daniel Hughes, Dr. Bessel van der Kolk, and others—we will explain how brain development plays an intricate part in parenting.

The Body Brain, Feelings Brain, & Thinking Brain

A neurotypical child is born with a fully functioning brain stem or a "body brain" that is connected to the spinal cord; this is the most primitive part of our brain and has been with us the longest in terms of our evolution. It is situated at the nape of our neck. It gathers sensory information from our bodies, which is relayed by the spinal cord. It also operates as a home base of the central nervous system. This is where our unconscious automatic responses come from. Your ability to blink, breathe, digest food, and regulate blood pressure all come from this lower brain area (see Figure 1.0). In a nutshell, the brain stem's job is to keep you alive, and it also always asks the question: Am I safe?

The second primary area of the brain that begins to develop after we are born is the "feeling brain" or the limbic system. The limbic system is situated just above the brain stem and under the cerebral cortex. The limbic system houses the parts of our brain that are essential for building relationships and maintaining attachments, as well as creating and storing autobiographical memory and where we experience and process emotions. It also partners with our brain stem to regulate physiological arousal, and it orchestrates and moderates the survival response known as fight-flight-freeze-collapse. The emotional brain asks the question: Am I loved?

The third primary area to develop is the "thinking brain" or the neocortex. As explained by Dr. Daniel Siegel, this area of the brain manages intricate mental processes like planning, decision-making, self-awareness, emotion regulation, empathy, and morality. Humans are born with an immature brain, and the neocortex really takes its time in terms of its growth (synaptic proliferation) and specialization (synaptic pruning), particularly the prefrontal cortex, which is involved in planning complex cognitive behavior, personality expression, decision-making, and moderating behavior and emotion. The thinking brain asks: What can I learn from this? or How can I solve this?

This area is not done maturing until we are twenty-five to thirty years old. Since the thinking brain takes such a long time to develop, it is no wonder children tend to be impulsive, emotional, and often lack the ability to make good decisions. Until approximately age four to seven, they primarily operate from their body brain and feeling brain, coined by Dr. Daniel Siegel as the "downstairs brain."

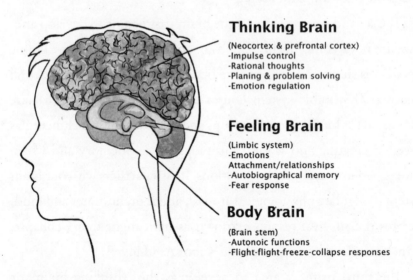

Thinking Brain

(Neocortex & prefrontal cortex)
-Impulse control
-Rational thoughts
-Planing & problem solving
-Emotion regulation

Feeling Brain

(Limbic system)
-Emotions
Attachment/relationships
-Autobiographical memory
-Fear response

Body Brain

(Brain stem)
-Autonoic functions
-Flight-flight-freeze-collapse responses

Left vs. Right Processing

The brain is broken up into two sides or hemispheres. The right and left sides of the brain are connected to each other through neural tissue called the corpus callosum. Each side has its own unique set of jobs. The right hemisphere is all about creativity, imagination, visual processing, emotions, empathy, social experiences, and processing and sending nonverbal signals. The left hemisphere deals with language, linear thinking, logic, cause-and-effect, and moral reasoning (right vs. wrong). Why do we mention this? Children's right hemisphere develops before the left, and they tend to utilize the right hemisphere more than the left. Anyone who has been around toddlers knows all about this. Happy one minute, melting down because they got the wrong color of cup, and back to playing in the fort fifteen minutes later, giggling away—it's a roller coaster of emotions. Children come by it naturally. They spend more time in their right brain, and the part of the brain responsible for logic, reasoning, and critical thinking is still under construction.

Since the right hemisphere is more active, it needs lots of nurturance and attention. It's also important that when we communicate to our children, we speak their language, which tends to be kinesthetic, play-based, and proximity-based interactions. This is why we recommend children under the age of ten engage in play-based therapies or animal-assisted therapies, and not talk therapy.

We love the idea presented by Dr. Daniel Siegel and Dr. Tina Payne Bryson in their book *No Drama Discipline*, in which they speak about the concepts "name-it-to-tame-it" and "connection before redirection." They are speaking about soothing children who are dysregulated (a process called co-regulation, which we will touch on later in this book) by connecting to and working with the part of the brain that is activated. By sending signals to this part of the brain that is activated during a meltdown, we can calm those parts. We calm the right brain (along with the emotional brain and body brain) by letting it know 1) we are not a threat; 2) we offer physical connection where appropriate and safe; and 3) we see them, understand them, and can help them better understand themselves by naming their emotional experiences.

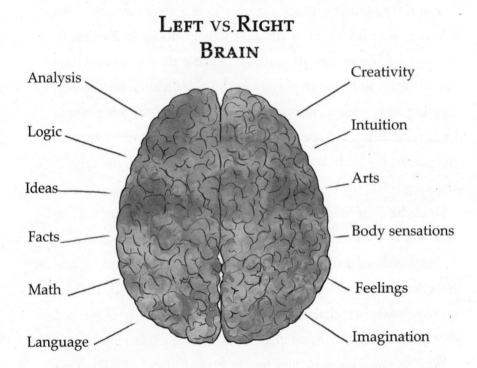

LEFT VS. RIGHT BRAIN

Analysis

Logic

Ideas

Facts

Math

Language

Creativity

Intuition

Arts

Body sensations

Feelings

Imagination

EXAMPLE

Your preteen wants to go over to a friend's house over the weekend, but you are aware there is no adult supervision as their friend's parents work. You are not comfortable with this, so you set a limit and tell her no. She screams at you that it's not fair, and you're the meanest dad in the whole world. She bursts into tears and runs into her room and slams the door. You give her a few minutes to calm down and then go into her room to check on her.

Right-Brain Connection

You sit next to her (may put a hand on her shoulder). "I can see you're really angry with me. It doesn't feel fair I said no. You were really looking forward to spending time with Macy."

Left-Brain Connection

(You hover over top of her with your arms crossed.) "Why are you overreacting like this? You know the rules. You can only go to someone's house if there are adults there. When you're ready to stop being so dramatic, you can come find me upstairs."

Integration

As Dr. Siegel says, the left likes to explain and the right likes to describe. In order to deactivate our preteen's emotional brain, we need to send calming signals to it. Once she is feeling seen and understood, we can then talk to her about what happened, then maybe come up with a plan to see her friend another weekend.

As children mature, these two sides of the brain will eventually work more cohesively together through a process called integration, which allows the brain to achieve higher levels of functioning. To help facilitate the connection between the two hemispheres, we recommend:

- Balancing activities that are left- vs. right-brain focused, not just one type of activity. Offer activities that promote movement (i.e., sports), expressive activities (i.e., art, music), and are logic, language, or problem-solving based (i.e., computers, learning a second language, Lego).

- When something highly emotional happens, especially experiences that are fearful, use a narrative-based approach. Have your child tell the story of what happened, with a concrete beginning, middle, and end. Have them focus not only on what physically happened but also engage their five senses. What did they hear, see, touch, feel, taste, or smell? What emotions did it evoke? And lastly, where did they feel that feeling in their body? This strategy is used by trauma therapists worldwide to integrate trauma memories so they don't stay stuck somatically in the right hemisphere. They must "integrate" with both sides of the brain.

EXAMPLE

On a cold winter day, my two-year-old son and I were driving to Edmonton to visit an indoor playground. The roads were very icy, and there was four inches of fresh snow on the highway. A large semitruck in the lane next to us lost control and jack-knifed in front of us, and it forced us off the road into the ditch. While we were physically fine, the experience was terrifying for both of us—probably more so for me than my son.

Knowing what I know about trauma, I took my son to my mother's (as I had to go file a police report) and told her to keep telling him the story of what happened using the script I had come up with shakily on the drive home: "A big truck came, and Mommy and Ayden hit the ditch. Mommy said, 'Hold on, Ayden.' It was scary, but we're okay. We drove out of the ditch and went to Grandma's house." I instructed her to tell him this story as long as she could keep his interest or have him tell this story as many times as he was interested in telling it. Had he been older, I would have asked him where he felt his scared feeling in his body, but at two this awareness is a bit beyond what he could express. My mother said in a span of three hours, he told the story himself at least half a dozen times, and she had told it three to four times herself. We continued to touch on this story a few times a day for about two weeks until I saw he was his normal, happy-go-lucky self.

CHILDREN ARE RULED BY THE EMOTIONAL BRAIN

Children are primarily ruled by their body brain and their emotional brain (along with the right hemisphere), which explains why younger children are impulsive, prone to emotional outbursts, and ruled by egocentrism, or as we like to call it, the "it's-all-about-me" complex.

Even when a child shows signs of a more developed thinking brain, the connection between the two areas is weak. If emotional and body brains sense a threat, communication is essentially cut off to the thinking brain. In short, a threat equals an emotional hijacking of the brain so that the brain can focus on protection instead of logic and reason (see Figure 1.3). When the alarm is sounded, the emotional brain sends signals to the pituitary glands to release such stress hormones as cortisol and adrenaline, and our bodies prepare for battle or escape. Then the brain focuses on protection instead of logic and reasoning.

Now children don't just become hijacked because they're having big feelings; they often become hijacked because their bodies do not feel safe. This is what Dr. Stephen Porges coined as neuroception of safety. If a child is hungry, tired, physiologically overwhelmed, disoriented, or sick, they are in a state of physical vulnerability, and this poses a risk to their body. When we are physiologically vulnerable, we are designed to move toward our tribe as there is safety in numbers. When your child's brain signals to them their bodies are facing a potential threat, it signals a fear response, and they move toward you. This fear can be disguised as a meltdown, tantrum, whining, clinging, or aggression. Any means to grab your attention to keep them safe. They are saying, "something doesn't feel right, and I need you to help me understand why I feel so overwhelmed and scared."

This emotional hijacking, while more frequent in children, is not unique to them. Many of us have been angry with our spouse and said something we wish we could take back or have been so overwhelmed by our children that we have yelled instead of keeping our cool. When our fight-flight-freeze-collapse response is activated, we are designed to go into self-protection mode, not to have a reasonable conversation or solve a complex problem. We will address parental emotion regulation in a later chapter.

It is important to understand why children, especially infants, toddlers, and preschoolers are so emotional. You cannot punish them out of this—they are simply equipped with an immature brain that lacks the skill set to regulate their feelings and to make good decisions when emotions run high. It takes time to develop the thinking brain, and every child's trajectory is different, but we assure you that the healthier the environment, and the more attuned and connected a parent is, the better and faster the brain will respond.

Imagine you want to grow some flowers in your garden. You get all the supplies you think you need—fertilizer, soil, mulch, and a hose to bring the plants water—and you plant the seeds deep in the earth in the perfect spot with just enough shade and light. You eagerly wait for weeks for the plants to mature and bloom. Perhaps this process takes longer than you anticipated, and you find yourself impatient. You wonder: When will my hard work pay off?

Do you think at any point in this cycle of growth that the flowers would bloom more quickly if you yelled at them or threatened them? Of course not. Plants, like children, have their own timeline for development. Our job as parents is to nurture our children and not to impede the developmental process. As Dr. Gordon Neufeld says, we must provide the conditions in which a child can realize their full human potential. This book was written to help you understand the optimal conditions needed so your child can become the best version of themselves.

Safety First, Growth Second

Humans have evolved for millions of years, and the brain can help us do magnificent things like write sonnets, engineer skyscrapers, or fly to the moon. However, the brain's alarm system that keeps us safe will always take precedence. Safety is the essential nutrient for growth. It has an intricate system built into place to keep us out of harm's way. The stress response, or the fight-flight-freeze-collapse response, helps you react to perceived threats and causes hormonal and physiological changes in the body, which enables you to protect yourself.

When your stress response is activated, the brain's watchdog (the amygdala) jumps into high alert. The amygdala sends a signal to the hypothalamus, which then stimulates the autonomic nervous system to release adrenaline and cortisol. These hormones are released very quickly, and your body responds by increasing your heart rate to bring oxygen to your major muscles. Your breathing speeds up to deliver more oxygen to the blood; you have changes to your vision to help you find a path to escape; your pupils dilate and let in more light so you can see better; your hearing becomes sharper; your blood flow to your major muscles increases, making your hands and feet feel cold; you may experience stomachaches or butterflies as your body stops digesting food to focus on other bodily processes. These changes in your body allow you to be faster, stronger, and more perceptive so that you can escape a dangerous situation. When a child's stress response is activated, they will either (1) freeze to survey the scene for an exit, wait for the danger to pass, or pause to decide on the next step of action; (2) avoid and try to remove themselves from the situation (flight); or (3) tantrum, hit, kick, spit, or yell (fight).

However, the fourth response is rarely understood by parents or many professionals. In the event a child stays stuck too long in fight-flight-freeze, they will move into what's called hypoarousal or collapse. Dr. Mona Delahooke refers to this as the blue pathway in her book *Beyond Behaviors*. The part of the brain called the ACT (anterior cingulate cortex) understands that staying in a state of hypoarousal is toxic and depletes the body's resources. In response to the stress and pain that the body is experiencing, it prepares the body to conserve its energy and prepare potentially for death.

When a child begins to experience this response, they may not be able to speak, and they feel detached or disconnected from their body. Their heart rate, blood pressure, and body temperature lower. A child in this response can have a "blank stare" as they become less aware of their internal and external world; they may even faint. There is a decrease in muscle tone, as the body is no longer attempting to fight or flee from the response. Emotionally, a person in collapse can experience hopelessness, numbness, depression, helplessness, shame, and defeat.

BOTTOM-UP VS. TOP-DOWN PROCESSING

When we are not in a hijacked emotional state, one of the mistakes we often make as parents is treating our children like mini-adults. We tend to want to communicate with our children in the same way we process information; we default to language and reasoning. This is what science calls top-down processing. We often try to use our left hemisphere along with our thinking brain to communicate with our children.

EXAMPLE

Honey, why did you hit your friend? Hitting is not kind. I want you to go to your room and think about what you've done.

Now this can sometimes work—if our children are older and their emotions are not running high. However, if emotions are elevated, and the younger the child is, the more this will backfire. This is because your child is engaged in what is called bottom-up processing as high-lighted by Dr. Bruce Perry's Neurosequential Model. Information flows from the bottom-up. We must work to first soothe the body brain, then the emotional brain, and finally the thinking brain.

Body Brain Asks: Am I Safe?

As we move to a bottom-up approach, we want you to understand that in order for a child to feel safe, you need to address the physiological overwhelm our children face: too many transitions, emotional sensitivity to others that might be experienced at school, feeling overwhelmed by loud sounds and lights from a celebration, etc. Without an outlet for movement, they struggle to release stress hormones, which can manifest in sleep deprivation or feeling overwhelmed. This can translate to emotional outbursts and a lack of impulse control. These all lead to the body brain feeling unsafe because your child's physiological resources are drained. They have been stuck in a stress response for too long, which takes a toll on their bodies.

Before we form a plan of action, we have to ensure we cultivate a safe space for them and give them grace when we know they are acting out of overwhelm, not in opposition. We have to decrease the noise of the outside world before moving to connection and problem-solving. This might mean providing quiet space, giving them nourishment for their bodies such as a healthy snack or water, moving their bodies if they have been cooped up all day, or inciting laughter to produce chemicals of closeness in the brain.

The Emotional Brain Asks: Am I Loved?

Once a child feels physically safe and isn't in a state of overwhelm, we move to the dance of attachment. This is where we ensure a child experiences our compassion, connection, and empathy. We mirror their emotional experiences, stay close, and ensure they know that regardless of what's happened they are still loved. This connection helps remove opposition and defensiveness, and it primes the brain for learning and initiates the will to cooperate. At this stage, we may offer cuddles, warm eye contact, a hug, name their feelings, or simply sit near them until the storm settles.

The Thinking Brain Asks: Am I Capable?

At this stage, we are working with consequences, problem-solving, or teaching. Often a parent's biggest mistake in discipline is they jump to the thinking brain and want to fix things and talk about what happened before a child feels safe and connected. This goes against how information flows in the brain. Here we may discuss consequences, offer other ways of interacting with their world the next time that happens, or have them make amends with someone they hurt.

PARENTING FROM THE BOTTOM-UP

Your son had swimming lessons in the morning and then attended a birthday party in the afternoon. They hadn't slept well the night before they were so excited about the party. When you return home from the party, your daughter wants to play with your son, but he gets frustrated with her and throws something at her for not getting out of his room when he asks her to.

1. **Body Brain:** Am I safe? You might ask your daughter to leave the room so your son and you can be alone, knowing he's overstimulated and tired.

2. **Feeling Brain:** Am I loved? You might validate how he feels by saying, "You are really frustrated with your sister—I can see you're tired and had a really big day. We don't always make great choices when we're tired." We might then offer a cuddle or hug and see what they have to say about what happened.

3. **Thinking Brain:** Am I capable? When you can see your son is calm and connected, we might say: "I think your

sister's feelings were really hurt. You can be mad at her, but you know in our family we don't use our bodies to hurt one another. What else could you have done to get her to give you some space?" After collaborating with him on some possible solutions, you might then move to, "I wonder how you can make it right with her?"

Am I safe? Am I loved? Am I capable? Are these not the questions we all ask throughout our lives? It starts from a young age, and far from just being an emotional response to the world, it is a neuro-development response. When those little faces look up to us, there is much more going on than meets the eye.

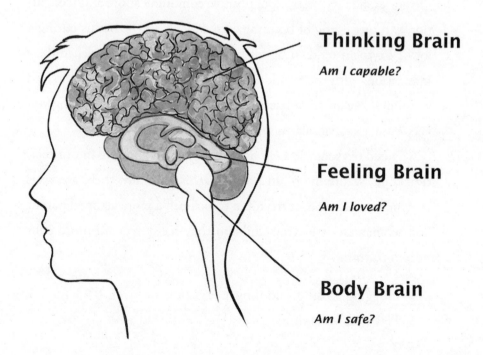

Thinking Brain
Am I capable?

Feeling Brain
Am I loved?

Body Brain
Am I safe?

CHEMICALS, PROTEINS, AND HORMONES AND HOW THEY INFLUENCE YOU AND YOUR CHILD

Oxytocin

Oxytocin is a neuropeptide produced in the hypothalamus and is secreted into the bloodstream by the posterior pituitary gland. In women, it is responsible for contraction of the womb (uterus) during childbirth and lactation. It also acts as a chemical messenger and has an important role in many human behaviors, including sexual arousal, recognition, trust, romantic attachment, and mother-infant bonding. In both our parent-child relationships and our romantic relationships having lots of oxytocin increases trust, empathy, positive memories, fidelity, relaxation, positive communication, and recognition and processing of bonding cues. Parents whose brains release a lot of oxytocin tend to be nurturing parents who experience their interactions with their children as highly pleasurable. Oxytocin also acts much like an antianxiety medication in your brain, helping you keep your amygdala alarm system calm.

We need oxytocin to help us feel connected and safe in our relationships. While the brain produces this naturally, there are ways in which you can boost oxytocin to be both a more attuned parent and to increase it in your child so they feel safer and more connected to you:

- Hugging, kissing, cuddling, eye gazing
- Play with your child
- Yoga

- Listening to music
- Massage
- Meditation
- Quality time
- Spending time with pets

The amygdala, the watchdog of our emotional brain, actually has receptors for oxytocin, and when these receptors are occupied, this has a quieting effect on the amygdala. Thus, oxytocin helps to inhibit our defensive reactions to our children and enables us to engage with our children in connected, attuned ways.

Dopamine

Dopamine is a neurotransmitter that is responsible for the reward system in our brains; it is released when your brain expects a reward. It is essentially a feel-good hormone, and it is ideal for learning, planning, and productivity. When dopamine is present, we feel alert, focused, motivated, and happy. If our dopamine is too low, we feel sleepy, distracted, bored, less motivated, and even have difficulty moving our bodies. Dopamine is important for good mental health outcomes and academic performance; it will make your role as the parent much easier—and your child's journey in life more balanced and joyful—if there are adequate amounts of dopamine.

So how do we ensure dopamine is maintained in a healthy way? Interacting with children can powerfully activate the brain's reward system. Spending time with our children—playing together, reading to them, cuddling, play fighting, and doing joint activities—can elevate dopamine. Research shows that our reward system is turned on by interacting with our children, and this is an extremely important process that helps ensure we will stay highly engaged and motivated to care for our kids. Other ways to increase dopamine in healthy ways include eating adequate amounts of protein and less saturated fat, taking a probiotic, exercise, getting enough sleep, listening to music, meditation, and adequate amounts of sunlight.

What is also worth mentioning is that too much dopamine is often at the heart of addiction in children and adults. If our children are flooded with it, they can become addicted to the activity that is associated with the high release of dopamine. Dysfunction in the dopaminergic pathway is responsible for addiction to drugs, alcohol, pornography, cigarettes, and many more substances and activities. One area in which we want to raise awareness is how overuse of screen time can be very addictive for anybody, particularly for children whose brains are vulnerable and still growing and forming. Studies have shown how overuse of screen time affects the prefrontal cortex of the brain, similar to the effect of cocaine. Screen use releases excessive amounts of dopamine, which creates cravings for the device in the same way a smoker craves a cigarette—it's highly rewarding and, thus, highly addictive.

We like to compare the amount of dopamine released when engaging in screen time to that of eating a sweet treat. While playing or exercising releases smaller, appropriate amounts of dopamine—like eating a bite-sized brownie—giving a device to a child or teen is like giving them the entire pan of brownies. This is why children exposed to high amounts of dopamine through overexposure to screens often declare "I'm bored" when they are forced to play outside or play with their toys. They are accustomed to a certain amount of dopamine, and small amounts no longer stimulate the reward-center of the brain.

We're sure you've also noticed how emotional they get when you take it away—screaming, pleading, crying, tantrums, and decreased impulse control. This is because screen time also turns on the sympathetic nervous system, the gas pedal of the brain. This is the same system that manages the fight-flight-freeze-collapse response. It directs the body's rapid responses to dangerous or stressful situations. An increase of hormones boosts the body's alertness and heart rate, sending extra blood to the muscles. Breathing quickens, delivering fresh oxygen to the brain, and an injection of glucose is shot into the bloodstream for a quick energy boost. This activation decreases the child's ability to access their thinking brain; subsequently, it leads to a decrease in emotion regulation and an increase in impulsivity.

Cortisol

Cortisol is a stress hormone produced in your adrenal glands and works with certain parts of your brain to control your mood, motivation, and fear. In terms of mental health, it is best known for fueling the fight-flight-freeze-collapse response. Normal (small to moderate) amounts of cortisol are not harmful; it is necessary to keep us safe from harm and has also been linked to higher levels of motivation. It also helps control blood pressure, increases the body's metabolism of glucose, and reduces inflammation.

It gets dicey when a person is exposed to large and prolonged amounts of cortisol: what doctors, researchers, and mental health professionals refer to as toxic stress. Toxic stress has been associated with volume loss in the prefrontal cortex (which involves emotion regulation, executive functioning, rational thought, reflective thinking, planning, etc.), reduced integrity of the anterior cingulate cortex (which involves empathy, impulse control, emotion, and decision-making), impairment of the corpus callosum (which allows the right and left hemispheres of the brain to communicate with one another), and volume loss in the hippocampus (which impairs memory and processing/mediation of sensory information).

In terms of caregiving, toxic stress can occur when there are no supportive caregivers around to safeguard a child's response to repeated stressful or scary experiences. Abuse, neglect, parental addiction, mental illness, violence in or outside the home, and chaotic environments all can be linked to toxic stress. Knowing how toxic stress negatively impacts the brains of children, it is crucial children receive attuned, loving, and safe caregiving.

Serotonin

Serotonin is the key hormone and neurotransmitter that helps stabilize our mood and increases feelings of well-being and happiness—good for parents and children alike. It also helps with sleeping, eating, memory, and digestion. If your serotonin is low, you can feel depressed or anxious; experience sleep and digestive issues, suffer from increased impulsivity or decreased appetite; or crave sweets and carbohydrate-rich foods. SSRI (selective serotonin reuptake inhibitor) and SNRI (serotonin and norepinephrine reuptake inhibitor) medication can stabilize mood, but there are natural ways to increase serotonin levels without these medications. Ninety percent of serotonin is produced in the digestive tract so it's also important that our children's diets are balanced to produce adequate amounts of serotonin.

- Food high in tryptophan: You can't directly get serotonin from food, but you can get tryptophan, an amino acid that's converted to serotonin in your brain. Foods high in tryptophan include poultry, salmon, nuts and seeds, dairy, oats
- Exercise
- Bright natural light
- Massage
- Supplements and nutrition (probiotics, St. John's wort, 5-HTP, pure tryptophan, vitamin B12, omega-3, zinc, magnesium)
- Massage
- Prebiotics (fiber)

The dance between love, security, attachment, and neurochemistry is intricate and beautiful. Our interactions with our children flood their brains with chemicals that impact how they feel both physically and psychologically. We may stumble, forget the dance steps, or be out of rhythm at different times in their lives. What matters is that we get up each day to dance, focus on the neurochemistry of love, and try again.

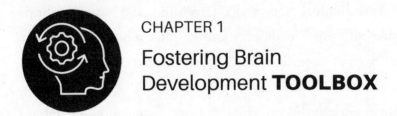

CHAPTER 1

Fostering Brain Development **TOOLBOX**

Body brain (the brain stem)

Rhythmic activities (i.e., rocking, swinging, hanging, and dancing)

Free play

Gross motor movement

Helping children understand how emotions are felt in their body (not just naming them)

Physical challenges to strengthen their bodies

Safe, predictable environments and relationships

Reducing overstimulation or too many transitions

Schedules

Adequate rest, sleep, balanced nutrition

Mindfulness, meditation, and yoga

Feelings brain (limbic system)

Attuned relationships (noticing and accurately validating how our children feel)

Co-regulation (using our calm to soothe their chaos) (more in upcoming chapters)

Encouraging autonomy but being available if they become overwhelmed

Being a safe caregiver, physically and emotionally

Not allowing a device to hijack you from your presence with your child

Fostering emotional literacy (teaching them about their
emotions and the emotions of others; books and movies, for
example, point their attention to how actions impact people's
emotions)

Thinking brain (prefrontal cortex & cortex)

Infants
Hide a toy under a cloth and encourage the infant to look for it.
Take turns with any activity that interests the child, such as
picking up toys, etc.
Talk to your infant as much as possible.
Songs or chants with simple hand motions.

Toddlers
Song games with many movements are also fun. Examples
include The Hokey Pokey; Teddy Bear; I'm a Little Teapot; or
Head, Shoulders, Knees, and Toes.
Provide many materials and opportunities to try new skills, such
as throwing and catching balls, walking a balance beam,
running up and down an incline, and jumping.
Games that require active inhibition like freeze dance (musical
statues).
Watching and narrating their play.
Talking about feelings.
Ask children to play a sorting game in which you take turns
sorting objects by size, shape, or color.

3 to 5 years
Provide many opportunities for children to test themselves
physically through access to materials such as climbing
structures, balance beams, seesaws, etc.

Play some music and have children dance really fast, then
slowly, and practice freezing

Imaginary play

Puzzles

Cooking

Encourage your children to tell you stories and act them out

5 to 7 years

Board and card games that involve strategy

Physical activities that require attention such as freeze dance
(musical statues), musical chairs, Red Light, Green Light, and
Simon Says

Fast-moving ball games: four square, dodgeball, and tetherball

Guessing games: I Spy With My Little Eye or 20 Questions

Imaginary play

8 to 12 years

Organized sports

Gross motor games that require attention: jump rope, laser tag,
and paintball

Playing a musical instrument

Dance

Brain teasers: crossword puzzles, sudoku, or Lumosity

Teens

Encourage teens to identify something specific that they want to
accomplish.

Getting involved in helping with social issues, such as
homelessness, domestic violence, or bullying, by volunteering.

Goal setting: write out short- and long-term goals.

Teach them about self-talk.

Help adolescents be mindful of interruptions such as electronic
communication such as email and cell phones.

Encourage them to journal.

Activities: yoga, sports, music (singing or playing an instrument), dance, theater, and computer games.

Right hemisphere

Play

Art

Physical activity

Dance and sports

Validating emotions and showing empathy

Naming emotions

Co-regulation (more in upcoming chapters)

Left hemisphere

Reading to your child or your child reading

Talking to your child

Puzzles and board games

Science experiments

Journaling and other forms of writing

Hypothetical scenarios and playful debate (when they're older)

Numeracy activities

CHAPTER TWO

BIG FEELINGS AND WHY THEY'RE IMPORTANT

A child's emotional system is central to their psychological and physical well-being. An emotional system ridden with stress can impact not only a child's mental health but also their immune system, the inflammatory response in the body, and even their mortality. There are no positive or negative emotions; all emotions serve a purpose and act as a guidance system for your child as they navigate the intricacies of life. Emotions are meant to be transient, to come and go like waves in the ocean. Our job as parents is to make space for these feelings, and with attunement and compassion, the emotions will gradually retreat back into the depths of the human experience. As Dan Millman says: "Life without emotions would be as calm as death, like a world without weather."

One of the greatest gifts that you can give your child is to create space for all feelings: delight, excitement, hope, anger, sadness, frustration, and disappointment. We always tell our clients that the more room we make for emotions, the less they take from us.

One of the ultimate goals of parenting is nurturing a safe space for our children to flourish. Stress and other overwhelming feelings, if not released with connection and compassion, can curtail this developmental process. When a child experiences feelings of overwhelm, translated in the body as "I am not safe," they need us to come alongside them. The safety of our presence will allow the crucial physiological release their body needs to return to baseline and brings the child to a state of physical and emotional safety.

One of my favorite anecdotes I give when I'm teaching our class on compassionate discipline to live audiences is the story of my son and the bathroom sink. I believe my son had just turned two years old, and like his momma, he loves the water. Now any working parent knows that getting ready for work with toddlers in the house is one of the most challenging feats of the day, and if done well, it is deserving of a gold medal in the parenting race. I try to choose my battles wisely and not sweat the small stuff as long as I can get to the office on time. I usually ask myself, "Is this the hill I want to die on today?"

When I would get ready in the morning, I would allow my son to play in the bathroom sink. He would splash around, pour water between containers, or play with his Paw Patrol figurines, teaching each one how to swim. Did this make a mess? Yes. Was it inconvenient? Yes. But it provided a good enough distraction, with the mess contained to a single room, while keeping my son in one place long enough for me to look somewhat presentable to clients.

That morning, my son had had a horrible sleep, had been sick for the past week, and he had also just transitioned from his father's house. Any parent from a two-home situation knows the mess that is the two-day transition process. It spawns irritability, testing, troubles waking up in a different bed, and more. I could see by his aversion to eye contact, his lack of concentration, refusal to eat his breakfast, his defiant "nos," and overall crankiness that he suffered from what I like to call "emotional constipation." He had bottled up his feelings, and the pressure was rising. This overwhelm made him feel unsafe and uncomfortable in his body.

I knew what he needed and dreaded having to give it to him because it would mean I would be late for work. What he needed was uncomfortable, loud, messy, and required every ounce of patience in my being as it went against what I was taught to do in my upbringing. The importance of the release with an overworked physiological and emotional system is kind of like handling a pressure cooker. You have to gradually give release by depressurizing it—otherwise you end up with an eruption hot enough to scald you with third-degree burns.

I did the most counterintuitive thing imaginable; I instigated a meltdown—intentionally. I set a limit when a limit was not really needed. After only five minutes in the sink, I stated firmly: "Ayden, I know you love the water, but we're done with water for today." I knew very well this would cause a classic meltdown as he was typically allowed to play in the water, and once this started, I knew I would not be able to pull myself away from it. He proceeded to cry, demand his return to the sink, and stomp his feet. I shut my bedroom door, begrudgingly sat on the carpet, and said to him:

"Sweetheart, I can see you're so mad at Mommy for ending your water time, but we are all done for today." That's it. This limit then seemed to escalate his tantrum.

He then proceeded to hit me—one of the only times my son has actually done that. Despite my blood pressure rising, I held his hands, gently but firmly, and I set another limit: "I can see you're so angry, but you may not hit me. You may yell or stomp your feet or yell, but you cannot hurt my body." Now he didn't go to hit me again, but he took my suggestion and ran with it—with gusto. He spent fifteen agonizing minutes yelling, banging his hands on the floor, crying, throwing my decorative pillows against the wall, and knocking over my garbage.

I sat in the same position, cross-legged on the carpet, and leaned in. I said a few phrases, such as, "Those are really big feelings. Mommy will stay here until they get smaller"; and "I'm not going anywhere." The whole time, I took big breaths and repeated internally, "this is the work of parenting; this is the right thing to do" so I wouldn't storm out of the room or scream back at him. Then, something happened. He paused, his eyes softened, his breathing slowed, and he looked over at me, as if to say, "now what?" I could see the anger in his face shift from frustration to utter heartbreak. I always stay long enough to look for that shift. I said, "You can come sit with me if you like. I have a hug here for you." I opened my arms, and he lunged into them and sobbed for a good five minutes. I rocked him and said, "See, your big feelings are going down. Big breaths, bud."

As the sobs subsided, he looked up at me and said, "You go to work now, Mommy. I go see Grandma." He hopped up like nothing had happened, ran downstairs, and lunged into my mother's waiting arms. My mother said you would have never known he had that kind of meltdown—and of course she never got to see them, as children seem to save these battles for their parents. It was like a different child—I had my son back.

Now, this was counterintuitive to how I was raised. Being punished or ignored for your feelings was common in my upbringing. Subsequently, my emotional connection with my parents never felt steadfast. I knew from my experience of being a child psychologist, and attending my own therapy, the importance of having someone to hold space for you when you are falling apart. Falling apart is a necessity to our emotional survival and our journey to self-actualization. We have to release the pressure, or it leads to dire mental health outcomes.

I tell this story for a few reasons. I'm not suggesting you intentionally trigger a meltdown every time. Your child will likely offer ample opportunities for this when you offer them the wrong color cup or their sandwich is not cut the right way. The more we normalize feelings in our children—and within ourselves—and allow them to express these feelings, the more quickly they move through them. It doesn't mean our children won't experience uncomfortable emotions; it just means they don't get stuck in those emotions for long periods of time. Remember, what we resist, persists.

It is important to stay emotionally regulated as a parent so you can share your calm. Your child's nervous system synchronizes to your own, so we want to dial into the right emotional frequency to help move them back toward a state of connection and safety. And emotions are pivotal to our children's survival. Children must learn that when life is hard or a need is unmet, they are to turn to others, not away from them. Our emotions give us this signal, and we are designed to move toward loved ones when we become dysregulated so we can stay safe.

You are in charge of caring for these little ones so their emotions serve as a beacon as where to take appropriate action. What my son learned was twofold: 1) when I feel overwhelmed, it's not a bad thing—my mom accepts my emotions, so they must be okay; and 2) when I turn to my parent, I am comforted, my body relaxes, my big feeling subsides, and I feel safe again. Take home: my caregiver is safe, and they are a source of comfort for me. They can handle me. This is my safe haven, my home.

THE ANATOMY OF EMOTIONS

Based on our chapter on the neurobiology of parenting, you will recall that emotions are held in the feeling brain (limbic system), but they are undeniably intertwined with our body brain (brain stem). The two centers of the brain work in a synchronistic dance to create our emotional world. It is believed, as with all mammals, that humans developed emotions as a sort of biofeedback mechanism that aids our survival.

Emotions are more than a sentimental notion found on the inside of a hallmark card. Their existence in our bodies and minds is hard science, and their purpose is hardwired into our anatomy. Let's look a little closer: we receive information from our external environment, such as a smile from our parent, a loud noise, our partner yelling, the feel of our child's arms wrapped around us, etc. Through our five senses, this information is conveyed to our body brain, processed, and then sent to our feelings brain for interpretation. This is what Dr. Daniel Siegel calls appraisal.

Internal and external events are assessed as important and worthy of our attention. Our brain relies partially on something called the hippocampus, which compares the event with other memories that have a similar blueprint. The brain then decides, based on this comparison, if the event is "good" or "bad." The emotion also drives further physiological shifts in the body (i.e., heart rate increases), which amplify and intensify the emotional experience. This loop between the body brain and feelings brain initiates the emotional experience, which tells us how to interact with our world and those in it. It gives a road map for navigating our lives: what to avoid, what we like and don't like, who is good for us and who is toxic, when to ask for help, when to improve our behavior, when to make amends with someone, etc.

Remember in our previous chapter we addressed the notion of integration. In order for your child to learn to tame their emotions on their own (emotion regulation), they need to be able to integrate the thinking brain with the feeling brain and body brain. They also need to be able to move back and forth between left and right hemisphere functioning. After a lot of practice, children and adults alike can talk themselves down from the ledge of a meltdown; however, this ability is not accessible in young children, especially before age four, and it takes time to develop (until you're close to thirty years of age).

Young children are driven by primarily their emotional brains, and when this area of the brain is attended to, and the amygdala is not consistently on high alert resorting to the fight-flight-freeze-collapse stress response, then the brain has the space to engage in the imperative work of developing critical neural connection in the thinking brain. Without an adequately developed thinking brain, a child will struggle with emotion regulation, even as an adult. Remember that the thinking brain is ultimately in charge of emotion regulation.

So you might be asking, if my child is young and lacking development of the thinking brain, is it hopeless to tame their emotions until they're older? Absolutely not. The amazing thing about parenting is we can help this process along and ensure healthy development of both the thinking and emotional brain. We also can help a child regulate their feelings by acting as a surrogate "thinking brain"—we help them with their emotions through co-regulation.

CO-REGULATION

Neuroscience confirms that children develop their abilities for emotional self-regulation through connections with reliable caregivers who help soothe and model emotion regulation in a process called co-regulation. Remember how activated our right hemisphere becomes when we are dysregulated and how the right hemisphere largely houses our emotional experience. If that part of the brain is activated, it makes sense that we send signals to soothe that part of the brain. This also means we must use our own right hemisphere to "feel" our children's emotions through awareness of our own emotional experiences and the feelings our children evoke in us. If a child is dysregulated, it also means their amygdala is activated, and the threat response is triggered. Our job in that moment is to connect through the right hemisphere and not further trigger the alarm system in our child.

Steps to Co-Regulation

1. **Keep your emotions in check:** How can your child trust it's safe to feel what they're feeling if you're losing it too? When little people are overwhelmed by big emotions, it's our job to share our calm, not join their chaos (L.R. Knost).

2. **Signal non-threat to the amygdala:** Ensure you are not towering over your child or raising your voice to evoke fear. Get on their level or lower, soften the tone of your voice, and open your body up (crossed arms indicate stress or threat).

3. **Name their emotion:** What is your child feeling? For example, you might say, "I can see you're so mad right now" or "you are so sad your sister won't play with you." If you get this wrong, your child will correct you, so no need to worry. If naming it doesn't quite do it, we can also label the intensity of the emotion and how big or urgent it is. For instance, "wow you're so mad; you're as mad as this whole room! Or maybe even the whole house!"

4. **Proximity:** Get in close. If your child will let you touch them, do that (i.e., hold them in your lap; give them a touch on the shoulder, a hug). There are some children who do not want to be touched. In that case, just stay close by so they can see you're there.

5. **Ride the wave:** Don't leave your child on their own. Stay with them until the storm calms. If your child insists repeatedly that you leave, stay near by checking in every few minutes. But we really urge you, try to stay in the room. Give your child time to learn to trust that it's safe to express emotion in the company of others.

HOW OUR BRAINS ORGANIZE EMOTIONS

Humans have an entire bank of memories, each organized by a specific feeling. We refer to them as emotional neuronetworks. It's kind of like a filing system. Memories then go into each file based on the specific emotion and are also flagged as being threatening or nonthreatening, depending on the history of how it was dealt with. For instance, in my file for "fear," I have yelling/aggression, snakes, rejection by a partner, and failure. For "happy," I have animals, nature, reading, my children, and traveling. No single person's files look exactly alike, nor are they good or bad—they just are.

The reason we bring this up is: 1) we want you, the caregiver, to be aware of which file you (and memories you and your child make) are going into; and 2) we want to help you to teach your child that certain files do not need to be tagged as threatening. These deposits into these memory files are vitally important to how your child will organize their emotional experiences around intimate relationships in the future.

EMOTIONS ARE NEITHER GOOD NOR BAD— THEY JUST ARE

Emotions are biofeedback, and we need our emotions to engage with our worlds. Our world would lack color and vibrancy without emotions. We were all once little humans, and in our own childhoods, we were often taught that certain emotions are unacceptable. Sometimes these messages are cultural (i.e., boys need to be tough and not show their feelings) and don't come from our caregiver directly. Our own beliefs about emotions will dictate our comfort level and reactions to our child's emotions, and how we handle our child's emotional waves will determine if those emotions are tagged as threatening or nonthreatening.

EXAMPLE

Imagine a little boy named Justin, whose father yells at him whenever he feels sad and cries. He will learn that sadness is a bad, scary feeling. The memories of his father now go into the sad file, along with whatever made him sad to begin with. He has also learned that feeling sad is a threat. It means he will be rejected, and he needs his father to love him, so it's unacceptable to go there. Subsequently, when something comes up that makes him sad, he will hide his feelings to avoid being yelled at.

Fast-forward thirty years, and the little boy has his own son, and his son cries. The cries of his son will trigger his own memories of being rejected by his father, and it will make it difficult to tolerate the cries of his son. He has no road map on how to deal with these emotions. All he knows is that sadness is bad, a threat, and can't be tolerated. There's a good chance Justin will act in a similar way to his own father and yell at his son, or check out from his son's pain (i.e., walk away). These intergenerational patterns of dealing with emotions are very common in families. Until we deal with our past, we are often destined to relive it.

In Chapter 5, we will go into more detail on how a parent's early experiences will impact their ability to parent their children. However, what we want you to take away most from this chapter is how important it is to make space for the feelings your child has. To foster emotional intelligence, you must befriend all of your child's emotions and make ample space for them to experience these feelings.

CRYING CALMS

When Tania or I conduct intakes with parents of new clients, one of the questions we ask is whether their child cries. It's always interesting to see the parents' reaction to this question; it tells us a lot about the parent's level of comfort with emotions and how healthy the child's emotional system is. I am relieved when a parent tells me that a child can cry and does so regularly—granted that this is followed by a parent explaining to us that the child accepts comfort from them and goes to them when distressed.

What is more concerning to me is when a caregiver states that they rarely see their child cry. Crying is Mother Nature's way of moving through emotions that are overwhelming and helps reset your nervous system. It helps rid the body of stress and recalibrates your stress response. When you or your child cries tears of frustration or sadness, it releases stress hormones such as cortisol and adrenaline.

Dr. William Frey, at the Ramsey Medical Center in Minneapolis, discovered tears shed from an emotional experience contain stress hormones that are excreted through crying. After studying the composition of tears, Dr. Frey found that emotional tears shed these hormones and other toxins that accumulate during stress. When you cry, your parasympathetic nervous system is also activated. This system is what revs the body down and stops the production of stress hormones. Oxytocin and endorphins are also released that help reduce pain (emotional and physical) and increase feelings of well-being.

As you can see, this process is so important for adults and children alike. Crying is part of our healing and the development of resiliency. We don't ever need to punish this in children. This only teaches children to hide their emotional experiences from their caregivers or eventually to numb them out entirely. The consequences of children not being able to have the space to process their feelings can lead to depression, anxiety, anger, and other mental health difficulties.

FEAR THAT DOESN'T SUBSIDE: TRAUMA AND THE BRAIN

When humans experience fear or stress, they're designed to stay in this stress response (fight-flight-freeze-collapse) for fifteen to twenty minutes, and then stress hormones begin to decrease naturally. It becomes concerning when an individual is stuck in a constant state of stress. This is called toxic stress. Prolonged elevated levels of cortisol and adrenaline have the potential to change brain chemistry, brain anatomy, and gene expression. In children, toxic stress weakens the architecture of the developing brain, which can lead to lifelong problems in learning, behavior, and physical and mental health.

CASE STUDY

Tommy is a five-year-old who lives in a home where there is constant yelling and verbal abuse. His dad drinks too much, and his mom is so preoccupied by the issues in their marriage that Tommy is often neglected. His dad is a source of fear, and his mom is nonresponsive. Tommy's brain spends all of its energy keeping him safe, and his stress response is on high alert, which causes damage to his developing brain. The overproduction of his stress hormones (cortisol and adrenaline) and the overuse of his body brain and emotional brain means that there is no more energy left for his thinking brain. As Tommy gets older, he starts to experience significant delays. He struggles with paying attention in school and staying organized, becomes explosive when angry, and easily gives up and retreats when tasks become too difficult—he shuts down.

This is often the case with children with trauma; they are wired for fear and often lack the fundamental "executive functioning" skills of the thinking brain. MRI images have shown a significant reduction in gray matter in the neocortex and deficits to the hippocampus in children who have experienced chronic stress or trauma. These children often struggle with cognitive delays, memory, flexible thinking, and self-control.

The classic landmark study by the CDC-Kaiser Permanente Adverse Childhood Experiences (ACEs) is one of the largest studies of childhood abuse and neglect and household challenges and later-life health and well-being. Over 17,000 Health Maintenance Organization members from Southern California receiving physical exams completed confidential surveys regarding their childhood experiences and current health status and behaviors. ACEs include physical, sexual, or emotional abuse; physical and emotional neglect; parental mental illness; domestic violence; divorce; parental incarceration; or substance abuse.

ACEs are not uncommon in our society, but it's when you have several of these experiences that long-term detrimental effects become evident. For instance, individuals who have experienced four or more categories of childhood exposure, compared to those who had experienced none, they are 4 to 12 times more likely to suffer from alcoholism, drug abuse, depression, and suicide attempt; are 2 to 4 times more likely to smoke; and are 1.4 to 1.6 times more likely to be physically inactive and develop severe obesity. And the higher the ACEs, the higher the risk for ischemic heart disease, cancer, COPD, asthma, chronic lung disease, skeletal fractures, and liver disease. Childhood trauma is not just a crisis of mental health; it's a health issue that impacts humans on every conceivable level (see Figure 1.2). Research shows that the single most protective factor against ACEs is to create and sustain a safe, connected, supportive environment for children. Change starts at home, with one adult who says, "this will no longer be my family's story." Let's raise children who don't have to heal from their childhoods.

The complex emotional worlds of children can be difficult to navigate, especially if we have a hard time tending to our own emotions. When we lean into discomfort with our children, when we breathe unconditional love and warmth into their most challenging moments, they learn that no part of themself is "too scary" or "unwanted." They embrace the full experience of being human and come to love the rich emotional landscape of their life.

CHAPTER 2

Emotions **TOOLBOX**

Co-regulation

Proximity

This how all mammals that live in groups seek safety. Numbers
equal protection. You don't have to force your child to hug
you, but suggest trying to be in the same room.

Name their emotion

Our children want to feel seen and understood—asking a child
infers that you don't actually understand how they feel. So
take a chance and name the feeling. Keep it short and simple
with your voice reflecting the tone of that emotion and the
urgency. i.e., "You're SO MAD at me right now!"

Keep your emotions in check

Learn some tools for self-regulation, so you can co-regulate
your child. Talk a walk, call your best friend, change the
narrative in your head about your child, exercise, or speak to a
professional.

Signal non-threat to the amygdala

Get on their level or lower, soften the tone of your voice, and
open your body up.

Ride the wave

Don't leave your child to manage their feelings on their own.

Make space for emotion

Play

Whether it's playing with our children or when they play on their
own, a child's language for processing feelings is through
play.

Setting limits

Often children who need to have a good cry and let out their
feelings do so after a limit has been set. Be careful not to
punish the emotion that ensues after the limit is set—
welcome it.

Give yourself space to share your own emotions

Make sure you have adults in your life who can hold space for
your feelings, in the same way you are holding space for your
child's. Your ability to be vulnerable with others will mirror
your capacity to hold space for your child's feelings.

CHAPTER THREE

THE DANCE OF ATTACHMENT

Humans are hardwired for connection and belonging. Humans stay with their parents longer than any other mammal on the planet, and as such, their relationship with their primary caregivers is pivotal to their physical and emotional safety. Children are by nature extremely vulnerable beings, and they rely on us to meet most of their needs. Babies and children cannot simply fend for themselves; they need us to comfort, clothe, feed, and, most of all, love them. This dependent relationship is the foundation for attachment: a deep and enduring emotional bond between two people in which each seeks closeness and feels more secure when in the presence of the other. Attachment is the hallmark of emotional well-being in humans, the antidote to trauma, and the catalyst of resiliency. On the other hand, insecure attachment style in childhood is related to an array of negative mental health outcomes and unstable adult relationships later in life.

A child's brain takes a significant amount of time to develop (up to thirty years of age), and their experiences with the outside world, including their attachments, greatly influence the architecture of their brain. We know that the higher the quality of attachments a child has with their caregivers, the stronger their brain grows, especially the thinking brain.

Something subtle but extraordinary happens when a child is in the right relationship with their caregiver. Little Amanda looks for her mother's nod, and she tries the monkey bars for the first time; Ayden's tears stop flowing as his father kisses his ouchy on his knee; Adam beams with pride as his mother throws him the ball and catches it while his father exclaims, "You did it, son!"

It is in these moments of connection when we feel seen, heard, valued, and loved that we feel like we can move mountains. These small moments accumulate over time to form a bond that provides our children the strength to persevere, explore, and connect with other people. We cannot think of a more valuable gift you can give your child than that of a secure attachment.

While most people understand that children need their basic needs met, such as food, clothing, water, and shelter, we now know that is simply not enough to raise a healthy child. In 1989 the fall of Romania's Ceaușescu regime left approximately 170,000 children in 700 overcrowded, impoverished institutions across Romania, and it prompted the most comprehensive study to date on the effects of institutionalization on children's well-being. Romania's Abandoned Children, the authoritative account of this landmark study, documented the devastating toll paid by children who were deprived of responsive care, social interaction, stimulation, and psychological comfort.

According to Nathan Fox, PhD, the babies lay in cribs all day, except when being fed, diapered, or bathed on a set schedule. They weren't rocked or sung to. Many stared at their own hands, trying to derive whatever stimulation they could from the world around them. After following these children for fourteen years, the results of this study were alarming and profound. The complete lack of connection with another human being impacted the children's development on multiple levels. Some of the symptoms these children demonstrated as they matured included: poor impulse control; social withdrawal; problems with coping and regulating emotions; low self-esteem; pathological behaviors such as tics, tantrums, stealing, and self-punishment; poor intellectual functioning; and low academic achievement. Children who are impacted by this kind of neglect show lower brain masses, deficits on tests of visual memory and attention, and delays in cognitive function, motor development, and language. Those children who were put into foster homes, especially before the age of two, fared much better but struggled with a variety of issues. This documented phenomenon is known as failure to thrive. It has been empirically studied around the globe and is a driving force in attachment research.

Now if you are reading this book, we doubt this is the fate of your child, but it does drive home the point that the relationship matters. Holding your baby when they cry matters. Kissing the boo-boos matters. Never doubt how powerful your love for your child truly is.

ATTACHMENT STYLE

Based on the landmark work of John Bowlby and Mary Ainsworth, children's early life experiences develop into four types of attachment styles. Their attachment style is a road map for how to navigate relationships with their caregiver and, later in life, with their friends, their partner, their boss, and their coworkers. This map begins to develop from their first moment on earth.

Does mom pick me up when I cry? Does dad turn away when I get angry? Does Mom gasp in horror when I climb a little too high? Does Dad yell at me when I have a tantrum? These small moments of connection (or disconnection) give our children a message about their attachments, their associations with their physical world, and their relationship with themselves.

Secure Attachment Style: Golden Retriever Children

Little Steven is an outgoing and sociable five-year-old. While his parents are divorced, he is always happy to see his mom or dad. He loves to climb, run, and play with other children. He navigates social situations well, and his feathers are not easily ruffled by other children. He speaks his mind,

and if he's not comfortable with something, he lets his parents know. His emotions are easily expressed, and if things aren't fair or he trips and takes a big fall, he cries big tears and goes to his caregivers for hugs and cuddles. Within a few minutes, he's back to his normal self and is able to carry on. When meeting new people, he hides behind mom or dad for a few minutes but quickly adjusts, and with a nod of approval from his parents, he begins exploring his new space.

Steven is the perfect example of what mental health professionals refer to as a secure attachment—it is the gold standard of healthy working relationships. Sometimes the jargon is lost on many of us, so we like to give something concrete for parents to remember. We affectionately refer to these children as having a golden retriever attachment style. If you've ever been around these lovely animals, you can see why they're utilized as service dogs. They are even-tempered, friendly, reliable, and resilient. They share these characteristics with securely attached children. A child with this attachment style is also resilient, has well-developed emotion regulation (or is easily co-regulated by a caregiver), and, overall, is psychologically healthy.

It doesn't mean they don't express sadness or anger, but overall, these emotions are fleeting and don't overshadow the child's overall disposition. Their amygdala, the alarm center of their brain, simply doesn't seem to be activated as much or as easily as other children's. They are children who miss their parents when they leave and rush to their parents' arms when they return. When things don't go their way and they become upset, they turn to their caregivers for comfort and are then easily brought to calm. Once they are comfortable in an environment, they easily explore and play well with other children.

Based on over fifty years of research, these children:

- Enjoy more happiness and less anger with their parents
- Do better socially with their peers
- Have stronger relationships with siblings
- Have higher self-esteem
- Are more optimistic
- Are more trusting of others
- Are more resilient
- Have stronger problem-solving abilities
- Have better emotion regulation
- Have stronger impulse control

What Are These Parents Doing Differently?

Parents of securely attached children are far from perfect, but they unmistakably have two sets of skills that set them apart from other parents. These skills come from the work of Kent Hoffman, Glenn Cooper, and Bert Powell and their groundbreaking work with Circle of Security International, as published in their book *Raising a Secure Child*.

They provide:

- **A secure base:** They are comfortable with their child exploring their world, and they delight in their child's adventures in the world.

- **A safe haven:** They are comfortable with their child's full array of emotions, provide co-regulation when the child is overwhelmed, and give ample amounts of connection to essentially keep their child's cup full until they are ready to explore again.

This sounds simple enough, but there are multiple moving pieces you need to consider.

SECURE BASE CHECKLIST

1. **Proximity:** You need to still be emotionally available to your child, and particularly when they're very young, you need to maintain some proximity until they have matured. This does not mean we helicopter over them (more on this later), but it does mean we are available should they need us. This requires you to allow your child the autonomy to explore and to make mistakes, but to be there when things inevitably start to come apart at the seams.

2. **Acknowledgment:** You have to be prepared to value and celebrate all the parts of your child, not just their accomplishments. Do you honor your child's quirks as well as their strengths? Do you see your child for who they truly are—not an extension of you but as their own person? Can you be with your child and find joy in the small moments while they navigate their world?

3. **Our own anxiety management:** As our children try
    new things and make mistakes, it can be horribly
    overwhelming. The "what-ifs" are a regular narration
    in many a parent's mind. It is imperative that we don't
    allow our own anxiety to prevent our children from
    investigating, playing, and problem-solving. It's primal:
    the minute your child senses your anxiety, they are
    programmed to stay close to avoid danger. This can be to
    your child's detriment. They need to go out into the world
    to learn about the world and themselves.

4. **Scaffolding skills:** Children need to try things, to make
    mistakes, and to try again to learn a new skill. Often, in the
    beginning, they need your support. You can "scaffold" by first
    modeling what it is they need to learn, have them try bits
    and pieces of the skill, and as they edge closer to competence,
    you allow them to do it on their own. In Canada, skating
    is a favorite past time. We often teach children to skate by
    modeling skating skills, positioning them behind a chair on
    the ice, and skating alongside them. We may then progress to
    skating while holding their hand. Finally, we have to let go.
    Yes, they will fall (likely many times), and there will be tears.
    We don't take off their skates and quit though. A parent who
    is also a good teacher will reinforce that falling down is part
    of the learning and support them as they pick themselves
    back up and try again. Support is followed by independence.
    Children aren't ready to dive into the deep end until they feel
    safe in the shallow end first.

5. **Play:** Play is so crucial to your child's development; we have an entire chapter on play. For now, we will mention that in terms of attachment, parents of securely attached children 1) allow ample time for play, and much of that is free play—not where you coach a child through a step-by-step craft you found on Pinterest; and 2) they play with their children. They roughhouse, dress up, build forts, ride bikes, play games, and speak their child's language while valuing their unique expression of play.

SAFE HAVEN CHECKLIST

1. **Protection:** Children need to know that you are their safe haven. It's essential that they feel that you can protect them from the dangers in the world. Granted you cannot Bubble Wrap your children, but they need to know that you are consistently in their corner when something scary happens and will do your best to keep them safe. Sometimes it means staying with them during an overwhelming moment, such as the first day of swimming lessons, when the neighbors scary dog barks loudly at them when they walk past, or as they climb the monkey bars at a playground for the first time and we stand below them in case they lose their balance. It doesn't mean we stop them from trying new things—they need to take risks to build their confidence—but they know we're available to them, whenever possible, and should there

be real danger, we will be there. If you do this enough when children are younger, they won't need your physical protection as often or as much as they become older and more secure in their attachment.

2.   **Co-regulation:** When a child's feelings get too big, it's normal for them to cry, tantrum, yell, become defiant, or withdraw. The important thing isn't preventing the meltdown but making it safe to have the meltdown in your presence. Remember, crying serves a biological purpose, and tantrums are common. Since children don't have a well-developed thinking brain that regulates their emotions; they need us to help soothe their feelings. The more we stay with our children during big emotional waves, the less frequent the waves and the smaller the storm. As Dr. Siegel and Dr. Bryson tell us in the *Whole Brain Child*, co-regulation helps build the staircase between the "downstairs brain" (the brain stem and the emotional [limbic] brain) and the "upstairs brain" (the thinking brain/neocortex). The more children utilize the staircase, the more quickly they can access the part of the brain that is responsible for emotion regulation. We must make it safe for our children to cry or become angry. Expression of emotion needs to be welcomed, not punished. This doesn't mean we don't set limits, but we want our children to know how they feel is always okay, and they won't be shamed or disciplined for experiencing an emotion.

3. **Connection:** Connection, like co-regulation, is about being present, warm, and attuned. It's not only about loving our children but also letting them know that we experience joy in being with them. How each parent maintains connection with their child depends on their communication style, interests, background, and comfort level. Perhaps connection is communicated through playing board games, taking walks outside, riding bikes, snuggles before bed, having family meals together, building a pillow fort, or family movie nights. However this is expressed in your family, what is important is how present you are.

   In this day and age, many of us are on the go—working multiple jobs, racing against deadlines, balancing several organized activities between multiple children, etc. We can't be "with" our children giving them our constant undivided attention all day long. But throughout the day, in small moments, you can give your child the gift of being present. Put down the phone. Move in close and make eye contact. Listen to what they have to say. Celebrate their accomplishments. Be there in the moment. Children don't need more things; they need more of us.

4. **Self-awareness:** Understanding your own emotions, the ability to regulate your emotions, and how your past impacts your ability to stay present and attuned to your children is a vital part of conscious parenting. When we

have a positive and healthy relationship with ourselves, it enables us to parent compassionately.

AMBIVALENT ATTACHMENT STYLE: KANGAROO CHILDREN

Little Rachel loves her parents very dearly but struggles with being on her own without them. When her parents leave her—whether it's school drop-off, soccer practice, or going to the day home—there are always big tears and clinging. She has a lot of worries, and it seems no matter what her parents do, they can't calm her fears. She often follows her parents around the house and struggles with playing on her own or even with other children. Bedtime is very difficult as she battles sleep—wanting another story or a drink of water—and she often requires her parents to sleep with her to fall or even stay asleep. Both of her parents are frustrated as their energy always feels depleted, and they feel like they can't do anything right.

Rachel is an example of an ambivalent attachment style. We affectionately call children who navigate the world through an ambivalent attachment style "kangaroo children" because they remind us of little joeys who cling to their mother's pouch. Kangaroo children tend to stick very close to their caregivers and are reluctant to explore their worlds. Play is often difficult for them, especially at home since they are very preoccupied with where their parents are. Attempted separation from the parent is often followed by begging, pleading, and clinging.

Now we don't want to mistake a slow-to-warm temperament for an ambivalent attachment style. Children who are naturally timid are weary in a new environment and are simply cautious when met with new faces and places. Once they are comfortable, they warm up and begin to explore and play. Even securely attached children demonstrate separation anxiety, particularly when put in a novel situation or meeting a new caregiver, like a babysitter or teacher. Kangaroo children struggle settling in and are often preoccupied with where you are and whether you are paying attention even in familiar situations. It's not uncommon for these children to continually request that their parent "watch me, watch me." Many families we work with describe these children as having an emotional bucket that can never be filled—like there is a hole in the bottom. Comforting these children can also feel futile. While they demand connection and physical comfort, when given, they do not calm easily and may resist your comfort.

If you are a caregiver of a child with this attachment style, it can prove exhausting. A parent once told me she felt that no matter what she did, it felt like she couldn't make her child happy— she felt helpless. Now here is where you take a deep breath. Of the three insecure attachment styles, we find our little kangaroos are the easiest to bring back to secure attachment.

How does this happen?

Ambivalent attachment comes from inconsistency in caregiving— the child just doesn't know what to expect or if their needs will be met, so their best insurance policy is to stay close. This can be caused by a few things:

- Two different caregivers are inconsistent in their caregiving. Maybe one parent is very strict and lacks warmth, while the other is more nurturing but struggles with setting limits.

- A parent was consistently available for a period of time, but there is a setback in their emotional or physical availability. Examples include the parents having another baby (and not being able to provide the older child with the same level of care), or a parent struggling with mental health issues such as postpartum depression, or parents newly splitting custody (where the child is used to having a caregiver there but now only has them 50% of the time).

- **Distracted parenting:** The parent isn't emotionally present in their interactions with their children, especially when the child is experiencing emotional dysregulation or needs a limit set (i.e., they are preoccupied with their cell phones or work tasks).

- **Anxious parenting:** A parent's own anxiety cues the child to cling. The child picks up on the parent's fear, so they feel afraid themselves.

- **Parental insecurity:** The child's separation from the parent cues the parent's fear that the child does not need them anymore, so the parent withdraws affection or connection or cues the child to come back every time they go to play or explore. Subsequently, the child clings for approval of the parent to maintain the attachment.

What Do They Need to Move Toward Security?

These children need more consistency and predictability. Forcing independence won't work, though. You meet them where they are at and validate how they are feeling—their anxiety and fears are real and overwhelming. That being said, they need to feel your confidence and leadership; you must convey to them that you believe that they can handle the world. You must encourage some autonomy, first in small ways, while in connection and proximity to you, and as they begin to trust they can handle small amounts of separation and healthy risk, you start to move away.

For example, we may practice by slowly moving away from our child while at the park or while engaged in play, perhaps every five minutes. We might try enrolling them in an extracurricular activity during which we first stand inside the area while they practice (if the child needs it), then just outside of it, and then we wait in the car eventually. We are constantly working on helping them to experience competency and confidence, independent of our presence. Providing too many accommodations to these children can be a detriment to their emotional well-being as we rob them of the experience of mastery and competence. A wonderful book to help you guide an anxious child toward more autonomy and confidence is *Breaking Free of Child Anxiety and OCD: A Scientifically Proven Program for Parents* by Eli R. Lebowitz.

AVOIDANT ATTACHMENT STYLE: CAT CHILDREN

Little Landon is bright and adventurous. He rarely seems scared of anything and easily plays on his own. Drops-offs are never an issue at school, and he's excited to try new things and meet new people. However, he struggles with being oppositional with adults. It's not uncommon for him to say "no" or become aggressive if things don't go his way. The only emotions he seems to show are happiness, excitement, and frustration. If Landon's teacher asks him about feeling sad or scared, he claims he doesn't feel those things. If he begins to cry, he is quick to hide his face or run out of the room. He rarely goes to his parents for comfort if he's hurt and tends to deal with things on his own.

Landon is an example of an avoidant attachment style. We nickname these children "cat children." If you have ever been around cats, you know they appear more independent than dogs. They march to the beat of their own drum. Some can be quite affectionate, but they can also claw and bite if they get too much affection or feel their space has been invaded. Their body language is often harder to read for most people than a dog's. While they need people, they often act like they don't. They are simply more solitary in nature. Parts of the cat's overall personality is reminiscent of your avoidant attachment style. These children don't appear to struggle with being independent, but they do struggle with their emotions, and they're more prone to default to anger than sadness or fear. Ironically, if we look at what is happening in their central nervous system, they actually experience more fear and anxiety than our kangaroo (ambivalent) children, but they don't display it outwardly. Studies have shown a child with an avoidant attachment has higher cortisol levels than children who are ambivalently attached. We like to call this good armor—they are excellent at hiding their emotions, but what's going on beneath the surface is anything but calm.

These children can be very challenging to discipline because they tend to act like they don't care, they don't ask for help (even when they need it), and they can become easily aggressive or angry, then retreat from you instead of moving toward you to deal with the issue. Unlike our golden retriever or kangaroo children, they lack the emotional vulnerability, big tears, physical affection, and softness that pulls out our nurturing side. They are more shut down and easily shut us out.

How does this happen?

As mentioned above, this attachment style is like armor for children. When parents or caregivers are largely emotionally unavailable or unresponsive, a majority of the time the child is too. These parents often demonstrate approval when the child plays, socializes, or achieves; however, when these children display what the parent perceives to be "negative emotions"—e.g., crying, feeling fear or anger—they are ignored or punished. This is likely because these emotional displays are often uncomfortable for these parents.

Children have an innate desire to be close and to be taken care of by the adults in their lives, and to maintain this closeness, they learn to suppress outward displays of emotion to adapt and to receive the approval and love they need from their parents. Using the analogy of the bucket, this child's bucket is turned upside down. They act like they don't have needs, but they are simply hiding their needs to stay connected to you.

What Do They Need to Move Toward Security?

These children need to know their emotions are safe. You need to work on validating their emotional experiences, naming emotions, and providing space for frustration. You have to try to gauge what stems beneath the surface with these children. Anger is usually a secondary emotion, meaning the true emotions of fear, sadness, and disappointment are at the heart of the matter. So when you go to "name the feeling," it might be a feeling that doesn't seem evident at first sight. For example, Tania was with one of her foster children, and he was experiencing overwhelming emotions. In a matter of minutes, his entire room had been destroyed as he poured water down an air vent. Tania mirrored back to him, "Jay, you must be feeling so sad right now." Jay looked at her and burst into tears and the destruction of the room stopped.

It doesn't always work so seamlessly, but often, if we can go to our own heart's center and connect with our child, it creates a shift in behavior. There are times when we may need to set a limit while creating space for an emotional experience. Maybe your younger son hit his older brother because he was worried that when they were wrestling, he would lose and become embarrassed. You might say, "I can see you were really overwhelmed by your brother. He is a lot bigger than you, and if he wins, that can make you feel really embarrassed. But I think maybe we need to think of some other ways to express our frustration."

Or your child lied and was caught. They deny doing it and show little emotion. Maybe this is because in the past, you would yell, and they don't want to evoke your anger. You might say, "I know telling the truth is hard because you worry I will yell. I want you to know I won't get angry if you tell the truth. I am going to try to do better, but I need us all to be honest with one another in this family so we can trust each other."

DISORGANIZED ATTACHMENT STYLE: PORCUPINE CHILDREN

Teresa is a little girl who tends to be in her own world much of the time. At day care, she is withdrawn and plays on her own much of the time. Her behavior confuses the staff as she cries when her mom leaves, but if the staff try to comfort her, she runs and hides.

Moses is a child who is very independent but appears callous. He seems to intentionally hurt other children to get a reaction from them. He also steals things from the teacher's desk and tends to lie if he's caught. He rarely demonstrates emotions or seems to form friendships.

Aria is a child who appears to easily attach to anyone around her. She prefers new people to her caregivers. Her parents communicate to the therapist that they fear she would go home with a perfect stranger.

The last of our three insecure attachment styles is often the most misunderstood and the most toxic: disorganized attachment. We call children who orient this way "porcupine children," as they are so difficult to form a relationship with. One foster mother described it to me as "hugging a porcupine." You want so badly to provide for your child what they need in the moment, but their responses toward you can make you want to pull away—it can feel very hurtful to care for these children.

These children just don't seem to have a healthy inner compass for forming healthy, reciprocal relationships, so they are "disorganized" in how they relate to caregivers and others around them. The way they present is varied and depends on the individual child, but some ways they may present include: consistently craving attention of caregivers, then frightfully respond to that attention with hiding or pushing the caregiver away; responding to the presence of their caregivers with tears, avoidance, etc.; nurturing others like a mother hen, but being unable to accept love or nurture themselves; or appearing antisocial, callous, and void of feelings.

How does this happen?

This often arises from a child being abused by a caregiver—emotionally, sexually, or physically. When a parent or caregiver is abusive, the child may experience the abuse and scary behavior as being life-threatening. The child is stuck in an awful dilemma: her survival instincts tell her to flee to safety, but safety may be in the very person who is frightening her. The attachment figure is the source of the child's distress. Ultimately, the child doesn't view the parent as a secure base because they cannot get their emotional or physical needs met. The child desperately tries to keep themselves safe in a world that has only ever been cruel.

What Do They Need to Move Toward Security?

These children need to feel safety—the kind that comes from consistency, predictability, and nurturance. They need to learn that people aren't going to hurt them, and it's safe to rely on adults in their life. This means setting up routines, ensuring we are predictable in our responses to them and that fear is not used as a discipline tactic. These children will often create chaos because their inner world is chaotic, and that is what is familiar to them. We have to repeatedly offer a new way of being calm, organized world where the child learns that they can rely on the steadfastness of their caregivers, that connection does not equal pain, that they can be vulnerable. After a child knows that feeling love is not a painful experience, that it is safe to trust their environment and those in it, the brain can begin to heal.

A BOAT ON THE WATER: A METAPHOR FOR MOVING TOWARD SECURE ATTACHMENT

If you have a little one with any of the three types of insecure attachment styles, we want you to know it is never too late to change that. Remember the brain has neuroplasticity, which means it can modify its connections and rewire throughout the life span. Repeated new experiences equal new connections, which equal new ways of relating. It is also possible for children's attachment style to vary from one caregiver to the next. So you might see your child behave one way with you and another way with a teacher or their other parent. Our goal is to see if we can foster that secure attachment with as many adults as possible in their life.

The Boat

Think about your child as a boat on the ocean on its way to a certain destination. Think of that destination as all the outcomes you want for your child. Most parents share that they want a child who is resilient, kind, happy, emotionally regulated, and self-sufficient. Now the journey to get to this point will have days where there is smooth sailing, days where there are waves, and days where there are hurricanes. Your child will still get to their destination as long as we're mindful of what they need to keep the boat afloat.

The Wind

Your job is to help your child keep sailing forward, to be the wind behind their backs. This involves our secure base checklist: proximity, acknowledgment, scaffolding skills, play, and managing our anxiety around their exploration of the world.

If we want our children to move mountains,
we first have to let them get out of their seats.

This requires the child to have connection but also autonomy; it's an interesting balance we have to strike. If we hold on too hard, they can't learn, move, or grow. Similarly, if we are frequently absent, distracted, or disengaged—they feel invisible and scared—they cling to us or numb out their feelings to cope with feeling alone.

The Anchor

Your child is new to this world, their toolbox is limited, and their brain has a long way to go in terms of development. The younger the child, the easier the boat rocks and becomes unstable. It's easy for a toddler to capsize.

Our job is to be an anchor for our children,
so when the waters are turbulent, they can stay afloat.

That means in the middle of a storm, we don't focus on the destination; we focus on preserving our child, and when things have settled, we return to sailing the course. Many parents get so focused on where they want their child to go, they forget to meet their child where they are at. An overwhelmed child cannot think straight, yet we expect them to stay on course during an emotional storm.

As an anchor, we need to be steady, predictable, and grounded in the moment to be a source of security for our children. This may mean co-regulating our children, gently but firmly setting limits, or providing an environment that is not a source of overwhelming waves that knock our children off course.

An anchor is only as strong as its ability to fasten securely into the ground. If you are not present, regulated, and in a place of connection with your child, it is very challenging to get your child back on course. The boat will remain unbalanced and prone to capsizing or sinking.

I have never met a child who wanted to be "bad." Children, like us, do the best they know how in the moment. Our primal and most urgent need is for belonging and connection, and the more disruptive the behavior or emotion, the more they need us in those moments. They are saying to you: "I'm drowning in emotion. I am overwhelmed, and I don't know how to do this without your guidance."

One of the greatest gifts we can give our children is our presence during hard moments.

Sometimes parents worry that if they connect with their child when they are struggling with a behavior or a "negative" emotional experience, that means "I accept your behavior." In reality, you're saying, "I accept your experience in this moment." True empathy is seeing the world as someone else sees it and accepting that they may feel differently from you, but still understanding how they could feel that way. Just because your child is in pain because of something you perceive to be trivial (i.e., they didn't get a turn on the swing at the playground) does not in any way make their pain any less real. Given their limited experience in this world and how vulnerable they are to big emotional storms, this experience hurts and feels unjust; it is significant to them. We ask you, in those moments, to join your child. Be with them and remember what it's like to feel seen, heard, and felt when you were in pain at some point in your life.

MIRROR NEURONS HELP ANCHOR OUR CHILDREN

Have you ever watched a movie in which someone has lost a loved one, and their tears bring tears to your own eyes? Have you ever felt thirsty after watching someone else take a sip of water? Have you ever watched one person's yawn set an entire group of people into yawning? Have you ever been to a sporting event in which the people in the audience cheer and holler, and when their team scores or a bad call is made by a referee, you could swear the goal or red flag impacted them personally? This is because of a group of neurons found in various parts of the brain called mirror neurons.

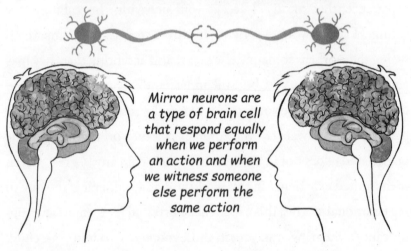

MIRROR NEURONS

Mirror neurons are a type of brain cell that respond equally when we perform an action and when we witness someone else perform the same action

The mirror neuron system directly links perception to action. Scientists believe the mirror neurons are the basis of learning in human beings. Mirror neurons allow us to learn through imitation—to reflect body language, facial expressions, and emotions. It's the monkey see, monkey do neurons—which is fitting since they were discovered by watching monkeys interact with one another.

Your mirror neurons fire when you observe someone else's behavior, and it feels as if that thing is happening to you. The same parts of your brain light up on an MRI scan as if you are completing the action you are watching. Why is this important to parenting? We are social beings. Our survival depends on our understanding the actions, intentions, and emotions of others.

Mirror neurons enable us to understand other people's minds, through conceptual reasoning and imitation—by feeling, not thinking. Children who feel connected to their caregiver will want to imitate them, and this imitation is needed for children to learn the skills—physical, cognitive, or emotional—required to be adaptive and resilient. We also believe that mirror neurons are fundamental to parenting because they are the foundation of empathy.

So much of what happens in relationships is about a process in which the emotional state of one person resonates in another. Children need to be able to understand their emotion, to understand the emotions of others. In order for them to know themselves, they first must feel seen, heard, and understood by their caregiver. You cannot teach empathy in a book. A story may strengthen empathy, but to foster empathy, a child must experience empathy.

EXAMPLE

Your two-year-old son is happily having a bath—splashing, giggling, and playing. You say it's time to get out, and you see a shift in your son. Tears come to his eyes, and he begins to cry—then a full meltdown ensues.

Here are two ways of responding. One activates the empathy centers, and one does not.

Activation

During his enjoyment of the bath, you say: "You're having so much fun! You look so happy in the tub" (mirroring enjoyment). When it's time to get out and he becomes distressed, you say, "You're so sad you have to get out of the tub. It's hard to stop playing when you're having fun" (mirroring his grief).

No Activation

During his enjoyment of the bath, you might say, "Honey, five more minutes, and then we have to get out." When it's time to get out and he becomes distressed, you say, "Oh sweetie, that's enough. I told you five minutes—that's enough."

If you can mirror your child's experience back to them (empathically reflect your child's emotions), this will activate and nurture the child's neuronal growth, and consequently, when your child sees another person in distress, they will know how they feel and are more likely to be compassionate. They understand when things don't go their way, or things have to end, they experience sadness or grief. This will resonate with them since they understand what that's like; they have walked a mile in that person's proverbial shoes. This increases the likelihood they will want to provide comfort to another person who is in pain.

Tantrums are never a fun thing for a parent, and they are much harder for some parents than for others; we will delve into this later in this book. Regardless, the takeaway for this section is that your child must feel accurately seen and understood by you in both the easy moments and the difficult moments. You need to be an accurate mirror reflection of their experience.

It is also important that you reflect your child's emotions not only with your words but also with your tone of voice and facial expressions. Much of what we communicate is nonverbal, so in the example above, it wouldn't work if your voice was angry and you had a scowl on your face as you said, "You're so sad." Those two things do not match. What's more likely is your child will mirror your nonverbal cues—your frustration—right back to you, and it will make the tantrum worse.

Often, this is what goes wrong during hard moments with our kids—if our emotions take over, they override our ability to be empathic. Inconsistency is often the source of misunderstanding between parents and children. The mirroring mechanism occurs much more quickly nonverbally than it takes to understand what someone is actually saying. When either the parent's emotional world is a bit of a mess, or the child feels the need to hide their emotions, neither person feels connected or understood. As a result, our children feel alone in their experience. This feeling of disconnection can result in a child acting out aggressively or pulling back and withdrawing.

A similar conflict can occur when the parent displays micro-expressions, which are fleeting facial expressions, of fear, anger, or disgust, which the child's mirror system detects, even though these aren't known to the parent or consciously processed by the child. Even if we try to hide it, our emotions tend to seep out. Children are sensitive to their caregiver's emotional state and quickly pick up on what's going on under the surface. To activate those mirror neurons and truly connect with our children, we have to put the oxygen mask on ourselves (more on this in a later chapter). We have to cultivate a deep understanding and inner awareness of our own emotional worlds to accurately connect with our child's. This is not always the most comfortable task, but a necessary one if you want to exercise compassion with your child.

You must be the calm you want to see in your child. If you have an angry or frustrated child, you do not want to meet them with anger and scream or shame them. Your tone must reflect their inner emotional state—a reflection of their frustration—and you may have to raise your voice enough so your child can still hear you amid the screams.

EXAMPLE

Your daughter is angry that her brother broke her Lego tower, and she comes to you in tears of frustration.

Mirroring

"Honey, I can see you're so frustrated your brother broke your tower! You worked really on that, didn't you?!"

This dance of attunement is a tricky one, especially when we are feeling emotional ourselves. Remember you cannot give your child what you don't have, so to be compassionate, you must also exercise this with yourself. You will never get this right every time, and we would never expect a parent to. This book was not written for "perfect parents." It was written for those who want to become better versions of themselves and who want to show up for their children.

We also want to note here that for highly sensitive children and those who are our little warriors with big personalities and really big feelings, simply naming the emotion can sometimes escalate them. What's important for these children is to high-light the quality and quantity of their emotional experience. For instance, a sensitive child who is angry with you won't be calmed by you simply naming their feeling—that feeling is so intense that the word "anger" doesn't come close to describing how unsafe their body feels.

They aren't struggling with floating in the water; they are in the deep end drowning in that feeling. In this case, you might try saying: "You are so angry it's as big as this entire room! You feel so mad maybe it's big as the entire house!" Or for a child who feels anxious you might not even name the feeling. You might just say, "Wow, I can see this is so hard for you, you feel like you can't even breathe. You just want to hide away till you feel safe. You just want it to go away." Focus on the overwhelm in lieu of simply stating the feeling.

But sometimes we are the storm

I learned this lesson the hard way when I was an elementary school teacher: the adult in charge is ultimately responsible for the emotional atmosphere of the room. If adults are a mess, the child is usually quick to follow suit. When we yell, criticize, belittle, become physically aggressive, or panic in front of our children, we have now moved from being an anchor to the hurricane that capsizes our children.

How can children learn to behave or regulate their emotions when the adults who are supposed to be leading them can't do the same? That's a tall order for our little ones.

How do we lead our children to a place of security if they are afraid of us? If we are to be their safe place, their anchor, we can't be the source of fear in their lives—we have to be a harbor of calm where they can rest.

There are a multitude of hurts and injustices that your child will experience. Your child will face rejection, cruelty, disappointments, failures, and loss at some point. Our hope is when they come home to you, they find refuge from not only the storms that exist within the outside world but also the storms that exist within themselves.

CHAPTER 3

Attachment **TOOLKIT**

WIND TOOLBOX
Play

- Every child needs ample time to play independently or with their siblings without the adults interfering.

- Spend time playing WITH your child utilizing our therapeutic play model (see Chapter 9).

- Parallel play can include your child helping you around the house. Young children naturally want to help.

- Ensure organized activities, sports, and screens do not replace child-directed play.

Coaching (Scaffolding)

- When your child is interested in something, allow them to try it first without your help. If they seem frustrated, empathize with them and then show them how to complete just one part of the skill. Let them practice that part independently, and then move on to the next part once they have it. Repeat until they can master the whole sequence.

- Allow them to struggle, fail, and figure it out by only providing assistance when absolutely necessary.

- Use words like: "You can do hard things" and "I believe in you, and I know you can figure this out."

- Remind your child that we learn the best when we make mistakes.

- Celebrate successes with specific language vs. vague language such as "good job." Focus on the effort it took to master the skill and the adversity they overcame. You could say: "You had such a hard time climbing the monkey bars. It was scary at first, but you kept trying until you figured it out. I am proud of you for not giving up!"

Physical Availability (proximity)

- Don't hover or helicopter; this makes children more anxious. Be near, but not so near that they can't move and explore on their own.

- Be accessible for when or if your child needs you.

- Let your kids know where you are if you aren't within eyesight, and pop in and check in on them sporadically with a hug or a kiss. You go to them (instead of only having your child seek you out).

- An insecure child will need more proximity than a secure child.

- If your child struggles with separating from you, engage in parallel activities nearby: cook, write, clean, and exercise. They will relax if they know that you are accessible.

- Celebrate accomplishments with specific language instead of vague language such as "good job." Focus on the effort instead of the outcome:

  - "I know math is really hard for you, but you stuck with it, and I can see you did much better this report card. How does that feel to see your grade improve?"

- "You figured that out!"
- "You did it!"

Acknowledgment

- **Empathy/right-brain connections:** Acknowledge their feelings regardless of the behavior you want or do not want to see. The emotion is always okay.

- Notice your child's quirks and talk to them about what you appreciate in them.

- Ensure you avoid sibling rivalry by doing these things with all your children.

- If you have a choice, choose to acknowledge positive changes your child makes rather than criticizing or shaming a child for the behavior you don't want to see.

Parental anxiety management

- Be the calm you want to see in your child

- Breathe

- Exercise

- Meditate or do yoga

- Imagine your child being safe

- Talk to someone when you feel overwhelmed

- Remind yourself that often children need to learn from the natural consequences of their actions; it's okay for them to experience pain

- Remind yourself that giving your child autonomy is a gift

ANCHOR TOOLBOX
Protection

- Keep them physically safe wherever possible (but still give them space to explore movement and their bodies to understand their limits through natural consequences).

- Have a zero-tolerance policy in your home for name-calling or physical aggression (i.e., hitting, spitting, kicking, biting).

- If your child cannot conduct themselves in a certain environment, it likely means they aren't ready to be in that environment until they have developed certain skills or are more mature. Rather than letting your child be wounded over and over, remove them from the situation until they're ready.

Co-regulation

- Stay with them during meltdowns until the storm begins to calm. If you have persistently tried to stay with them, and they STILL insist that you leave, stay close by, and check on them often. Let them know you're available and not going anywhere.

- Validate feelings when they come up—even the feelings that make us uncomfortable (i.e., anger) i.e., "You're so excited to go to the birthday party!" i.e., "I can see you're so frustrated it's time to go to bed."

- For our warrior children or highly sensitive children, describe how the feeling might feel for them; focus on their impulse to fight or run away while acknowledging how big that feeling is and how overwhelmed it makes them feel. Don't simply name the feeling; enter into it with them experientially.

Connection

- Spend quality, one-on-one time with your child each day, even if it's just for fifteen minutes.
- Get to know your child. How do they uniquely experience love? Look up Gary Chapman's *5 Love Language for Kids*.
- Cultivate screen-free time for your whole family (i.e., in my home, we have tech-free days, so no devices at mealtimes or after 6 p.m. unless it's a movie night).
- Develop special rituals that are unique for your family or for you and your child (i.e., family games nights, evening walks after supper, reading together before bedtime).

Self-awareness

- Journal about your emotions and triggers.
- If you are overwhelmed, speak to a counselor or therapist.
- Practice mindfulness to better understand how to work through your emotions using the present moment and your breath.
- When your child's behavior is upsetting, think of a time you were your best self as a parent. Try your best to get in touch with that part of yourself or imagine yourself as a child. What did you need in moments like this?
- When you notice yourself getting dysregulated, take a moment to yourself, away from your child, until you are calm. Ensure your child knows it's not a punishment and you'll be back in ___ minutes (make sure you come back!). If this is a strategy you plan to utilize, try talking to your child about your need to self-regulate prior to challenging moments. It is far easier for your child to comprehend what is happening in a challenging moment if it has been discussed calmly beforehand.

CHAPTER FOUR

REACTIVE PARENTING
Understanding & Healing Our Wounds

Tania and I have never met a parent who didn't love their child and want what was best for them. A lack of love is not the issue when it comes to parenting. Everybody has ghosts, past experiences that may have been counterintuitive to healthy development. We may have been taught to hide our tears to avoid shame, to lash out with anger when we felt scared to physically protect ourselves, or to avoid conflict in order to preserve our connection to our loved ones. Some of us have minor scars, while others carry the burden of grievous trauma. Without critical reflection of our early experiences, our past can unconsciously script our responses to our own children and loved ones, and then unhealthy patterns are passed down from one generation to the next.

MEMORY

Whenever we sit with new clients, one of the things we ask parents is how the child fared during their early years and if there was any adversity during this time, including the mother's birth. The common reaction is: "Does that really matter? My child wouldn't remember that anyway." This response does make a lot of sense—do you have many memories from early childhood, before the age of five? Probably not in the way most people perceive memory.

Most people think of memory as "the story of what happened to me." This is one type of memory known as explicit or autobiographical memory. It is all about what you saw, your feelings about the event, your thoughts, and interpretations, and it involves integration of the five senses. When you use this type of memory, you recall something from a specific moment in time, almost like watching a movie on a screen. You start to form this type of memory after age two, and fairly unreliably until after age five, but since the hippocampus—the associated part of the brain—is poorly developed in the early years, we can't coordinate all the pieces to create a story.

The other is known as implicit memory, which is more about what happens perceptually to us, which is why a lot of people call it muscle memory or body memory. When it is retrieved, it lacks an internal sensation of being recalled. It doesn't require conscious attention to encode it. This type of memory uses past experiences to help us remember things without thinking about them. For example, if you've ever learned to ride a bike and don't get back on for fifteen years, your body remembers how to push the pedals and balance. Another example would be how certain smells or tastes can bring you comfort without recalling any specific experience linked with it. I feel this way when I smell banana bread baking in the oven as I associate it with my mother's comfort and the feeling of being home.

You might wonder why memory is important in terms of parenting. Of course, you want your children to have positive memories of their childhood—that's a given. But we want you to understand how your memory system can interfere with or strengthen your ability to parent, as well as how you can cultivate a stronger bond with your children by understanding how memories are formed.

From the beginning of life, our brains are able to respond to experience by altering the connections among neurons, the basic building blocks of the brain. A phrase was coined by neuropsychologist Donald Hebb that illustrates our point beautifully: "Neurons that fire together, wire together." When neurons become active at the same time, links are made so that if a dog bites you when you hear fireworks, your mind associates both dogs and fireworks with pain and fear. While the fear of dogs may make sense to you as an adult, the fear of fireworks will likely seem irrational until you have examined the memory.

Similarly, in my example of banana bread, I have many positive memories of my mother growing up, and one of things she would often make is banana bread. My brain learned to associate my mother with the loaves baking in the oven. The original smell of banana bread isn't in itself an emotional experience—it's the affection, safety, and connection I felt when I was with my mother that coincided with the smell of banana bread. This created a link between them to make it emotional. Neurons that wire together do so because of what Dr. Eagleman calls timed activation; they become located close to one another and fire up at the same time.

This is exciting news for you as a parent. It means you can create a brain that's wired for compassion, positivity, and empathy. The more experiences we give a child in which these feelings occur, the more associations the brain makes, and the more resilient our children become. If you understand the notion of neurons that fire together, wire together, you become more conscious and deliberate in the experiences you give your child. When they see you, what associations have they made? Do they feel safe, heard, comforted, loved, and connected to? If your child is wired for these associations, then even in hard parenting moments, your child will default to their strongest connections. There will be moments where your child will be angry with you or disappointed, but those moments will not define your parenting experience.

This being said, sometimes we struggle with our parenting journey. Maybe your story is defined by more moments of hostility and conflict rather than that of connection. We want to give space for that. This doesn't mean you're a "bad parent"—chances are, you have had some pretty difficult moments in your life that simply interfere with your parenting. Unfortunately, this can mean that your child may associate you with fear, rejection, or disconnection. When this happens, discipline and daily interactions can feel like you're walking uphill until everything feels like a battle. Breathe in here. Hope is not lost.

This is where neuroplasticity comes in. Our brains are wired to change and adapt. The neural networks in our brains can change through growth and reorganization. It takes time to do this, and the younger the brain, the easier it is. However, regardless of your child's age, you can rewire their brain for more positive connections if you are intentional about the experiences you give them.

Exercise

When you interact with your child, pause and ask yourself this question before you offer any response: is what I'm about to say or do coming from a place of love and compassion or from a place of fear (i.e., anger, helplessness, guilt, inadequacy)?

The work of world-renowned American psychological research-ers Drs. John and Julie Gottman provides an interesting number for you to contemplate. In their work studying couples, they found that secure and healthy relationships have a ratio of five to one: five positive feelings/interactions for every negative interaction/feeling during conflict. Psychological wellness and harmonious par-ent-child relationships are nurtured when parents express positive feelings toward their children significantly more often than nega-tive expressions, such as scolding or criticism. When your words, emotions, and behaviors toward your child consistently convey the message "you are good, loved, and wanted," the child absorbs those feelings and develops an internal voice that consistently says, "I am good, I am lovable, I am wanted."

A positive sense of self buffers a child against many of the risks and dangers of being a child in this complicated time. It also allows children to rely on you as a compass to guide their behavior. Since they associate you with safety and acceptance, they are much more willing to accept your influence in all aspects of their life. In a recent interview with Jay Shetty in 2020, Dr. John Gottman high-lighted that in everyday interactions, outside of conflict, the ratio should increase to 20:1. That's a tall order for many of us, but these micro-positives do not need to be big-ticket items. A smile, laugh, snuggle, acknowledgment, or hug all count here.

Lastly and probably most importantly, we want to highlight how your own memories of your childhood can interfere with your par-enting. Many of our experiences with our children "activate" our own memories from childhood—the good and the bad. These can be implicit memories, which simply evoke a feeling or reaction, or explicit memories where we recall moments where we experienced something similar to our children. We will be doing a deeper dive into this in Chapter 5, but we want you to know that you are not alone if you feel triggered by your child. This is often your memory system being activated and there is a call for healing here—an opportunity for self-compassion.

As an example, we often see parents who find their child's crying to be intolerable. Crying is completely normal, and we are designed to be distressed by this, so we go to our children. However, if your child's crying feels intolerable and evokes a response that urges you to yell (fight), run away (flight), or check out (collapse), this typically signals that your own cries were ignored or punished. You were not met with the compassion and the attunement you needed. Herein lies the opportunity. You have the ability to make sense of this experience and to move forward with awareness and conscious intention—giving your child the gift of presence and empathy.

WHEN WE CAST OURSELVES AS VILLAINS

Rechelle was so excited to be a mom. She had a rough upbringing; her mother was an alcoholic who was emotionally abusive. Her father was distant and disengaged from his children. The only time she saw her parents engage was when they were fighting about money or her mother's drinking. Jane was lucky that when her parents divorced, her father remarried a kind woman whom Jane loved very much. While things were always strained with her father, she felt blessed that her stepmother had come into her life when she was a teen.

Rechelle knew she wanted to do things differently than her parents. She didn't want to scream or bring her children up in a home of chaos. So when she met her husband Dan, she truly hoped things could be different. While they had a peaceful five years before having children, things changed rapidly when their son Carson was born. Carson's screams made her want to run from the room, or she ignored them altogether. She struggled with postpartum depression and connecting with her son—at times she thought he would be better off without her.

As he got older, it became more challenging. She struggled with staying engaged with her son when he would cry or tantrum—sometimes she would yell, and other times, she would ignore him and lock herself in her room. She was plagued by thoughts about being a horrible mother, that she wasn't cut out to be a parent. Rechelle had always struggled with low self-esteem, trusting others, and she was well acquainted with anxiety and depression. She had thought she had that under control until she had children, but it just seemed to come back with a vengeance.

We all have a storyline that flows through our lives; it's shaped by our experiences, our interpretations of those experiences, and the voices of significant people in our lives. For some, this narrative is empowering. These kinds of people know their worth and are aware of the gifts they have to bring to this world—particularly when it comes to raising their children. While they are not self-assured all the time, deep down, they know their lives are meaningful and they have something to offer their children. Chances are, when they were growing up, they had significant adults in their corner who taught them to love and respect themselves, showed them compassion and respect, and helped form a lens in which they could see the inherent good in others and the world.

Unfortunately, this is not always the case for so many parents. Many parents feel trapped by the voice in their mind that tells them they are unlovable, not good enough, or broken, while others are scary and untrustworthy. Those adults often see circumstances as threatening and worry about what they stand to lose rather than feeling grateful for what they have. Emotions can be difficult, overwhelming, and burdensome. If this sounds like you, please understand that this is not who you are but a story someone long ago started writing for you. Maybe it was an abusive family member, a dismissive parent, the school bully, or another trauma you endured as a child. We do our best to adapt from adversity, but sometimes these negative childhood experiences shape our behavior to such an extent that, without our awareness, they start to become "who we are," and our life story becomes written for us, not by us.

Many of us are trapped in our childhood wounds, and while we thought we could bury them, they often rear their ugly heads once we have our own children. The little child in you comes back and reminds you of your pain. Your children's cries may feel unbearable, their tantrums can enrage you, and you may find yourself speaking in the same unkind words your father spoke—despite swearing up and down to yourself that you would never do that to your children.

A childhood in which you experienced your caregivers as unresponsive or inconsistent, or where your needs went unmet altogether, will influence your response to your children's pain. Recent brain imaging studies comparing the brain reactions of parents with secure versus insecure adult attachment show differences in brain activity when listening to recordings of their children crying. Parents who experienced a secure attachment in their own childhood appear to activate their reward pathways in response to the sounds of distress, making it easier to move toward their child and provide comfort. Insecurely attached parents show a more complicated pattern of brain activity in which they appear to activate conflicting systems of approach and avoidance. Part of them wants to comfort their child, while part of them is highly stressed by their child's distress, which makes them want to pull away. We carry our attachment styles into adulthood, so in other words, a healthy attachment style drives a parent to care for their child, and providing that comfort to a crying infant is gratifying. An insecure attachment style may drive a parent to go to their distressed children but also send them into a flight response—you experience your child's distress as a threat. A part of you knows you need to be the calm, but part of you feels like you are under siege.

Parents who spent much of their own childhood in a state of protection, experiencing adults as scary or not meeting their needs, are more likely to perceive hard moments with their children as threatening, making connection more difficult. These parents' amygdalas, especially on the right side of the brain, are likely to be enlarged and exquisitely sensitive to potential threats compared to those parents who grew up in a nurturing environment. Other regions of the brain that are essential to staying calm and grounded shrink from exposure to chronic or acutely excessive stress.

A parent with a history of developmental trauma is more likely to personalize the experiences of a child acting out rather than understanding that the child's behavior has more to do with a natural expression of emotion or developmentally appropriate limit testing. They may feel like the child is doing it intentionally or that they are a bad parent. It is difficult to be our best selves if we assume our child's behavior reflects who we are—particularly for those parents who look at themselves in the mirror each morning and despise who they see.

If you recall, earlier in this chapter, we discussed how memories are stored both explicitly and implicitly. Often when you find yourself disengaged or in battle with your child, it is because you are battling with yourself and your implicit memory system. When these memories are triggered, just like your child who cries because they do not want a certain outcome, you default to your emotional brain and body brain. Dr. Daniel Siegel and Dr. Tina Payne Bryson would say you "flip your lid," and as the compassionate, logical part of your brain loses its ability to steer the ship, you are hijacked by the emotional brain. You become the storm. You may yell, criticize, shut down, resort to physical punishment—most likely whatever was modeled to you as a child. This sends you further into self-contempt and shame because you feel like a failure as a parent. You become the person you never wanted to be.

When we become triggered by our parenting, we become flooded by feelings such as fear, sadness, or rage. Intense emotions can lead you to have knee-jerk reactions instead of intentional responses. It makes it difficult to maintain nurturing communication and connection with your child. When parents carry their difficult experiences from childhood into their own parenting, they may behave in ways that are alarming for their children. Parents with unresolved, stress-inducing memories from their past or parents who are experiencing current high levels of stress are likely to express this in ways that are primarily nonverbal while interacting with their children. These include avoiding eye contact, a negative tone of voice, closing off their body, and leaving their child alone to deal with hard emotions.

This kind of communication leaves a child feeling scared, confused, and on guard. A child will often mirror the parent's stress or rejection, which then triggers the parent to move further into their defensive position, which intensifies the negative dance of dysregulation for both the child and parent. Both feel alone and broken—nobody wins. Brain imaging studies show feeling this kind of rejection from our children activates the same pattern in the brain as feeling physical pain. In other words, emotional pain and physical pain are processed similarly in the brain.

Being rejected by your child is painful, but that voice—that negative emotional current of shame that follows you like a dark shadow—can be changed. You have the power to rewrite your story and give yourself a new, hopeful ending.

CALMING YOUR OWN STORM: HEALING EXERCISES FROM THE THERAPY ROOM

Rome was not built in a day. Changing our patterns of behavior and thinking takes time and focused effort, so be gentle with yourself if you are embarking on this journey into self-healing. What we want you to be able to do is engage the part of the brain that manages reflection and logic—your thinking brain. This is where your empathy and reasoning skills lie. Here are some things you can do to help calm your storm and become more compassionate with yourself, as well as your child.

Become an Observer

The ACT (anterior cingulate cortex) is in charge of the processing of pain, as well as negative, rigid thinking. If this part of your brain lights up you are more likely to be flooded with negative thoughts about yourself and your child.

> "If I don't get this child under control, he'll turn into a spoiled brat."
> "I am the worst mom in the world—I'm turning into my mother."
> "Why does it always have to be like this?"

"I just yelled again; my kids are going to hate me."

"How dare she take that tone with me; I'll show her."

"After all that I do for them, they can't even listen this one time. They are such entitled children. I need to fix this now."

Do any of these sound familiar? These are the thoughts that come from our pain. The stories we tell ourselves about our parenting and about our children when we feel triggered. They are not true.

Pay attention to the thoughts that arise when you are feeling triggered during your difficult parenting moments. Don't judge them—that just makes them worse. Make space for them. Imagine you are observing your thoughts as a third-party bystander. Maybe you can't do this in the moment but can do this after the fact—that's fine too. What we are about to describe next are a series of exercises. We suggest taking your time with these. If you are working through complex childhood trauma (i.e., sexual abuse), we suggest you work with a mental health professional directly.

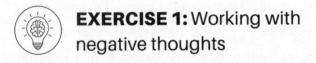

EXERCISE 1: Working with negative thoughts

What are the thoughts you have about yourself or your child when you are at your boiling point? When we are in pain our brains naturally exaggerate the thoughts until they can become cognitive distortions (i.e., "my son NEVER listens to me" or "If I don't get this under control my child will end up being a criminal!"). These questions, or a variation of these questions, are often used in Cognitive

Behavioral Therapy, or Dialectical Behavioral Therapy, and can also be found embedded in the innovative work of author Byron Katie.

Once you know what they are, try these five steps:

1. Is that thought true? Can you be 100% sure that thought is true?
2. Who are you with that thought?
3. Who are you without it?
4. Think of the opposite thought: Is that thought true? Is there evidence substantiating that thought?
5. Now name the more accurate thought and notice how it makes you feel.

EXAMPLE

You're exhausted and have had a horribly stressful day and your child is throwing a tantrum AGAIN because you won't give them a sugary snack before dinner. You think, "My son is always so angry; I can't handle this!"

1. Is that thought true? Are you 100% sure that thought is true? No, my son is not always angry. Just this morning he was so wonderful getting ready for day care. And he was so goofy on the drive home.

2. Who are you with that thought? I feel like a bad mom.

3. Who are you without it? A tired mom.

4.   Think of the opposite thought: Is that thought true? Is there evidence that substantiates that thought. My son is not angry all the time (list times in your mind he is sweet, kind, silly, affectionate, etc.).

5.   Now name the more accurate thought and notice how it makes you feel. My son is angry in this moment because he's hungry and he's been away from me all day—his cup is empty. I'm struggling because I'm tired too. In fact, I would love to have a good cry right now too. I need rest and he needs connection and food.

 EXERCISE 2: Get reacquainted with your inner child

1.   Ask yourself how your own parents dealt with you when you were struggling with big feelings. Did they yell? Spank? Shame you? Walk away?

2.   How did their response make you feel? Did it cause you to fear them? Resent them? Respect them? The answer doesn't have to be negative. Maybe your parent's response was warranted, and you felt safer because of the limits they set. But there is a chance it's not how you wanted them to deal with the situation.

3.   What did you need, in that moment? What did that little girl or boy need from their parent? What do you wish they had done differently?

4.   Think of a hard parenting moment you've had recently.

EXERCISE 3: Calm your own nervous system

Learn how to calm the reactive parts of your brain to gain access to the thinking brain before you respond to your child. We want to engage the parasympathetic nervous system—the brakes of the brain and the system that helps to calm us. You will then see a reduction in stress hormones such as cortisol and adrenaline, which will make you less reactive and more flexible.

Ideas:

- Reach out to your village: Engage with another adult whom you are connected with who has a calming presence on you. The ventral branch of the vagal: this is the branch that serves the social engagement system. The ventral vagal nerve dampens the body's regularly active state.

- Move your body: This releases GABA, the inhibitory neurotransmitter that inhibits activity in your nervous system. The more large muscle groups you incorporate, the better. Push-ups, running on the spot, stretching, walking, etc.— whatever gets the job done.

- Breathe through your stomach or diaphragm: This stimulates the vagus nerve, which also helps with regulation. Ten breaths won't do; you need to give yourself at least ten minutes, if at all possible. Always breathe in through your nose, out through your mouth. The out breath should be one or two seconds longer than the in breath. It may also help to listen to a guided mindfulness or meditation app when you are doing this.

- Remove yourself from the situation and listen to calming music for five minutes to inhibit the production of stress hormones.

- Cold water: I often suggest this to people with PTSD or to those who are struggling with panic attacks. Fill up a sink with cold water. Take a deep breath in through your nose, and place your face underwater for the out breath, exhaling through both your nose and mouth. I recommend you do this for a full five minutes.

- Screaming: This can be cathartic as long as it isn't directed at someone else. We recommend going into your vehicle or doing this into a pillow.

 EXERCISE 4: Processing

The next exercise combines some processing strategies from EMDR therapy (a popular type of trauma treatment I am trained in) and Kim Payne's Compassionate Response Meditation. We highly recommend his book *Being at Your Best When Your Kids Are at Their Worst*, in which Kim has a wealth of knowledge regarding parent emotion regulation.

If you prefer guided mindfulness and you have the paperback version of this book, go to **myparentinghandbook.com/ch4audio**, where you can find a recorded audio guide to walk you through each step.

Positive Memory Installation 1

Find a moment alone in which you can engage in this exercise first to solidify a positive memory.

Step 1: Sit back in a comfortable position, and practice deep breathing for five to ten minutes. You can also engage in a guided meditation or mindfulness of your choosing.

Step 2: Now, imagine a moment in which you were your best self as a parent—when you and your child were synchronized, connected, happy, and peaceful. Watch this moment play out almost as if you were watching it on a big screen. Watch yourself engage with your child like you are a third-party observer. As you recall this memory, pay close attention to what you see, smell, hear, and feel.

Sensations Connected to This Memory:

Step 3: Notice how that feels in your body and what emotions arise. When I think of this memory, I feel _____, and I can feel it in my _____ (where in your body).

Step 4: What thoughts come to mind when you think about this memory. Formulate a concrete positive and empowering thought that starts with "I am _____" (i.e., I am competent, I am strong, I am kind, I am a good mother). When I think of this memory: "I am _____."

Step 5: Engage in the "butterfly hug" for twenty seconds as depicted below. As you recall the memory, state the "I am" statement from above, either in your mind or out loud, and tap for twenty to thirty seconds.

Give myself a butterfly hug using alternate hand taps
(Left, right, left, right)

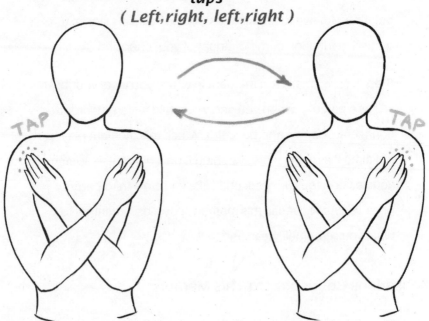

Imagine that your hands are a butterfly,
flapping one wing, then the other.

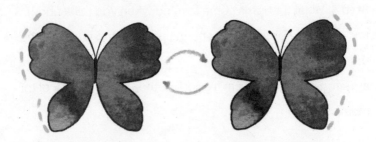

Positive Memory Installation 2

Step 1: Sit back in a comfortable position, and practice deep breathing for five to ten minutes.

Step 2: Imagine a time where your child was their best self. A moment where you felt proud, content, or simply connected to them. Maybe it's when they are playing joyfully, snuggling before bed, a memory from a family vacation you cherish, or the thought of them engaged in their favorite activity. Like watching a film on the big screen at a movie theater, watch this memory play out. Watch yourself engage with your child like you are a third-party observer. As you recall this memory, pay close attention to what you see, hear, and feel.

Sensations connected to this memory:

Step 3: Notice how that feels in your body and what emotions arise. When I think of this memory, I feel _____, and I can feel it in my _____.

Step 4: What thoughts come to mind when you think about this memory? Formulate a concrete thought that starts with "My child is _____" (i.e., my child is kind, loving, creative, compassionate, talented). When I think of this memory: I think "My child is _____."

Step 5: Engage in the "butterfly hug" as depicted above for twenty seconds. As you recall this memory, say the "my child is _____" statement from above in your mind or out loud.

Working Through a Shameful Parenting Memory

Step 1: Now think of a memory where you were your worst self as a parent. A memory you wish you could go back and change. Maybe you are yelling at your child for not cleaning up their playroom or shaming them for not doing well on a test at school. As you think about this memory, pay close attention to how you feel, both in your body and your emotions. Like watching a film on the big screen at a movie theater, watch this memory play out. Watch yourself like you are a third-party observer. Notice what you hear, see, and feel as you watch this memory unfold.

Sensations connected to this memory:

Step 2: Notice how the sensations feel in your body and what emotions arise. When I think of this memory, I feel _____ and I can feel it in my _____.

Step 3: What thoughts come to mind when you think about this memory? (They are probably not true, but be honest about what judgments arise.) Formulate a concrete thought that starts with: "I am _____" (i.e., a bad mom, just like my dad, mean, a failure).

Step 4: Now scale that feeling from zero to ten, with zero being "the memory doesn't bother me at all" and ten being "the memory is very upsetting." My number is _____.

Step 5: Now think of installation 1. As you think about the negative parenting memory, switch the picture on the screen to that of the positive one where you are your best self as a parent. Think of how that memory feels in your body and the positive emotion that washes over you as you watch the memory play out. Recall the powerful positive thought associated with the memory (i.e., "I am competent" or "I am compassionate.")

Step 6: Engage in the butterfly hug as depicted for twenty seconds. Once you recall the memory, in your mind, or out loud, state the positive statement you chose from the above installation (i.e., "I am competent"). When I think of this memory, I think: "I am _____." (Butterfly hug twenty seconds)

Step 7: Now take a deep breath in. Now recall the negative memory again, and give it a number to indicate how distressing it is. My number is _____.

Step 8: If your number is above two, recall the negative memory again, and switch to your positive one. Go through steps 5 through 7 again until the distressing feelings are reduced to a zero or one.

Step 9: Once you are at a zero or one, engage in the butterfly hug again for twenty seconds. Imagine yourself engaged in the same situation with your child, but this time, you do something different. Add the same positive thought you had before and tap for twenty seconds. Notice how the new situation feels in your body and the emotions that arise. When I think of this memory, I feel _____, and I can feel it in my _____.

Working Through a Triggering Behavior

Step 1: Now recall a memory in which your child was on their worst behavior. Maybe your child was having a horrible tantrum at the grocery store, yelling "no" at you, or had broken a beloved object in your home. As you think about this memory, pay close attention to how you feel, both in your body and your emotions. Like watching a film on the big screen at a movie theater, watch this memory play out. Watch yourself like you are a third-party observer. Notice what you hear, see, and feel as you watch this memory unfold.

Sensations connected to this memory:

Step 2: Notice how that feels in your body and what emotions arise. When I think of this memory, I feel _____, and I can feel it in my _____.

Step 3: What thoughts come to mind when you think about this memory. (They are probably not true, but be honest about what judgments arise.) Formulate a concrete thought that starts with "My child is _____," (i.e., challenging, driving me crazy, stressing me out). When I think of this memory, I think: "My child is _____."

Step 4: Now scale that feeling from zero to ten, with zero being "the memory doesn't bother me at all" and ten being "the memory is very distressing." My number is _____.

Step 5: Now think of installation 2 above. As you think about the challenging behavior memory, switch the picture on the screen to that of the positive one where your child is their best self (for example, my son is sharing his toys with his little sister, and they are laughing and playing without fighting). Think of how that memory feels in your body (i.e., "I feel a warm sensation near my heart"). Let the positive emotion wash over you as you watch the memory play out (i.e., grateful or happy). Recall the powerful positive thought associated with the memory (i.e., "My child is so loving").

Step 6: Engage in the butterfly hug for twenty seconds. As you recall the memory, state the positive statement from installation 2, in your mind or out loud. When I think of this memory, I think: "I am _____." (Butterfly hug twenty seconds)

Step 7: Now take a deep breath in. Now recall the negative memory again and give it a number to indicate how distressing it is. My number is _____.

Step 8: If your number is above two, recall the negative memory again, and switch to your positive one. Go through steps 5 through 7 again until the distressing feelings are reduced to a zero or one.

Step 9: Once you are at a zero or one, engage in the butterfly hug for twenty seconds. Imagine yourself engaged in the same situation with your child, but this time you do something different. Add the same positive thought you had before, and tap for twenty seconds. Notice how the new situation feels in your body and the emotions that arise. When I think of this memory, I feel _____, and I can feel it in my _____.

In the future when you are presented with a situation that is triggering you, all you need to do is ground yourself and think of that moment when you were your best self as a parent or when your child was their best self, and recall the specific powerful thought associated with it to help de-escalate yourself or at least inhibit you from engaging in the behavior you want to change.

What we want you to take away from this chapter is how our memories, experiences, thoughts, and personal narratives impact our ability to parent. While it's probably easy to accept and understand the reasoning for your child's behavior, we often neglect to take the time to get to know the "why" we parent as we do.

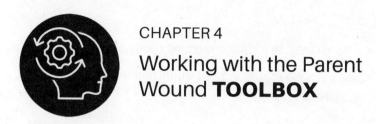

CHAPTER 4

Working with the Parent Wound **TOOLBOX**

Thought stopping

- Ask yourself if this is about your history or your child's actual actions in this moment (i.e., Am I uncomfortable with their crying because my parents shamed me for crying?)
- Question your thoughts; search for evidence that substantiate the thoughts—can you be sure this thought is true?
- Try a thought that's the opposite and see how that fits.
- Who are you with the thought?
- Who would you be without the thought?
- Reframe the thought to allow for compassion for your child and yourself.

Reach out to your village

Engage with another adult with whom you are connected who has a calming presence on you. This activates the ventral branch of the vagal; this is the branch that serves the social engagement system. The ventral vagal nerve dampens the body's regularly active state.

Exercise

- Releases GABA to turn off the cortisol production
- Releases mood regulating neurotransmitters such as dopamine and serotonin

Engage the vagus system

- Deep breathing
- Yoga
- Mindfulness

Cold

- Submersion in cold water (face or body)
- Walk in the cold air
- Sip cold water

CHAPTER FIVE

REFRAMING DISCIPLINE

Jennifer, a mom in her thirties with three boys, sat in my office looking utterly exhausted as she slumped on the couch. She worked full-time, as did her husband. With a business and busy household, she found it hard to keep up.

Most of the time she felt like she was balancing the role of the judge, the jury, and the executioner in her home—none of which she enjoyed. She described her boys as battling for her attention or battling each other—sometimes literally. The eldest was smart and sociable with other children but oppositional with her, her husband, and nearly every adult. Everything felt like a battle, and no amount of negotiating, bribing, time-outs, or yelling seemed to work.

Jennifer said, when it came to her eldest, she felt like her worst self as a parent. Her younger two are a little easier. The middle child was kind and sensitive but demanded her constant attention. He clung and fussed over everything; tattling and tears became her soundtrack to parenting him. The youngest was more mischievous but more carefree than the older two. While he seemed to be less emotional, she experienced him as impulsive and destructive. He spent more time in time-outs for breaking things around their house than playing with his brothers.

Jennifer came to me to learn how to effectively manage their behaviors and reduce the hostility in their home. I asked her a question I ask almost any parent that I work with: "What does discipline mean to you?" Her response was similar to many parents we work with: "It means to take something away or scare enough so they learn a lesson and know who's the boss."

Does Jennifer's exhaustion resonate with you? When you think of why you may have decided to pick up this book, the words "how do I discipline my child effectively" may have crossed your mind. We want you to ask yourself the same question as I asked Jennifer in my office: What does discipline mean to you?

For some parents, words like time-outs, sticker charts, grounding, taking things away, or yelling may come to mind. For a large majority of the world, discipline is code for punishment—inflicting some discomfort or pain to get a child to comply or change their behavior. For my parents and grandparents, spanking, the belt, or a switch were not uncommon, even in schools. I know I was spanked and even slapped on one occasion as a child. However, this was what parents were taught to do. This was the norm. And in many parts of the world it is still the norm.

We are not here to chastise or judge your parents or how they raised you. This was what they knew, and they did their best with the limited tools and knowledge they had. Maybe you're thinking:

See, you're like me. You were spanked, and you turned out just fine. We hear that more often than we like to from parents, and we like to offer this analogy:

For decades, we drove vehicles without seat belts. Did everyone who rode in a vehicle without a seat belt end up dying or suffering a brain injury from an accident? No. Did more people die or suffer injuries before seat belts? Absolutely. When the research came out that demonstrated the preventive nature of seat belts, they mandated them.

We live in a golden age where we have concrete research available at our fingertips to do better by our children. Thanks to fifty-plus years of research, we now know how harmful spanking and corporal discipline is on the brains and psychological well-being of children, so it is no longer encouraged and in many cases is illegal. When we learned not wearing a seat belt could be harmful, we changed our laws—we did better as a society. When you know better, you do better.

We will assume every parent wants to do better by their child. The following three chapters aim to teach you a new way to view discipline, to provide you with tools to guide your child in a compassionate way through difficult moments at all stages of development, while always honoring your relationship with them.

PHYSICAL PUNISHMENT

While this form of discipline (i.e., spanking, paddling) was common for centuries, we know that spanking and hitting children is ineffective and proves extremely damaging to children's development and emotional health. These consequences can be far-reaching and have lasting effects that include increased aggression, antisocial behavior (criminal behavior and delinquency), disruptions in moral development, and the onset of depression and anxiety disorders. What might also be surprising to some parents is that, in the long term, spanking is associated with less compliance than other forms of discipline.

Physical discipline has an adverse impact on the brain. One study points to a change in neurological functioning in response to perceived environmental threats compared to children who were not spanked. Their findings demonstrated that spanked children exhibited greater brain response, suggesting that physical discipline can alter children's brain function in similar ways to severe forms of maltreatment. Physical discipline has also been shown to reduce gray matter in the brain. Gray matter is the connective tissue found between brain cells that is essential for healthy neurological development. It plays an essential role in emotions, intelligence, learning, speech, muscle control, and memory. The United Nations Committee on the Rights of the Child issued a directive in 2006 calling physical punishment "legalized violence against children" that should be eliminated in all settings through "legislative, administrative, social and educational measures." Thankfully, we are seeing a decline in the use of such punishment.

The core of this issue, as it pertains to the child-parent relationship, is that when we choose to become a source of both love and fear, we create a paradox—a puzzle the child cannot solve. How are you supposed to be the person they turn to for comfort when you are also a source of fear? Now if discipline is all about teaching our children, what is the lesson they have really learned from being spanked?

"It's okay to be physical with people when we're angry."

"Two wrongs make a right. Physical aggression should be met with physical aggression."

Remember, to be an impactful and effective parent, we must be the calm. We are meant to be a harbor of safety—not the storm.

YELLING

My father was a recovering alcoholic, and without whiskey numbing him out, the mood swings were completely unpredictable. Whenever we'd hear the back door slam shut, my whole body tensed up, and I would run to my room. I don't even recall what he would yell about—all I knew was the fear I felt. How he would cower over us and how his screams seemed to echo off the walls in our small farmhouse. I loved my father very much, but I was terrified of him when he was in a bad mood. His anger and harsh words are the reason I still freeze if I encounter another adult who demonstrates that kind of hostility. I feel like a little girl again. I can't speak; I can't even move. I become powerless and helpless.

What you do speaks so loudly that I cannot hear what you say.
—RALPH WALDO EMERSON

We believe yelling is often a last resort for parents and not necessarily an intentional discipline strategy. It's a result of the parents' own dysregulation; it comes from a place of futility. It's what we grasp at when nothing else seems to work and sends us into a shame spiral after the dust has settled.

Shouting may have replaced hitting in many households, but the long-lasting effects are worryingly similar.

Yelling at children creates a similar impact in the brain to hitting; it creates a fear response, which can cause children to comply. This compliance comes at a cost. Research shows us that children who are subjected to yelling have lower self-esteem, higher rates of depression, and increased aggression.

You also run the risk of moving to a trajectory of escalation: the more you yell, the more desensitized your child becomes; essentially, increased amounts of yelling are required to get the same response. If a painful stimulus is applied frequently and predictably, a child eventually learns to tune out and numb out from the pain of the yelling and develops tolerance. This only intensifies the frustration you feel as a parent, and it decreases the overall effectiveness of your discipline.

TIME-OUTS AND OTHER FORMS OF SEPARATION-BASED DISCIPLINE

Since the mid-1990s, with the movement away from physical discipline, we have seen a surge of parents who utilize "time-outs" as a form of discipline. If you aren't familiar with this strategy, it is where you have a child sit in isolation until they calm down or think about what they did. We see two errors right off the bat: 1) Children, especially young children, do not self-regulate effectively, if at all; they need co-regulation with a safe adult to help soothe their limbic system. 2) Young children do not have a reflective capacity to consider how their actions are impacting others or how they will modulate their behavior in future. This sophisticated cognitive skill is not developed until the cortical brain starts developing and specializing. You know that isn't until much later—after the age that a time-out would be typically employed.

Now we are not here to argue with whether time-outs do or do not work. We have seen them work for some children, but probably not for the reasons those parents want them to. It's common knowledge that separation from a caregiver during times of distress actually increases anxiety, and the act of demanding they leave a caregiver's presence would also register for many children as rejection. In terms of what occurs in the human brain, rejection registers quite similarly to physical pain. Thus, we have a child with increased levels of anxiety and one who is likely motivated to decrease the pain they feel from the parental rejection. This would motivate many children to change their behavior.

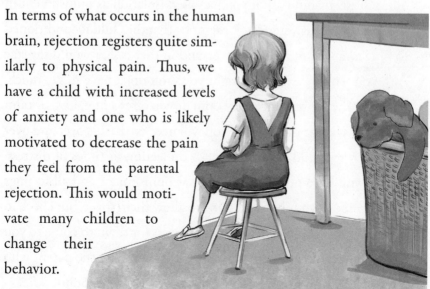

We are using our child's biggest fear against them—fear of separation and disconnection from the parent. This is a primal response. Children know we are their source of love, shelter, protection, and nurturance. When we forcibly separate them from us when they misbehave, we create an innate fear that 1) their needs might not be met; 2) love is contingent upon "good" behavior; 3) their emotions are not welcome and cannot be tolerated. They conclude: I must hide my feelings from my parent to receive approval and love. We highly doubt any parent wants to convey these messages to their children. We also run the risk of developing an avoidant attachment style, which will cause children to hide their feelings from their caregiver rather than risk punishment.

Now, we get asked this question a lot: "My child wants to be alone when they are upset; should I not allow them time to calm down if they ask for it?"

I would respond with a follow-up question if you were sitting in my office. First, I would ask if you had used isolation as punishment in the past. If the answer is yes, it might be that the child is conditioned to hide away from their caregiver, and in that case, I would say stay with your child even if they fight you. You don't have to say much, but sit in the room. Once they calm down, offer a hug, kiss, or calm words. To change that wiring, you will need to do this over and over to show your child it's safe to seek connection in times of distress. Now if you have not used isolation as punishment and all feelings are welcome in your home, it's fine to allow them space, but check in on them every few minutes, and don't wait for them to come to you to reconnect. When there is a rupture, it should be the parent who seeks connection from the child, not the other way around.

Think of it this way: Imagine you are furious with your partner, and you have a big fight. You go to your best friend's house for support. When you get there, you still feel very upset. You're saying some not-so-nice things about your partner, your voice is elevated, and you might be using colorful language. As your friend allows you to finish, she turns to you, looks you right in the eye, and she says, "I don't think that language or tone is appropriate; I want you to go into my guest room to calm down. Don't come out until you're ready to speak like a calm, rational person!" Can you imagine how that would make you feel? Yet we use this logic with our children all the time.

GROUNDING AND TAKING THINGS AWAY

Speaking as someone who spent a large portion of the tenth grade being grounded for a variety of transgressions—and after examining research on grounding—I can verify that this is an ineffective strategy. Not that grounding can't be used, but under most circumstances, it's used ineffectively and inappropriately. Often, parents utilize these strategies to create pain for a child so they won't engage in a behavior.

But remember, you want to teach a skill, not hurt your child. When we chronically use pain to get what we want from our children, they start to emotionally harden and resent us. If you have a teen, I assure you they aren't sitting in their room thinking how to rectify the situation; they're stewing in their room, thinking about how unfair you're being. What we don't want for you is to foster oppositionality or rebellion in your child, and these strategies can create the perfect storm for that.

Now if grounding or taking things away are used as logical consequences and for short-term purposes (I always recommend never more than one day in duration), it could work—but that means this consequence is related to the offense—it has to make sense to the child why you employed it. This includes taking away technology. If we take away our teen's phone or Xbox for every infraction, the consequence eventually loses its impact. Initially, it is a power move by the parent to take away a child's screen, but eventually the tables turn. Our clinical work has taught us that teens always outsmart their parents when it comes to technology. They use a friend's phone, have a hidden extra charger, or utilize school resources. Technology should only be removed when it is directly related to your teen's behavior.

EXAMPLE 1

Your daughter breaks curfew, so the next night, they don't get to go out or they have to come home much earlier than their curfew.

EXAMPLE 2

Your son hits their sibling with a toy, so the toy is gone.

EXAMPLE 3

Your teen spends all night on their phone. The phone is removed.

All of these consequences are related to the behavior. There is a rational link between the behavior and the consequence.

REFRAMING BEHAVIOR

Have you heard any of these statements?

- "Your child is just manipulating you."
- "Just ignore them; they're looking for attention."
- "Time-outs force children to think about what they did wrong."
- "You need to show them who's boss or they'll walk all over you!"
- "If you give a child attention when they're having a melt-down, you're reinforcing the behavior."

What all these statements have in common is: "Children are inherently bad, deceptive, and manipulative." When this is the underlying narrative that guides our discipline and overall parenting, we are defensive, harsh, and punitive. We are scared, and we parent from a place of fear.

We are scared we will be judged as a bad parent; fearful our children will become spoiled; terrified that they won't turn out the way we had dreamed; afraid we will lose control. How we perceive our children determines how we relate to them and scripts our responses, especially under times of stress. If our perception is stained by fear, we will act harshly. Our anxiety will trigger us to try to regain control at all costs.

However, control is an illusion. You cannot "control" a child. You can overpower a child, break their spirit, and scare them into temporary compliance, but control implies you can police their every move or mold them into doing exactly what you want in each moment. We believe parents who fall into the mindset of control set themselves up for failure.

Your child is their own person with a unique set of experiences, thoughts, feelings, and a journey that differs from yours. They need to forge their own path in life, be allowed to make mistakes, to feel every emotion, and to know all the while they can lean on us for support. It is our privilege to walk that journey alongside them.

KIDS DO WELL IF THEY CAN

Many of us are taught to believe children lack the will to behave well, but science has taught us that they lack the skill to behave well.

Whether this is a social, cognitive, or emotional skill that is missing, they do the best they can. This mindset changes everything. You no longer see the child as manipulative or deceptive but in need of assistance in growing as a human being.

Children often experience a sense of overwhelm in their bodies; their brains and nervous systems are still under construction. This overwhelm may be caused by a lack of connection, sensory overload, too many transitions, or an underdeveloped thinking brain. Children often communicate their struggles through "misbehavior" or meltdowns. The fight-flight-freeze-collapse stress response is responsible for a bulk of issues pertaining to discipline issues in children, and so much of this is out of a child's hands if their lower brain regions are hijacking the logical parts of the brain.

A child's emotional life is like a digestive system. The system extracts nutrients from food and not a thought goes into it. They are nourished, but not everything they eat can be digested. The body takes what it needs and has a disposal system for the rest. The elimination process is frequent and inconvenient for several years, and it's not the most pleasant stuff to deal with, but the body was designed to do it. Children eliminate the parts of their life that are difficult to digest through tantrums, crying, laughing hard, and playing. The emotional disposal process, while not always pretty, is vital in moving through life and ensuring that the emotional mind and body are functioning properly (adapted from Patty Wipfler & Tosha Schore). Your child is trying the best they can to reduce the discomfort they feel in their body by dispelling stress. This is a natural process we are often uncomfortable with, but when we realize it's Mother Nature's imperative to initiate this response, we can make more space for it.

THEY AREN'T ATTENTION SEEKING; THEY'RE CONNECTION SEEKING

We can love our child desperately, but sometimes the rigors of modern life pull us from being present, and our children's bids for connection end up being communicated through misbehavior. These bids are often misinterpreted, and our reactions can actually escalate the behavior until the child feels seen and heard.

If attachment is a child's preeminent need, it makes sense a child will do almost anything to connect with us, even if it means getting in trouble. The opposite of love is not hate; it's indifference. To experience indifference from a caregiver means a child feels utterly invisible. It means if danger ensues, a parent might not be there to protect them. It means that a parent lacks concern or interest in them, and they are all alone in this world. If a parent yells or hits a child, the parent shows some emotion. Now we aren't advocating for either of these, but understand a child will do almost anything to feel seen by you, even if your response is in anger. So whether it's misbehavior due to dysregulation in the brain or a child's misguided attempt to connect with you, they are doing the best they know how to cope with stress and fear. Our job is to separate our children from their behavior and hold space for them being human as they grow and learn how to cope with overwhelm.

TEACHER VS. TYRANT

Too often we forget that discipline really means to teach, not to punish. A disciple is a student, not a recipient of behavioral consequences.

—DANIEL SIEGEL

Discipline comes from *discipulus*, the Latin word for pupil. Discipline means you're guiding your child through a learning process. Learning implies that your child is either lacking a skill that has yet to be taught (i.e., the capacity to share or not knowing how to use their words to express their frustration with a family member) or learning to trust that you will understand that their behavior is a cry for connection or an expression of an unmet need. Maybe they are tired, overstimulated, feeling ignored, or struggling at school but don't have the words to explain that to you. It is our job as the adults to see through the behavior to the heart of the issue.

Think back to grade school. Can you think of a teacher that stands out to you in a positive way? What probably stands out to you isn't what they taught, so much as how they made you feel. They probably made you feel seen, heard, and valued. You felt safe with that teacher, and it made the learning experience memorable. You probably did very well in that teacher's class in contrast to other grades, or at least worked harder. This is the key to any effective leadership. Whether you are a teacher, boss, or parent, your success is correlated with how connected you are to the people you are trying to lead. If they feel valued, respected, and that you legitimately care, they want to be better for you and for themselves.

Now think of a boss or even your own parent with whom you had a poor relationship. A "leader" who used coercion or fear tactics to get what they wanted from you. Maybe they yelled, threatened, or criticized you. How did this make you feel? Did you feel valued or seen by this person? Did you feel safe with this person? I'm sure the answer is unequivocally no. While these tactics may have worked in the short term, they probably left you extremely unhappy or wounded.

The brain doesn't learn or work well when in a state of fear due to the fight-flight-freeze-collapse system. If you are always preoccupied with your physical or psychological safety, it makes it difficult to encode new information or access your creative potential. Your brain is in survival mode and can't afford the luxury of accessing those sophisticated tools. Most children (and people in general) tend to be "allergic" to coercion, which means they naturally resist it (especially young children). Feeling tricked or forced over the long term creates opposition, not compliance.

Children generally follow our lead when they are in a right relationship with us, when there is a secure attachment in place. To be an effective teacher, we must ensure their attachment instincts are primed because our children naturally look to us for security and leadership. Before we try to tackle the issue of discipline, ask yourself: "Am I in a safe, attuned relationship with my child?" If the answer is no, you must work on the attachment before you can be effective as a teacher.

CO-REGULATION OR CO-ESCALATION

Remember our analogy of the anchor and the storm. In any given moment, we need to pause and ask ourselves: "Am I anchoring my child or escalating them?" Without our calm, grounded presence, we have no chance of moving our child to emotion regulation. Calmness requires self-awareness and giving yourself grace. If we are reactive, we dump gasoline on the fire; we move away from being a safe harbor and become the storm.

If you need a moment to collect yourself, take it. If you need to tag your spouse in, do it. If you need to put your child in front of the TV for ten minutes to have a good cry in the bathroom, march on in there. You are of no use to your child if you are falling apart. You need to take care of yourself so you can take care of your child.

H.E.L.P. IN DIFFICULT PARENTING MOMENTS

Your job as a parent is to teach instead of punish. But sometimes when emotions are high, we need something to hold onto to guide us. We have developed an acronym to help guide you through this process regardless of your child's age: H.E.L.P.

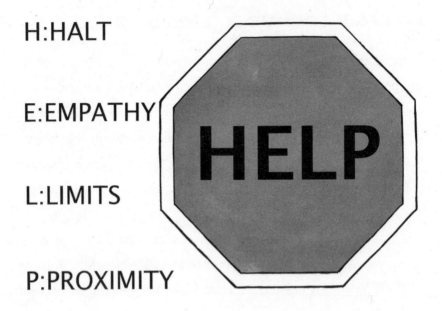

H:HALT

E:EMPATHY

L:LIMITS

P:PROXIMITY

HALT

Before you act, stop what you are doing and ask yourself: Where is this behavior coming from?

We truly believe that no child wants to be "bad." Why would a child, or anyone for that matter, want to fail and subsequently disappoint a person who means the world to them? They don't. Children want to make us happy, and they want to succeed. But there are biological limitations of your child's developing brain working against them. An underdeveloped thinking brain, paired with an overactive emotional brain and a lack of perspective, leads to chaos and poor decision-making. An immature brain produces immature behavior.

In hard moments, our anxiety tends to interfere with seeing our children's behavior for what it really is—a need that is unmet or a skill that has yet to be learned.

The reflection is paramount to becoming a successful and compassionate parent. As Dr. Daniel Siegel and Dr. Tina Bryson state in their groundbreaking book *No Drama Discipline*, you must chase the why. Being curious is a cornerstone of effective discipline.

Your child is not their behavior. Their behavior is simply a form of communication that a parent is meant to decode.

What My Child's Behavior Might Mean

Hungry

Tired

Overstimulated

They feel unwanted, rejected, sad, scared, lonely, angry, or ignored

Confused about expectations

Needing more freedom

Seeking connection

Feeling inadequate

Needing a limit set

They don't understand

Getting sick

Stressed about school, day home

Too much screen time

Not enough play

Not enough movement

Needing time outdoors

Diet isn't balanced

Struggling with a transition

When we can reframe the behavior as an unmet need or a skill that needs to be learned, we are less reactive and more empathic, and we parent from a place of intention.

As outlined in our last chapter, the second part of "Halt" is to ask yourself: Is this about my emotional baggage (i.e., I can't stand my child's crying because my parents didn't allow me to cry and it overwhelms me), or is this a reasonable response to my child's behavior (i.e., my child yelled "I hate you," and my feelings are hurt)?

This step is what will set you apart from many other parents and help you in your evolution as a person. Your self-awareness will save you from falling into old patterns you adopted from your own family of origin and allow you to act from a place of compassion and intention.

Lastly, in the case of older children, we often want to take time to be intentional about how we will respond, knowing we have some critical lessons we have to teach. Our own reactivity might get in the way, so we may talk an entire day or sleep on it before moving on to the next three parts of our acronym.

EMPATHY

When little people are overwhelmed by big emotions,
it's our job to share our calm, not to join their chaos.
—L. R. KNOST

Depending on your child's age, this is where we would employ a time-in or active listening skills (more about this in the next two chapters). This is all about a right-brain connection and taming the body and feeling brain; ensuring our children feel safe, seen, and heard before we move on to limit setting, teaching, or problem-solving.

Empathy is less about what we say and more about how we say it. This requires you to be accepting and fully present with your child's emotions, as well as aware of what is going on inside of you. Empathy is not feeling bad for your child, fixing a problem, being overwhelmed by their emotions, overidentifying with your child and assuming their experience is just like yours, or a time to discipline or lecture. Empathy means aligning with your child, getting alongside them, seeing their world as they see it, and believing them when they show you how they feel.

EMPATHY 101

Welcome Feelings with Our Bodies
- Lean in
- Get close
- Make eye contact
- Get on their level
- Open up your body language

Acknowledge and Validate Feelings

With a soft tone, acknowledge how they are feeling:
- "I can see you're feeling so _____."
- "You must be feeling so _____."
- "You're so ____ with me right now."

REALLY Listen (more in Chapter 7)

Summarize and/or paraphrase: What did you hear them say?

i.e., "So what I'm hearing you say is your friends ignored you all day, and you felt really lonely."

Clarify: Check for understanding. "So no one talked to you at lunch and you felt really sad, am I understanding you correctly?"

Don't Judge

- Conflict in relationships is normal.
- Feelings are neither good nor bad; they just are.
- Your child is not their behavior.
- While behavior may not be acceptable,
  their feelings always are.

Don't Try to Fix It

Allow for the crying, screaming, or verbal unloading. This is about your child being seen and heard, not fixing the behavior or problem.

Less Is More

- Talking too much overwhelms kids. If you are talking a lot, you are likely speaking to the wrong hemisphere (left).
- This is less about what you say and more about your presence.

Regulate Your Own Emotions

- Notice how you feel.
- Breathe and take a moment (or several) to compose and ground yourself.
- Ask yourself if your reaction is about you or your child.
- Think about giving your child a gift—maybe one you never received yourself.

LIMITS

This can be used at any age, and it is a simple way to draw boundaries with our children, create structure, and, most importantly, teach more appropriate behavior. Use simple statements that employ as few words as possible, but convey that the behavior is not acceptable, validate how your child is feeling (we will expand on limit setting more in the next chapter), and offer alternatives.

EXAMPLES

"Honey, in our family we don't use that kind of language. I know you're angry with me, and if you need to we can talk later, you can write down how you feel, or you can take a walk and then we can meet in twenty minutes to determine a solution."

"You are so frustrated, you can't have the cookie before dinner, but you know the rule—no dessert before supper. You can have a glass of water or a piece of fruit, or you can put the cookie on a plate and save it for later."

"You feel like it's not fair we won't let you have screen time after supper, but that's the rule in our family that everyone follows. You can go outside and play or draw in your room."

PROXIMITY

Often after we have empathized or set a limit, there is an unloading process that happens. Our children negotiate, plead, or bargain, and when they realize your answer is still the same (i.e., "honey, I still have a no in me"), they will become upset. This is where we are often tempted to walk away as we either are overwhelmed by their response, or we feel like we are being permissive indulging their drama. Please remember our chapters about the brain and the role of emotions. This process is completely healthy and normal. For our children to become successful at self-regulating, we first have to co-regulate them. Even grown adults don't enjoy suffering alone.

Connecting during hard moments is wired into our biology. To help calm your child, stay close. I always tell parents to look for the moment in which your child's anger or frustration shifts into sadness. This movement into vulnerability is the golden moment of connection. We don't want to miss this moment as it is the key to children learning that they can be vulnerable with people and show them their authentic self.

Whether you are seated on the floor inside the bedroom, parked on the floor in front of their bedroom, sitting with them at the kitchen table, or cuddled up with them on the couch or in their bed, never underestimate the power your physical presence holds.

CHAPTER 5

Discipline **TOOLKIT**

Reframe during hard moments

Kids Do Well If They Can
- They're not attention seeking, they're connection seeking
- Discipline means to teach, not to punish
- Focus on co-regulation or you get co-escalation

H.E.L.P. your child

H: HALT
Pause and ask; be curious

E: EMPATHY
Connect to the part of the brain that's over-activated. Name the feeling but be mindful how many words you speak, and just listen to your child or allow the tears to come. It's not about fixing it; it's about being in it with them.

L: LIMITS
A: Acknowledge the behavior
C: Communicate the limit
T: Target an alternative

P: PROXIMITY

Move in close or at least stay in the room, get down on their
level, don't hover or cower over top of them, and open up
your body.

Empathy is key

- Welcome feelings with your body
- Regulate your own emotions
- Less is more
- Don't try to fix it
- Don't judge
- Use active listening skills (teens/tweens)

CHAPTER SIX

DISCIPLINE: TODDLERS TO SEVEN

With such an underdeveloped brain, we can only expect so much from our littles. Our role in the early years is to focus on establishing rhythm, predictability, allowing ample play and exploration, and being armed with knowing that they are mostly governed primarily by their emotional brains. They are easily overwhelmed and governed by what is happening in front of them. The cortex in the brain may start to come "online" for children as young as four, but that typically occurs between the ages of five and seven.

Our main objective is to show them our love is unconditional, as well as to be consistent with our limits and expectations. This demonstrates that we will provide ample structure and routine, that we will make most of the "big" decisions for them (i.e., bedtime, mealtimes, calls about safety). This is where we focus on co-regulation and structure, allowing our children to become acquainted with their outer physical worlds and inner emotional worlds.

*Effective discipline might be the red light on a behavior,
but there should always be a green light for your child's feelings.*

One Thanksgiving, we had our entire extended family over for
the holidays. There were at least twenty people in our home, and
the night before Thanksgiving, we ordered Chinese food. My son,
who is normally a very good eater, refused to sit down or eat his
food. In agitation, he threw his fork across the table and screamed
"I'm not eating this!" I was very embarrassed by his behavior, as this
was not the way my son normally behaved. I felt anger bubbling up
in me, but instead of yelling or scolding, I paused. I thought "what
could be causing this behavior?"

It was fairly obvious he wasn't accustomed to having that many
people in his home. He was overstimulated, and he hadn't slept
well the night before because he was so excited to see his cousins.
I decided to use the strategy I teach all my clients. 1) I paused and
reflected on why he may be feeling this way. 2) I used empathy. I
leaned in close, got his gaze, and I said, "honey, I can see you're so
frustrated right now, you don't want to eat your dinner." He softened his expression and tears started to well in his eyes. 3) Then I
said, "But you need to have three bites of dinner before you can go
play" [limits]. He then exploded into tears. I knew this wasn't working. He needed quiet and connection from me if I was going to get
any food into his body. I quietly carried him into his room where
he proceeded to scream "I don't want to eat my dinner" for what
felt like an eternity. I sat cross-legged on the floor and validated
and mirrored his distress: "You're so angry right now. Those are
really big feelings. I am going to stay right here till those feelings go

down." After three or four minutes when the angry words stopped, and I could see the downshift into sadness—he softened.

I opened up my arms and said, "I wonder if you want to sit in my lap for snuggles?" He nodded and crawled in my lap and proceeded to weep for another five minutes or so. When he was done, I asked for his eyes and said, "I know you want to play with your cousins, but you still have to have three bites of dinner. Are you ready to eat, or do we need to stay in here for a little while longer?" My son nodded his head and told me he was ready to have his three bites. He bounced down the stairs, holding my hand, and I sat with him until the three bites were gone. It was like a reset button hit. Oh, the magic of a good cry.

CONNECTION BEFORE DIRECTION

Before asking your child to do anything, we suggest you prime their attachment instincts and avoid inadvertently using your size or stature to trigger fear or opposition. I learned this from being an elementary school teacher. Children take direction best when you connect with them and then ask them to complete a task.

Tips

- Don't ask from across the room—get in close.

- Enter their world: if they are playing, enter their play with them for a few moments or make a positive comment about something they're doing.

- Get their gaze and say, "eyes on me" or "can I have your eyes."

- Give an affectionate light touch, such as a touch on the shoulder, a hug, or a kiss.

- Say something positive to get a smile or a nod (i.e., "that's a beautiful picture you drew").

- Then ask them for the thing you want them to do.

CONSEQUENCES

Natural consequences occur without any enforcement on the part of the parent (i.e., if you don't wear a coat you get cold). Logical consequences involve specific action taken by the parent, wherein a logical consequence is applied, and that consequence is related to the error (i.e., if you break something, you pay for it; if you violate your screen time limits, you forfeit screen time the next day). Children at this stage do not do well with logical consequences. Logical consequences are more appropriate for children eight years and older (although it may be appropriate under certain circumstances, such as taking a toy away if two siblings are fighting over it). In this stage, natural consequences are most effective.

Natural consequences occur automatically as a result of actions. They are things that happen to the child as a result of their behavior, without parental involvement.

EXAMPLES OF NATURAL CONSEQUENCES

A child who does not play by the game rules with other children will not be asked to play in the next game.

If your child does not wear a winter coat, they get cold.

If your child runs too fast, they fall.

"Yes, it hurts a lot when we fall. You were running too fast on the slippery floor."

Of course there are times in which natural consequences are not appropriate. We don't want to employ a natural consequence if it is dangerous or harmful to our child (i.e., allowing the child to play in the street when she might be struck by a car); if the natural consequence is delayed for a long period after the behavior (i.e., the child leaves a bike in the yard and it rusts); or if the natural consequence isolates the child and causes problems for others (i.e., missing the bus results in a parent having to drive the child to school).

If we know time-outs are not the best choice for our relationship with our child or their psychological health, what is the alternative? In stage 1, we recommend utilizing time-ins and limit setting instead.

LIMIT SETTING

Parenting without boundaries and limits is like allowing a child to run across a suspension bridge without handrails.
—BRENÉ BROWN

Limit setting is one of the most essential tools you will have in this stage. It not only teaches appropriate behavior but also carves out safety for our children, both physically and psychologically. Children need to know we're watching, we're in charge, and we can keep them safe. Limit setting let's children know we're present and points them toward respectful relationships, learning, and protection.

We recommend Gary Landreth's ACT model for redirection:

A: Acknowledge the feeling
C: Communicate the limit
T: Target alternatives (or solutions)

Using this model means we have a target behavior we are not comfortable with and want to modify. To start, we want to connect with our child to engage their attachment instincts and to disarm the emotional brain by acknowledging their feelings. We also recommend getting down on their level. This does not work well across the room or if you're hovering. Then we use a strong, warm, assertive voice to set our limit on the unacceptable behavior. Last of all, we teach. If discipline is about teaching, then we need to give them acceptable alternatives to the behavior. Your child is not bad; they lack some of the fundamental skills to resolve the issue.

EXAMPLES

Your child is having a wonderful time drawing all over your kitchen wall with a marker.

A: "You are having so much fun drawing."

C: "But you may not draw on the wall."

T: "You may draw on this paper or on your chalkboard."

Out of frustration, your child throws their dinner plate across the table when asked to eat their vegetables.

A: "You are so angry we asked you to eat something you don't want to."

C: "But you may not throw things when you are angry."

T: "You may tell us that you're angry or take a quick walk and come back, but I need you to pick up your plate and come and eat your vegetables."

Note: With a child four years of age and older, you can also employ rectifying their mistake after targeting alternatives. In the first example, you may have your child help you wash the wall.

TIME-INS

Imagine your children are playing with Lego together and your six-year-old daughter knocks over your four-year-old son's Lego tower. In frustration, your four-year-old hits your daughter. Now we have two children who have acted out, but one is so dysregulated they act out aggressively. We would suggest you come back to your daughter later to make amends regarding the Lego, but our attention will be on the child who is acting out aggressively so that they don't escalate further. This also acts as further protection for the daughter who has been struck.

Steps

1. We would set a limit: "In our family, we do not hit."

2. Take your child away from the environment where the difficult moment happened (i.e., take your son to his room or any room nearby that is quiet and away from the other child).

3. During this time, you would use empathy to attune to their feelings and tame their right hemisphere and emotional brain: "You were so mad at your sister when she knocked down your Lego," stay close (maybe sit on the floor next to him), show warmth and connection (give him eye contact, lean in, use a soft tone/voice, and get down on his level).

4. The child is allowed to express their feelings through crying, stomping, shaking, screaming, talking, etc. until they have calmed down. This is part of working through the fight-fight-freeze-collapse survival response. It's a normal biological response when we feel scared, anxious, or angry. You could say, "you are having a really

big feeling" or "Mom will stay here till that angry/sad/big feeling goes down." It's important to notice as your child begins to regulate and draw attention to it; emotions are just as much in our bodies as our minds, so it's important for them to see they do not last forever and there is a light at the end of the tunnel (i.e., "I can see your feelings are getting calmer and your breathing is slowing down"). Limits may be set if the child is hurting the parent or themselves, and you may need to hold your child to prevent them from harming themselves (i.e., "Mommy is not for hitting" and hold his hands still until the impulse to hit is gone).

5. If the child is older (usually four years or older), once they are calm, the caregiver can then teach the skill that is needed to be successful in a future incident (i.e., "When you're mad at your brother, I wonder what we could do instead of hitting him? Hmmm?") Then allow the child to think and provide a solution or offer a few of your own (i.e., "Maybe you could come tell me what happened or tell him, 'I don't like when you break my Lego tower.' Let's practice saying that.")

6. Move on without grudges or future lectures. Children need our grace and forgiveness. Once the incident is over, we do not keep bringing it up. Trust your child understands it was not okay and give them the benefit of the doubt.

DIFFUSE WITH PLAY

My son, like most children, is often reluctant to get ready for bedtime, especially if he is engaged in something enjoyable with his family. In these moments, I know I could resort to threats or coercion (i.e., "if you don't get up to get ready for bed, I will carry you there, and you won't like it" or "no books if you don't get ready for bed"), but what is often more helpful is when I can make it a game. I smile and say, "I bet you I can beat you to the bathroom. I'm faster than you!" Ninety percent of the time, he smiles mischievously and says, "No way, Mommy! I'm faster than you." We're then off to the races. I usually have him in the bathroom, smiling, in thirty seconds.

As play therapists, we know how laughter, novelty, and silliness connect children with adults and soothe the nervous system. Play is also a child's language and a way to authentically connect with them on their level. But until we read the work of Lawrence Cohen, Patty Wipfler, and Tosha Schore, it never occurred to us how play can be applied to discipline. The research is clear that laughter reduces cortisol and the brain is drawn to novel experiences. When you can incorporate these elements into difficult parentings moments, discipline "strategies" do not need to be implemented.

We will give you a few examples of this in the chapter Toolbox, but we recommend reading Patty and Tosha's book *Listen* and Lawrence's book *Playful Parenting* for more examples.

The idea is to use the game or shenanigans to diffuse the resistance and emotional buildup in your child, and use the positive dynamic you have created through play to prime their natural attachment instincts. When they feel calm and connected, they are less likely to be resistant or oppositional.

CHAPTER 6

Discipline: Toddlers to Seven **TOOLBOX**

Play to diffuse resistance

Chase me

Run around and have your child try to catch you and tackle you to the ground. You can use the tackle as an opportunity to be physically close to your child by hugging or kissing him while you're on the ground. Adjust how hard or easy it is to catch you based on your child's age, strength, and temperament.

I can get there faster

Challenge your child to race to get to a destination first (i.e., to brush their teeth, get in the car to go to school)

You can't push me off the bed

You invite your child onto your bed, get on your knees, and pretend to be very strong and say, "Nobody will ever be able to push me off this bed!" Then let your child try to push you toward the side of the bed. Make a big deal about how strong they are. Adjust how hard or easy it is to push you based on your child's age, strength, and temperament. At the end, playfully take a tumble off the bed.

Pretend you can't do it

If your child doesn't want to engage in activity such as getting dressed or brushing their teeth, you adopt the role, but in a playful way; you mess it all up and do it wrong.

Example 1: Child does not want to brush their teeth. Instead of "brushing your teeth," you pretend to use the toothbrush to brush your hair, fingers, ears, elbows, and say, "Let me show you how to do it." Your child will hopefully giggle and then you say, "well, I wonder if you can show me how to do it?"

Example 2: Child does not want to get dressed. Instead of forcing your child to get dressed, you playfully say something like, "I'm so happy you don't want to get dressed. I was wanting to wear these clothes today!" Then you put the clothes on in a ridiculous way. You put the shirt over your head like a hat, the socks on your fingers, or pull the pants over your arms. You then can say, "Does this look right?" Your child will likely giggle and say, "No, Daddy, you're silly." Then you invite them to show you how to do it.

Follow the leader

Do everything that your child wants to do, even if it is uncomfortable (crawling on your knees all over the house), unpleasant (pretending to eat worms), or nerve-racking (making loud screaming noises).

Your child wants to find out if you really will follow his lead! If it is truly unsafe, you will need to modify it, but this isn't common. Then ensure you switch roles, and don't be afraid to be ridiculous.

Pillow fight

When engaging your child in pillow fighting, follow their lead. Only hit as hard as it takes to get laughter from your child. Make a big show of it when you fall over after your child hits you, and, as always, adjust how hard or soft you hit based on your child's age, strength, and temperament.

Time-ins

Remove a child from a situation when they are having a difficult moment and have them sit elsewhere with a caregiver. Validate their feelings, but don't try to lecture, argue, or provide solutions. Just be in the room with them until they become regulated.

Connection before direction

Get on their level, in close range, make eye contact (if culturally appropriate), and get a smile before making a request.

Small choices

As young children are developing autonomy and trying to master their world, they need some control to feel capable. Since the adults still need to be in charge of big-ticket items, you can give your child small choices to empower them.

Examples:

- The red cup or the blue cup with dinner
- Brush their teeth or use the potty first
- Picking the book they want to read before bed
- Choose what they want to wear for the day

Therapeutic play

(See Chapter 9)

Ensure you are getting enough one-on-one time playing with your child to stay connected and to help facilitate positive mental health outcomes.

Routine

- Ensure you have a solid sleep, bedtime, and mealtime routine in place.
- Review their day in the mornings regarding what's happening that day, and give them a preview of the next day before bedtime.

Emotional coaching

- Teach your child how to identify emotions in themselves and others.
- Point out characters' feelings in books and movies.
- Name what they are feeling in the easy and difficult moments (i.e., "you are so excited to go swimming"; "you're so frustrated when you can't figure that out").

Natural consequences

Allow your child to feel the consequence of their behavior without interfering. Gently point out how the two are connected (i.e., "See, we get cold when we don't put our coat on.").

Limit setting

A: Acknowledge the feeling
C: Communicate the limit
T: Target alternatives (or solutions)

Low screen time

- Notice how your child behaves after you take away the screen; meltdowns, pleading/bargaining, irritability, and increased impulsivity.

- Create a media plan that works for the family and look at doctor-recommended guidelines.

CHAPTER SEVEN

DISCIPLINE FOR OLDER CHILDREN & TEENS

Once our children's thinking brain is well underway in terms of its development, the discipline game changes. Our role starts to shift from benevolent leader to copilot, with the child flying their plane more independently as they move into adolescence and young adulthood. At the beginning they need a lot more guidance, but we can't expect our children to move mountains if we don't let them get out of their seats. This is the stage where their thoughts, perspectives, and desires really need to be heard and taken into consideration— they need to genuinely feel they have a voice. In order to become good decision-makers, they need the opportunity to make real decisions, and a safe space to make mistakes and course correct where needed. Know your child wants their life to work out, they simply need our help to navigate the complex social nuances that life presents and acquire the skills necessary to be successful. At this age, good discipline is about imparting knowledge in a way that your child will accept your influence, while allowing ample opportunities for your child to grow and strengthen their capacity for critical thinking and problem-solving.

One day after school, my then eleven-year-old stepdaughter declared she wanted a YouTube channel because so many kids in her class had one. Even though I am not her biological mother, everything in me screamed "heck no!" We have a lot of limits around screen time, and while YouTube can be a wonderful platform, we had reservations about the types of adults who often prey on impressionable and vulnerable children on these platforms (among many other reasons). Instead of an outright "no," we said, "We're willing to hear you out, and we will have a family meeting tomorrow. Before our meeting, we need two lists from you. One is a list of reasons why you think it's a good idea. The second is a list of reasons why you think we might say no." My stepdaughter prepared her lists, and we met the following night. Her list looked something like this:

Reasons I Should Have a YouTube Channel	Reasons My Dad and Tammy Think I Shouldn't
YouTube is awesome.	My Dad and Tammy don't like YouTube.
Some of my friends have one.	There are some bad videos and people on there.
I can make things on there, so it's fun to show people what I made.	I'm not supposed to be on my iPad all the time.

We then went through this list with our daughter. We agreed that she was creative, and she had some pretty cool things to offer the world. We acknowledged it's normal to want things that her peers have so she can feel "the same." Then we processed the reasons she shouldn't based on her list, and we added a few of our own. We told her how much we enjoyed YouTube as well and how I had videos on there for work. We then took the opportunity to talk about how screen time impacted her brain and that if she spent all her time on YouTube, she might neglect the art she was so skilled at creating on paper.

We discussed how some adults prey on children and that we worry about her being taken advantage of. The disappointment on her face was unmistakable, and she knew our case for not having it was stronger than her case for having it. We acknowledged her feelings and how hard it was for her to feel different from her friends. Then we told her it was a "no for now," but we promised to revisit it in two years if she was still interested. We also found a more appropriate app with which she could still make the videos she wanted but not air them in such a public manner.

> *Effective discipline means that we're not only stopping a*
> *bad behavior or promoting a good one, but also teach-*
> *ing skills and nurturing the connections in our children's*
> *brains that will help them make better decisions and*
> *handle themselves well in the future.*
> —DANIEL SIEGEL

At this stage of development, our children need some autonomy and to know they have a voice. They are their own person. They need to know their thoughts and feelings are taken into consideration by their parents, and it's not a dictatorship. By this age, many children also have the capacity to understand others' feelings and perspectives, but this is something they often need help fostering. They also have a strong desire for belonging and feeling like they're part of something, so we need to ensure our discipline takes this into consideration when we frame things.

In most cases, by this age, we are working with a functioning cortex—a limited one, but nonetheless, one that is starting to be utilized more substantially. Some children as young as seven are ready for stage two, but only you know the maturity of your child. Some children who are seven or eight will need stage 1 discipline because their emotional maturity is lagging. Before deciding if you should move on to stage 2, ask yourself:

1. Can my child understand how other people feel when it differs from their own?

2. Can they reflect on their behavior and understand how they impact others?

3. Have they moved past black-and-white thinking (i.e., do they understand how a villain in a movie can have both enduring and negative qualities)?

4. Can they have mixed feelings (ambiguity) during heated moments (i.e., when they're mad at you, can they acknowledge they can love you and feel angry at the same time)?

If you're answering yes to these questions, your child is ready for this stage of discipline.

CONNECTION BEFORE CORRECTION

Before thinking about implementing a consequence or setting a limit, you should engage the attachment instincts of your child first. Get their eyes, a smile, or get in close. Just like we wouldn't want our spouse to jump on our backs if we made a mistake, we would rather have a calm and loving conversation in which we didn't feel attacked or shamed.

Connection is not a fluffy strategy. It's science; it's about aligning with our child's emotional brain and calming their nervous system before engaging the more sophisticated regions of their brain. It's about connecting to that right hemisphere and speaking the same language as our child, instead of defaulting to the left side and lecturing, nagging, or trying to explain to a child why they shouldn't do something—in other words, speaking Latin to the right hemisphere.

Now your older child or teen may not want to crawl on your lap for a good cry, but they might be receptive to you sitting next to them on the bed or offering a hand on the shoulder. By offering proximity, you say to your child, "I can handle you, and I'm here for you." Next, you want to ensure you choose words that speak emotion, not reason. Show your child you really "see" them. You recognize they're struggling, and their pain has not gone unnoticed (even if you don't agree with their behavior).

EXAMPLES

"I can see you; you're so mad right now."

"Wow, that must have really hurt when your brother said that."

"I can see you're really hurting, or you wouldn't have said those things."

"It's frustrating to stop your game when you're so close to finishing."

Then stop talking. Allow your words to sink in. See if you notice even a subtle shift in your child's demeanor. Don't just launch into a consequence or lecture. There is plenty of time for that. Now is the opportunity to be your child's ally instead of their opponent. Children this age want a voice. They want to be heard.

COLLABORATIVE CONSEQUENCES

Here is where your child needs to feel like they have a voice, like their thoughts are at least considered. We would say this strategy carries on into the teen years as well. Now we don't make any guarantees a nine-year-old will be overly innovative when it comes to deciding on an appropriate consequence for sneaking their iPad into their bedroom at night, but that's not the point. The point is you're starting to plant the seeds of self-reflection and accountability.

STEP 1: Wait until both you and your child are calm. Remember, you are the anchor, not the storm. Connect with your child, and then simply point their attention to the mistake they've made.

EXAMPLE

You know that there are no electronics after suppertime.

STEP 2: Give them a chance to speak to what's on their mind and be curious about why they did what they did.

EXAMPLE

"Can you help me understand why you did that?"

Granted, children at this age don't often understand why they did what they did, but this gives them an opportunity to feel heard.

STEP 3: Give them a chance to course correct this and apply a measure that's appropriate. If it's off base, you can guide them to a choice that might be more appropriate, but give them an opportunity to own it.

EXAMPLE

"Sounds like you really wanted to finish making your character on that app, but you knew that was a wrong choice. When we make mistakes, there are consequences. I want you to think about the mistake you made and what you think needs to happen. We can talk about this tomorrow after school."

"What do you think would be an appropriate consequence for ripping up your sister's art?"

"What do you think needs to happen now that you made that mistake?"

If the consequence that they come up with is inappropriate (i.e., your child states they need electronics time after supper so they don't sneak the iPad late at night when your house is electronics-free after dinner), remind them of the rules in your home, and let them know "that's not going to work for our family." Then give them a few options you came up with and allow them to weigh in and choose one of them. The point is they have a voice, and they are beginning to practice autonomy and reflective decision-making. It's a win-win—accountability and brain development all rolled into one.

MAKE IT RIGHT

This is probably my favorite strategy for my eldest two children. I piggyback on the collaborative consequences, but I add this simple caveat: "How are you going to make this right?" This not only makes your child think, but it focuses on repairing relationships and social accountability.

EXAMPLE

"You were so angry, and you ended up saying some things that were really hurtful to your brother. I know you know that in this family we don't use words like that. I think we need to take a break and cool down. In an hour, I'm going to come back down here, and I want you to think about how you are going to make this right."

WHO WAS IMPACTED BY THEIR CHOICE

Perspective taking is not easy, even for adults who are dysregulated. However, it is a necessity for the development of emotional intelligence and empathy. When your child makes a poor choice, simply and gently point their attention toward the impact it had on the other person. You can also draw a parallel to a time they felt the same way. This alone empowers a child to take it upon themselves to make it right without much intervention on your part.

EXAMPLE

"I know you were so mad at your brother for interrupting your time with your friend. You don't get to see Charlie very often. You also know we don't use our bodies to hurt one another in this family. Can you see the tears rolling down his face? That really hurt him when you punched him in the arm."

EXAMPLE

"I know you want to be alone with Charlie, and it's frustrating when your little brother tags along. But remember when you wanted to play with Tessa (older sister), and she kicked you out of her room and called you annoying? Do you remember how much that hurt your feelings? This is just like that."

ACTIVE LISTENING SKILLS

As parents, we tend to explain, nag, and preach to our children. But it's rarely effective and often leads to escalating a situation or shutting a child down. Now we believe that too much talking is inappropriate to the dysregulated child, especially young children. But there is a time and place for it when our children begin to mature. When we use language, we are very intentional about how we use it.

Like any good therapist will tell you, people need to be heard and feel seen. This is the foundation of change. So here are some great tools to promote better listening skills as a parent, spouse, or friend.

AFFIRM: Let the person know you understand their emotional experience.

EXAMPLE

"That must have been so frustrating" or "I can see when he did that how sad you felt."

PARAPHRASE: Restate what the person is saying but using different words.

EXAMPLE

Your child tells you her brother took the cupcake she saved all day to eat after supper, so she hit him because she was mad. You might say, "You had been patiently waiting to eat that all day, and you're mad because your brother took it without asking you if it was okay."

CLARIFY: Clarifying shows you are following what the speaker is saying and eliminates any confusion. This skill typically follows paraphrasing.

EXAMPLE

"Am I hearing that right?" or "Is that what happened?" or "Did I understand what you are trying to say?"

SUMMARIZE: A summary is what you give after the speaker is completely done talking. It includes all the skills above wrapped into one. It shows you heard what they said and how they felt, and it allows the speaker to add any additional information.

EXAMPLE

"So what I heard was you are so hurt you weren't invited to Sydney's birthday party. You have always invited her to things, and you spend lots of time together in school, so it's hard to understand why you didn't get an invite. Is there anything I'm missing, sweetheart?"

FOSTER BELONGING

We will speak more to this in Chapter 12, but ensuring your child feels like they are a contributing member of the family unit will be key to cohesion in your family. I know in my own family unit we use words like "in this family, we . . ." and "it's important we all _____ in our family" and "you are an important member of this family." It is a sociological and biological imperative that we "belong" to a group. Our survival depends on it. The more a child feels like they belong in their family unit, the more cooperative they will be.

This isn't just about language, though. You must walk the walk as well. This means you don't just order your child to do things; you do them together, as a family. Whether it is a movie night, cooking a meal, or chores, children thrive and will be more cooperative if the whole family engages in the activity together.

OTHER DISCIPLINE TIPS

Wait and regroup

If you feel like you're going to flip your lid, or you think the moment is too heated for your teen—wait, always wait. Come back to the issue when you're both calm and collected. This strategy is also important for tweens as well. Set a time for when you will meet to discuss the issue at hand, even if it's the next day (i.e., "We're both upset right now. Let's talk about this after supper when we've both cooled off.").

What did you learn

Our teens make lots of mistakes. Don't look at this as failure. They are supposed to make those mistakes while they are safely still in your care. A lot of parents miss the opportunity to point their teen's attention to what they learned from their mistake and what they can do differently next time.

To a teen who struggles in school, you might say: "I know your grades are important to you, and you didn't get the grade you normally did on your math test. How do you feel about that?" (Let's assume your teen says they feel disappointed.) "What did this experience teach you? What do you think needs to change so you can do better next time?"

Notice, not nag

Instead of demanding your teen clean up the basement or unload the dishwasher, point their attention to the issue at hand and give them the opportunity to step up to the plate.

EXAMPLES

"Wow, this basement is a mess."

"The dishwasher is full."

"I see coats and backpacks by the front door."

If they don't step up to the plate, remind them that everyone in the family needs to help each other out for things to work. While you work really hard to make their life better, you need their help so things run smoothly in the house.

Don't assume, be curious

Sometimes we assume the worst or jump to a conclusion, when our teen might have been trying their best. We also don't always get to see the whole picture, and only a piece of the conflict. So stay open and be curious. This will make you less defensive and your teen will feel more heard.

EXAMPLES

"I know you know it's not okay to _____, so I'm wondering what happened?"

"I saw you snap at your sister, who you know adores you. Looks like today is a hard day for you. Is there anything you want to share about what's going on?"

"I've noticed every time we get ready for soccer, you hide in your room, and we always end up being late. I wonder if something is going on? Maybe something happened on the team or you just aren't feeling this anymore. Can you help me understand?"

Author's Note: This book was written primarily for parenting children two years to twelve years, so this section of the book is brief. We will include references to books that we recommend at the end of the section for parenting teens.

TIPS FOR DISCIPLINING A TEEN

Haley was slumped over on my couch in my office. She was both sad and angry with her parents. She shared with me they had been fighting again, and now she was grounded for being disrespectful, and her phone was taken away for a week. "My parents just don't get me. They want me to play ringette, get good grades, and take care of my little brother. I'm not perfect, and I'm sick of them thinking I should be perfect. I don't even like ringette! I told them I want to focus on my art and take graphic design in college one day, and they keep telling me I'll never make any money, and I need to study hard so I can go to university and get a 'real job.' If they don't care about me, why should I care about them?"

Haley is similar to hundreds of teens Tania and I have worked with. They are beautifully messy, opinionated, creative, and have a fire in them that makes most parents panic. They are so misunderstood, and the parents I often work with are so busy grieving the loss of the "little boy or girl," they can't see the amazing young adult blossoming before them. Raising a teenager is hard—but being a teenager is hard too. Which is why our kids need someone they trust to lean on, to come to for advice, and to share their lives—the good, the bad, and the ugly. Having a front row seat in our kids' lives is a far better place to be than on the highest bleacher (**raisingteenstoday.com**).

We feel many of the strategies from earlier in this chapter can be used with teens, so we don't want to relist them here; however, there must be an understanding that our role as parents radically shifts once we have a teenager. Parents forget that we need children who will become adults who are "self-disciplined," and our role is to cultivate many micro "teachable" moments so our children have the skills necessary to navigate life's challenges and effectively modify their own behavior.

The teen brain also goes through a renovation of sorts, which leads to a great deal of behavioral changes, all of which seem to create contention between teens and parents. It's common for parents to resort back to a place of reactivity instead of parenting with intention.

BECOMING SEPARATE

Children who enter the teen years are beginning the process of individuation. This essentially means they are psychologically preparing to leave the nest, to form an identity that is unique and separate from their parents. This is also where their peers become more important as they begin to form romantic relationships and seem to pull away. This process is necessary from an evolutionary standpoint but utterly painful for parents.

A child who once wanted to snuggle before bed and to spend evenings riding bikes with their parents now spends countless hours locked in their room listening to music, begging for time with their friends, and rebuffing their parents' requests—or at least dramatically saying, "Ugh! Why?" whenever they are asked to unload the dishwasher. This process is utterly painful. (I know because I have a fourteen-year-old living in my home). But I assure you, it does not last forever. Please don't discredit your importance, though. We don't believe teens are meant to pull away from parents entirely— your relationship is just as important now as it was when they were five years old. It's just their bids for connection can be less obvious, and their social world has expanded.

What is most important is that you take an interest in your teen. It is the parent who often needs to work on finding a connection point with their teen. Don't leave it up to your teen. Take initiative. Show up in a million different ways. Keep knocking. Explore their thoughts, opinions, and interests. Ask about their video game (and maybe even play with them), play the music they are into in the car, let them paint their room whatever color they're into, allow them to weigh in on heated topics, and ask them what they think about it. All they want is for you to notice that they are their own person, that you value this person they are becoming. Give them the independence (within reason) they so desperately want.

ORGANIZATIONAL CHAOS OF THE TEEN BRAIN

They may walk and talk like adults, but don't let them fool you. Their brain is nowhere near where it needs to be. So in addition to being undeveloped, there are also many neurological changes happening in the teen brain that make it challenging for parents to connect with their teens.

If you recall in our chapter about the brain, teens undergo myelination. Myelination in the cortical (thinking) brain is an important part of the maturing process for adolescents; it allows for the brain to strengthen neural connections and allows messages to travel faster in the brain. A parallel process called synaptic pruning allows the brain to essentially cut out those parts of the brain it no longer needs to support this optimization process.

Now this takes a lot out of our teens—their brains are undergoing significant changes, and this overhaul demonstrates how much energy their brains require to undergo this process. This partially explains why they need so much sleep and why they feel so irritable if they don't get it. Also noteworthy, melatonin—the chemical that makes you sleepy—is released later in the evening in the teen brain than in children and adults, which explains why they like to stay up too late and sleep in. Fundamentally, their sleep clock gets pushed back. Additionally, changes in both the levels of the neurotransmitters dopamine and serotonin in the limbic system make adolescents more emotional and more responsive to rewards and stress (i.e., during the teen years, dopamine levels may have implications for adolescent risk-taking and vulnerability to boredom).

Lastly, this process also includes a flood of sex hormones to help our children to reach sexual maturity (i.e., estrogen and testosterone), which can contribute to the "moodiness" and sexual exploration we see in our teens.

PARENTAL ROLE REDEFINED: MENTORSHIP

As a parent of a teen, I know I want my child to make the right decisions even when her dad and I are not looking; we want her to be self-sufficient. But with the oppositional nature of teens and their need for autonomy and independence, we can't force her to make good choices. As they say: "You can lead a horse to water, but you can't make them drink."

This is the stage where you start highlighting your family's values, your teen's personal values, and whether the decisions they make are aligned with them. This is a collaborative conversation you must have with your teen. This is where we strive to empower them to make the right choices while giving them grace when they inevitably stumble and make mistakes. Then it becomes a question of what they learned from that mistake and what they can do differently next time.

This doesn't mean we don't have consequences for our teens, but their voice in this process is vital. This is where collaboration is key to effectively disciplining your teen. The more control we try to assert, the more oppositional or shut down they will become.

CHAPTER 7

Tween & Teens **TOOLBOX**

Connection before direction

- Make sure you are calm before you try to connect.
- Get in close and validate their feelings; i.e., "I can see you; you're so frustrated with your sister right now" or "Wow, it sounds like you felt really embarrassed when I made that comment in front of your friends."

Collaborative consequences

- Proceed when calm and connected
- Let them share what's on their mind
- Ask them to share with you what consequence they think should be appropriate; share your thoughts and meet in the middle

Make it right

- Point your child's attention to the impact their behavior had on others
- Ask them to think about how they are going "make it right"

Active listening

- Affirm: Let the person know you understand their emotional experience.

- **Paraphrase:** Restate what the person is saying but using different words.
- **Clarify:** Ask a question to ensure you accurately understood your child.
- **Summarize:** Using your own words and in one to two sentences, summarize what your child has said, including how they felt.

Don't assume, be curious

Ask them what happened. Get to know their point of view and remain open and curious.

Wait and regroup

Don't proceed until everyone is calm. It's okay to wait several hours or until the next day.

What did you learn?

Mistakes are going to happen; it's how our children learn. So when things are calm, talk about the mistake, and what the lesson is, and what things they can do differently next time.

Notice, not nag

Point their attention to the issue at hand and give them the opportunity to step up to the plate.

RECOMMENDED READS FOR PARENTING TEENS

- *You're Ruining My Life* by Jennifer Kolari
- *How to Talk so Teens Will Listen and Listen so Teens Will Talk* by Adele Faber and Elaine Mazlish
- *Brainstorm: The Power and Purpose of the Teenage Brain* by Dr. Daniel Siegel

CHAPTER EIGHT

CULTIVATING RESILIENCE

Children don't need perfect parents; they need compassionate parents who are actively working on their own imperfections. When a child feels loved, they are more likely to learn from a challenging situation. This is the heart of resiliency. Take a minute to think about the one burning parenting question you have. For many parents, the question will be a variation of: "How do I help my child to be brave, to be strong, to be kind, and to approach life's challenges with courage?"

Research demonstrates that the single most common factor for children who develop resilience is at least one stable and committed relationship with a supportive parent, caregiver, or other adult. For a moment, reflect on who you are to your child. Are you their person? When they think about you, what comes up for them? Who you are to your child is more important than what you say or how much parenting "knowledge" you have.

Who you are is based on the "relational credits" that you have built up over time with your child. Relational credits are gained when a child feels seen, heard, and loved. These credits are accrued when you're least aware—when you're reading a book to a child, emanating warmth and presence as they tell you about their day, or lying on the floor and playing with them. This gradual buildup of relational moments creates an anchor for a child during life's storms.

When my husband and I first began living with our foster children, I was consumed with how to connect with them, how to get them to truly trust me. It is in hindsight now that I recognize that trust was built up over micro-moments—daily interactions over time.

When we encounter life's inevitable storms, our children need us to be an anchor. The anchor is primarily nonverbal and needs to be the standard we strive for in all difficult interactions with our child, regardless of their age. It is in our ability to remain present, to keep our voice warm and resonant, our bodies open and relaxed, and to use touch and gestures in a manner that elicits trust.

Often we rush to "fix," and in lieu of calming the stress response, we accelerate it. Your child needs you to slow down and calm your thoughts and your body. When you do this, your child's alarm system is calmed, and their thinking brain is nurtured. This differs greatly from the parenting model we have seen in the recent past. Instead of emphasizing "teaching," the emphasis is on "connection."

Throughout this book, we have emphasized the vital role of caregiving in cultivating resiliency, but what about the role of genetics? Don't some children come into the world a little more robust? The Center on the Developing Child at Harvard explains that individual characteristics and environment both play a role. Certain genes may make a child more sensitive to their environment. These genes turn up or turn down the expression of chemicals in the brain and in the body that govern our responses to stress, anxiety, and depression. However, when nurturing experiences dominate, children learn coping skills, and resilient outcomes become more likely. As a clinician, I cannot change a child's genetic backing, but I can actively help caregivers become aware of the types of experiences that build resilience. These experiences fall under three different pillars: purpose, belonging, and hope.

PILLAR 1: PURPOSE

Purpose is our ability to live with intention and to focus on goals that bring meaning to our existence. This is a big topic and is at the core of what drives us to seek fulfilling relationships, to engage in passionate pursuits, and to set value-driven goals. There are times when we find ourselves clocking in and out of a job that we hate, or investing in unfulfilling relationships, or living in a manner that differs from who we want to be in the world. In reflecting on my own life, I am deeply aware of periods in my life when I felt as if I was on the outside looking in, instead of being deeply present and driven. Usually, these periods were marked by feeling either overwhelmed or underwhelmed by the events in my life. Balance and awareness were lacking.

There are also times when we feel alive, driven, connected, and motivated. Michael Stegge, director of the Laboratory of Meaning and Quality of Life at Colorado State University, says: "The sense that your personal life is meaningful to you is a cornerstone of psychological wellness. Purpose is unique, and will is a shapeshifter. It will morph as our child develops and [their] life circumstances shift." I like the way Richard Ledier breaks down purpose. He states that the equation for purpose is (G + P + V) = P (gifts + passions + values) = purpose. Let's take a closer look at how to nurture purpose in our children's lives.

Some theorists believe that we are born with innate talents and abilities, while others believe that innate talents are skills that are practiced and honed over years. As an example, in the book *Peak: Secrets from the New Science of Expertise*, Ericsson and Pool argue, "The belief that one's abilities are limited by one's genetically prescribed characteristics manifests itself in all sorts of 'I can't' or 'I'm not' statements." They argue the key to extraordinary performance is "thousands and thousands of hours of hard, focused work."

We would argue that gifts are the result of individual characteristics of the person and the environment in which the gifts are nurtured. Helping children explore many interests and intentionally fostering a growth mindset helps them to become lifelong learners. For elementary school children, Steger suggests that parents help children figure out what their strengths are and point their attention toward the times they had a positive impact by relying on these qualities. Let's turn to one of the countries in the world with the happiest, most well-adjusted, and resilient children—Denmark. One of the reasons researchers believe Danish children are so well-adjusted is that in Danish culture, children are valued for who they are and for their innate, individual gifts and qualities; a child is not asked to be someone they are not.

For example, in Denmark, a child who struggles academically but excels in art would not be pushed into tutoring so they could excel in math. The adults in that child's life would recognize that the child derives a sense of accomplishment and confidence from engaging in their natural talents, which foster self-efficacy and confidence. As a result, the child feels valued and like they are an important part of their families, schools, and communities.

We can start doing this for our children too. In lieu of projecting onto our children who we "think" they should become, let's see them for who they are—unique humans with innate gifts, talents, and strengths.

When children can say that they "love to snowboard" or that they bake cookies for all of their neighbors, it serves to anchor them in how they feel about themselves, others, and the world. Passion is a window into the soul and will morph, change, and develop in complexity. Here are some ways we can help children nurture their passionate pursuits.

WORKING ON PURPOSE WITH YOUR CHILD

Foster interest

This is the beauty of nondirected play. Allow your child ample space to explore and grow without limitations or pressure. Unfortunately, in the race to arm our children with skills, we unwittingly rob them of the natural work of childhood. The freedom to explore their worlds without the undue pressure to perform or win some accolade or move to the next level will allow your child the space to discover what they are truly passionate about. Psychologist Peter Gray explains the importance of non-pressured time: "That time is needed to make friends, play with ideas and materials, experience and overcome boredom, learn from one's own mistakes, and develop passions".

Exposure to a wide range of activities, through which a child can discover new experiences, is more important than a one-track investment. Expose your child to art, sports, nature, cultural experiences, and music. See what lights a fire in them. Often, we unknowingly push our children into certain activities because they either interest us, not necessarily our children, or we feel that we missed out on something when we were younger, so we feel the need to live vicariously through our children. Be mindful of either of these dynamics before enrolling your child in an activity. To help battle this, it can also be beneficial to actively involve your child in exploring what interests them. Have them participate in choosing what structured activities they want to enroll in. This also helps empower our children into being more autonomous decision-makers rather than passive participants in their lives.

Creative Exploration

Tammy and I both love nondirected exploration. In our own homes, we have a range of different arts, crafts, and materials that are readily available to our children to explore, create, and express in any way that is meaningful to them. It is through this process of self-directed discovery that children begin to discover who they want to be in the world. We can ask our children to share their creations once they are complete, but it's important we don't critique or praise the end product.

Turn down the pressure valve: According to the National Alliance for Youth Sports, 75% of children quit organized sports around the age of thirteen years old due to burnout and lack of interest. This is a devastating number as this is the time that a child is most likely to benefit from sports, which enables them to develop critical thinking skills and grit, learn to work on a team, and hone their physical abilities.

Research indicates that organized activity proves beneficial for children because it is a vehicle to explore new interests and skills. As a parent, when we see our child is interested in an activity, we have to carefully nurture their interest while also ensuring we are not throttling their innate joy. When we put too much pressure on our children, they become more likely to disengage from an activity. In helping a child to discover their passion, you are not the leader. The child is the leader, and you are the support team. It is important to prioritize relationships over activities. If you or your child are struggling, it may be time to explore if your life has become too pressured and what could be eliminated from the schedule.

Let them help

There are many wonderful reasons why children should be engaged with household chores. When we look specifically at discovering passions, chores can be a window into nurturing passion—and hugely helpful for us as parents to share the load of running a household. If a child never helps in the kitchen or in the garden, how will they know they love to cook or grow vegetables? "Let them help" truly means let them help; don't pay them to help maintain their home. Research demonstrates that when we reward children for an activity, over time, their innate desire to participate in the activity decreases.

Although children may grumble about chores, chores are integral in defining family culture and in skill building, as well as exposing children to activities that they may not naturally gravitate toward. The sooner we get children helping, the better. Children are natural-born helpers as young as eighteen months, but we often ignore this desire because when they do help, they seem to make more work for us. If we can reframe their helping as fostering passion and altruism, then we're more likely to capitalize on excitement to lend a hand in the backyard or kitchen.

Talk to them

As mentioned, it's so important that we speak with our children about our own passions, about how we feel when we engage in them and how we feel when we do not. Using books and movies is another beautiful way to teach passion. Even if their dreams seem unrealistic, they enable us to see who they want to be in the world. Be authentically curious without pushing your own agenda—this is a tricky one for many parents. While you share and listen, be creative, and be open to how their vision unfolds. As passion is unique, your child's experiences may push you to reevaluate, reconsider, and see the world in a different way.

Using books and movies is another way to really help your child to explore who they want to be in the world. Through the medium of story, we can talk to children about complex topics like passion in simple terms. In the movie *Moana*, for instance, she has a passion for sailing and being in the ocean. In this beautiful scene, we see Moana's love and passion come to light despite the obstacles and discouragement she faces. If we are using this movie as an example of how to begin discussing passion, we might say to our children:

- "How does Moana know she belongs in the sea?"
- "I wonder what about the sea is so important to her?"
- "I wonder if there is anything in your life you feel that excited about?"
- "How does she use her passion of the sea to help her family?"

When we quieten all the noisy chatter in the world, and we foster who our child wants to be—a creator, a strategist, an advocate—we say yes to their spirit and no to a world that is often too hurried to celebrate the value of authentic living.

It's in the Micro-moments

As technology invades every area of our lives, parenting has unfortunately become increasingly distracted. We miss out on watching our children discover the world around them, on being delighted by our children, on those "aha" moments when we see our children connect with something that they love. So often we focus on turning the phone off at dinnertime or keeping it out of the bedroom—which are good starting points—but what about the moments in between? Nothing can replace presence. In our own lives, both Tammy and I have started to enforce strict restrictions around use of our phones because we were losing too many precious moments that could not be regained.

We believe that this is among the reasons why play therapy with children is so impactful. In the play therapy room, the experience is embodied with generosity of time, presence, and curiosity. A seed of a dream can be joyfully explored. Slow down with your children, and take time to watch the snails—within that time, seeds are given the space to flourish.

SAVORING MOMENTS ACTIVITY

We encourage parents to journal, even if it's via their notes app, to help them slow down and explore moments of awe that they have experienced with their child—after the moment passes, of course. What did you notice about them, how did they engage with their world, what were they drawn to, and what emotions did you or your child experience? This activity has a secondary gain as well. When you have a hard parenting moment and struggle to see your child with compassion, pull up these notes and remind yourself of these precious moments of connections and presence.

Fostering a Growth Mindset

As children discover their gifts, it is important that we constantly help them to understand that being strong in a specific area—painting, reading, or climbing—is just a starting point. Our strengths need to be nurtured and developed over time. This is called a growth mindset (i.e., I need to put in effort; I learn when I persevere). Carol Dweck's work has shown that children from a growth mindset home believe that interests can be developed, which leads to a desire to learn and a tendency to embrace challenges, to persist in the face of setbacks, to see effort as the path to mastery, to learn from criticism, and to find lessons and inspirations in the success of others.

As a result of this mindset, they reach higher levels of achievement, and this gives them a greater sense of free will. On the other hand, children who grow up with a fixed mindset (e.g., I'm smart or not; I'm athletic or not; I'm creative or not) tend to believe that gifts are innate, which leads to a desire to "fit the label" and a tendency to avoid challenges, to give up easily, to see effort as fruitless or worth, to ignore useful negative feedback, and to feel threatened by the success of others. Carol Dweck outlines five strategies to help children develop a growth mindset:

1. **Focus on process praise.** We want to focus on effort instead of the final outcome. For example, we may say, "It was incredible to watch how much energy you put into that assignment" or "Wow! You've really been figuring out how to balance those blocks to make a taller and taller tower." We want to avoid praise like "you're so good at math" or

"you're so smart." This teaches children that although they can't always control all outcomes—like being chosen for the hockey team—they can control how much effort they put into different activities. The focus is always on growth.

When we focus on praising an outcome, we run the risk of our child engaging in an activity to please us or others. This leads to extrinsic motivation or motivation to participate in an activity based on meeting an external goal, seeking out praise and approval, winning a competition, or receiving an award or payment. Process praise puts the focus on intrinsic motivation: the "doing" of an activity for its inherent satisfaction.

Generic Praise	Process Praise
You're so smart.	You put a lot of effort into that assignment. How do you feel about it?
Good job!	You figured that out. It was really hard at first, but you kept at it. You must feel really proud.
You're such an amazing dancer.	You seem to love dancing, and you work really hard at it. I see your face glow when you get on stage.
Way to go.	You've practiced that move in soccer at home all week, and your hard work sure paid off!

2. **Make praise specific and sincere.** Children's desire to learn needs to be intrinsically motivated, not motivated by a desire to please or to perform for praise. Be deliberate and authentic when praising a child. When praise is manipulative or lacking in integrity, our children begin to doubt not only the praise itself, but the source of the praise. Think before you praise.

3. **Teach children about the brain.** We spoke about this in a previous chapter, but understanding how the brain works empowers children to understand that the brain can grow and develop over time. Teaching children about the brain needs to be an ongoing conversation within the home. Aside from emotion regulation and "flipping your lid," one of the most important concepts we can teach children about the brain is that it is constantly changing with experience (neuroplasticity).

    One of our favorite programs to teach children about the power of effort on the brain is an online program called Mindset Works. This program provides an e-learning platform that offers growth mindset training and programs to develop abilities and intelligence. We also love the growth mindset journals from Big Life Journal.

4. **Accept mistakes as learning opportunities.** Many of us may respond to this with an eye roll. It seems pretty obvious; however, research indicates that a large percentage of people cannot tolerate making mistakes. There are both physiological and psychological reasons for

this. Our body's response to failure is often experienced as actual physical pain. The same areas of the brain that are activated when we experience emotional injury are activated when we experience physical injury. So not only do we physically "feel" mistakes, but we experience shame as a result of an error, and we feel like something is wrong with us if we can't get something right.

Shame is one of the most potent and painful emotions we can experience, and people will do whatever they can to avoid feeling this way. As parents, it's important that we take time to help our children talk about how it feels to make a mistake and let them know there is nothing wrong with them. They aren't bad, stupid, or a failure. They're human, and perfectly imperfect.

But it's not just our child's relationship with the pain of failure that prevents them from taking appropriate risks. It's our relationship with our children's pain that gets in the way. We so badly want to protect them from failing because this pain is uncomfortable for us and our children. This is why parents jump in and complete their child's homework or science project for their child or why some parents pressure the teacher to allow their child to take a test in school repeatedly to get the grade they want when they simply didn't study. But pain is where children and adults alike experience growth and is the catalyst for molding integrity and character. Struggle is the ashes from which our children rise to become strong capable human beings. Our job isn't to remove their pain or protect them from making mistakes by solving problems for them. Our job is to be present with pain and lean into it. Our job is to say to our child: "I see your pain from this mistake. It is real and overwhelming, but I also see your courage, and it's bigger."

We have created a world in which children receive minimal exposure to the stress of making mistakes. A decade ago, faculty at Stanford and Harvard coined the term "failure deprived" to describe the emotional struggles that students faced when met with simple challenges. Many of our youth enter college or university without having experienced failure, and when they get out on their own and they now are competing for an A with 500 students instead of 25 peers, it's completely crippling. They have no relationship with pain to understand it's not actually a threat; it's their greatest teacher.

Children need to know that mistakes are an opportunity, not a dead end. It takes time and practice to get good at something, and we develop grit from picking ourselves back up after we fail. I always remind my children they weren't born walking. They had to sit up, crawl, stand, fall, walk, fall some more, and then run. Competence is not built overnight, and it takes a lot of falling to get it right.

We also need to be aware of how we talk about our own mistakes and how much space we give for learning and developing, which involves slowing everything down. Often, we don't communicate enough with our children. In our home, I intentionally focus on modeling the importance of making mistakes to our kids by saying, "This is hard. I will need to do it many more times before I get it right." Children will often see a parent's end point—the job, the degree, and the house—without knowing the backstory. Tell your child about the journey that got you to where you are: the assignments that were forgotten, the job interview you were not prepared for, and the budget that failed. These conversations build a growth mindset. We learn more from the journey than we do the final destination.

Dinnertime is a great time to share conversations around, "What's your oops?" As the parent, start the conversation by saying "This was my oops today." Lean into discomfort and vulnerability with your children. When they share their "oops," don't try and fix it or problem solve—you can do this later if needed. Think about the emotional experience under their story and then validate. So for instance, we may respond with "that sounds incredibly frustrating" or "you tried so hard, and it didn't work out." Be mindful of not filling any resulting silence with more words. Let your children sit with being uncomfortable. By nurturing this at home, you give your children the gift of courage—the ability to take a risk, to persevere when they want to quit, to lean into the discomfort of making mistakes, to recover, and to move forward in a way that harnesses new learning and understanding.

NEURON TRACE ACTIVITY

One activity we love to do with our own children or the children we work with is to take a piece of paper and have them write a mistake on it. You then crumple up the paper and smooth it out. You will see hundreds of little white lines all over the paper. Ask your child how they feel about that mistake and then color each line with a

different color. Explain that each line represents new neurons growing in their brain—a mistake is their brain growing and learning
and is not bad. Their brain has learned something, and it can build
on that mistake to make a new choice.

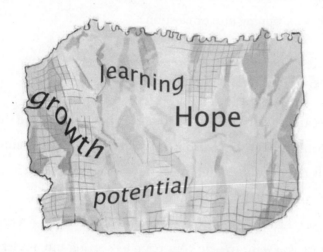

5. **Understand the role of emotion.** We have a whole
   chapter dedicated to understanding the role of emotions,
   but when we look specifically at developing a growth
   mindset, healthy stress—referred to as eustress—is
   inevitable when we operate at the edge of our abilities.
   As parents, our perception of stress determines how our
   children understand stress. When we construe stress
   as "bad," the negative connotation creates a snowball
   impact. Our body experiences a stress signal, and we
   interpret the signal as negative, which spawns more stress.
   However, when we perceive stress as a signal that we are
   being challenged, that we are growing and learning, that
   others are there to support this growth, then we open

ourselves up to deeper levels of motivation and creativity. Eustress has to be accompanied with healthy lifestyle strategies like sleep, nutrition, limited screen time, leisure time, healthy boundaries, and secure connections to prevent tipping into exhaustion.

SAMPLE DIALOGUE

Stress and anxiety are designed to keep us safe from bad things happening, but they're also there to help us be better people! Small and medium amounts of stress are good because it makes you want to do things that are hard but make you stronger. It's like when you want to do well at soccer, you feel nervous, because you want to help your team by scoring and not let them down. Your stress makes you practice harder, and then you get to be a better soccer player, and you score more goals. Can you think of another time you felt stressed about something, but it helped you try harder?

Lean into talking about difficult emotional times: One thing we loved about the book *The Danish Way of Parenting* is the author's explanation that in Danish culture—which has some of the happiest people in the world—rarely shy away from dark themes and tragic endings. Why? Danes believe that we learn more about our own character from suffering than we do from success. Stories about hardship, struggle, and conflict enhance social-emotional skills because they communicate truths about the human experience and help children identify with the feelings of others.

One way we can do this is by simply reading classic fairy tales by Hans Christian Andersen. These stories bring difficult, and even painful, topics into family homes in developmentally appropriate ways that don't overwhelm children. In a guided reading experience, we can talk to children about what elements of the story move them. In sitting with difficult moments, our children start to tap into the exquisite richness of being human.

PILLAR 2: BELONGING

The second pillar that we are going to look at is belonging. We looked at the importance of attachment in an earlier chapter, and in this chapter, we will focus specifically on how belonging builds resilience. Many of us are so pulled by the demands of everyday life, and in the frantic pursuit of perfection, we end up desperately trying to turn to experts, parenting books, and Facebook groups to figure out "how to parent." Yet all that our children need from us is to trust our gut, to listen to the wisdom we already carry, and to be the answer.

Instinctively, you have enough, and you are enough for your child. To be the answer, we need to slow down, be present, and begin to trust our inner wisdom. According to Dr. Neufeld, "We have been educated out of our instinct." We have lost our way in understanding and connecting with our children. Many families live far away from "their village" or network of extended family and close community. Often the strain of a world that is too fast and too pressured distracts us from what is important. The beautiful rituals of sit-down meals, bedtime stories, and lazy family-focused Sunday afternoons are quickly disappearing.

Dr. Gordon Neufeld does an excellent job of explaining how often we end up focusing on socialization over security. In Western societies, there is a drive to teach children rules, to have them "learn" to be in groups of other children, and to start teaching academic material earlier and earlier. Dr. Neufeld argues that if we focus on security first—prioritizing bonding activities and creating societies where children can spend as much time as possible with connected adults during the formative years—they will grow up feeling more rooted and confident. Once a child feels secure, socialization comes more naturally.

Think back to the chapter about the brain. You will recall that the thinking brain is more likely to be activated when a child feels safe and connected. Conversely, the amygdala in the feeling brain is more likely to be activated when a child feels threatened. From a neurological perspective, resiliency is the ability to quieten the stress response during a challenge and tune into a "thinking brain response," which helps us consider different perspectives, problem solve, or adapt to the challenge. The ability to activate the thinking brain during stressful moments is nurtured through repeated experiences of a child feeling safe, supported, and loved as they journey through life's ups and downs.

The foundation of resiliency is built on connection and belonging. Brené Brown says, "belonging is being part of something bigger than yourself. But it's also the courage to stand alone and to belong to yourself above all else." When we slow down, when we focus on what's important to our family, it helps our children to realize they are a part of something bigger. It is within this warm, connected space that our children can start to explore who they want to be in the world. As our children move through different developmental phases, our focus is always on connection and ensuring that the compass returns to the parents.

Children need to feel they can belong at home and have the space to be who they are without judgment, before they can truly experience the feeling of belonging to themselves. How do we foster belonging?

Our children need to know we fully and unequivocally value them for who they are, not what they do or achieve. They are worthy just by existing. This means we focus on effort vs. outcome (as explained earlier in this chapter), allow them to pursue their passions without judgment, and make room for all their feelings without shaming or punishing.

When children experience unconditional love and acceptance, that is the essence of belonging.

Use phrases such as:

- "You belong in our family."
- "No one could ever replace you."
- "I love you just the way you are."
- "You have special gifts to share with the world that are unique to you."
- "In our family, we don't hurt one another's bodies."

Fostering Belonging with Stories

Every family has a unique tapestry of traditions, rituals, family history, culture, relational joy, and practices. Your family culture is what makes your family unique. As human beings, we have a deep, innate desire to belong. When we intentionally create a strong family culture, we create a natural place of belonging for our children and for ourselves.

When children are not anchored to their parents, they search for belonging in other places. In the adolescent years, the pursuit of independence and peer group identification is a natural developmental stage, but when children have a primary sense of belonging with their family unit, the family unit remains an anchor through all the shifts and changes of life. If you want to read more on this specific topic, Dr. Gordon Neufeld and Dr. Mate co-authored a beautiful book, *Hold On to Your Kids: Why Parents Need to Matter More than Peers.*

What is your family's Story? A portion of our family culture unfolds naturally, but when we add intentionality to our stories and the lives of our children's stories, we breathe life into our tremendous power to narrate what these stories may or may not look like. Our history—and the generations of people in our family who came before us—play an integral role in how we come to define and understand family.

In the chapter "Compassionate vs. Reactive Parenting," we explore how triggers from our childhood will be activated in our parenting journey and how these triggers are often "stress/trauma activators" that have been passed on from generation to generation. Similarly, value systems tend to be passed down. For some families, we may actively work at moving away from generational value sets, while other families may hold onto value sets.

One of the best strategies to enhance family resilience is to give your child a strong family narrative; help them understand where they came from and what influences have shaped who they are today. One smaller study found that when a child knows about their family's history, they have higher self-esteem, a stronger sense of control, and a better understanding of how their family functions. Look at family photo albums, tell them stories about your life, about growing up, and about the generations of people that came before them.

Be intentional about the ingredients that we want to include in our family's essence. How do we want to explore stories with our children? When do we want to explore different stories? How have we explained stories to ourselves? To our partner? Which aspects of our history do we want to embrace more? Let go of? Don't underestimate how powerful stories are in fostering belonging.

Fostering Belonging with Ritual

Rituals are quickly becoming an area of great interest within the field of psychology. They can be defined as a series of actions that are performed in a customary manner. Often, rituals are referred to in a religious or spiritual context, but this can also refer to a family's pattern of making pancakes on a Saturday morning, walks after dinner, or special greetings. Rituals are a safe container in which children can immerse themselves in familiarity, belonging, and expression; rituals bring a rhythmic quality to a child's life.

Rituals also give children a sense of identity and can prove soothing when they face transitions in other areas of their life. They are a powerful vehicle to teach values as they focus on maintaining and threading what is important into a child's life through tangible, repeated experiences.

Who a family is, is not necessarily about increasing activities and experiences. It's about repeating what is important so it becomes an indelible part of their family culture. Family rituals also often create continuity, passing values down among generations, and they may link us to family members who are no longer with us. It is important not to confuse "ritual" and "routine." A routine is about getting things done, while a ritual is about doing things in a way that expresses a family's connection in a unique way and often leaves an emotional imprint. Spagnola and Fiese distinguish further by stating that when routines are disrupted, they create a disruption, whereas when rituals are disrupted in a family, they threaten family cohesion. Rituals bind us together and prove instrumental in helping us navigate life's ups and downs.

When your children look back in fifteen years, what rituals will they remember? My adult clients are far more likely to tell me about a childhood ritual—such as the smell of pancakes on a Saturday morning, family swims every Friday night, or a special bedtime ritual—than they are to tell me about an expensive holiday they went on as a child. Some adult clients struggle to recall any family rituals, and this is usually an indicator of larger family stressors.

Be intentional about creating and sustaining ritual and weave it into the fabric of your family's life. These are the moments that build your child's character, and one day, they will contribute to your child's inherent understanding of belonging and love.

Fostering Belonging by Creating a Cooperative Family Culture

In these families' relationships are prioritized over things (i.e., your children are fighting over a toy, and you say, "this relationship is more important than your toy. We will bring it back once everyone has had time to cool down"). Respect for one another is valued above all else. In our family our children know that disrespectful language (i.e., name-calling) and being physical when upset is never acceptable, and a line is always drawn if that value is violated in any capacity. Children and adults participate in maintaining the house and preparing meals. Family time is a priority; in our family, that includes watching movies together with popcorn on the weekend, walks after supper, swimming, and family game nights. Lastly, a cooperative family culture includes a focus on actively listening and engaging in mutual conversations versus simply talking at one another. Adults model this by focusing on validating emotions, paraphrasing what children and their spouse have said, and asking questions to show interest in what the speaker has to say.

PILLAR 3: HOPE

Hope is the final pillar of resiliency. Hope is the desire or belief that circumstances will change for the better. In her book *Fostering Resilience and Well-Being in Children and Families in Poverty: Why Hope Still Matters*, Dr. Maholmes states that hope is a major

contributing factor for our children being able to lift themselves out of poverty. She defines hope as a mixture of planning, motivation, and determination. When our children struggle at school, at home, or within the community, it is essential to utilize a multifaceted approach to help them bounce back.

As clinicians, when we work with a child, we often engage other influential adults within the child's social system to help create a shift. With parental consent, we speak to teachers, day care providers, and coaches. Our children need a village, and they need at least one adult who can see through the storms, to look at entire environments to ask: "What can we do to create a shift? What stressors can be reduced? What relationships can be nurtured? How do we foster hope for this child?" Our children need to know that life can and will be better.

Part of having hope is to internalize the idea that the world is truly a good place. While tragedies, adversity, and suffering are inevitable, when we have hope, we are able to hold on to the belief that we are all interconnected, that humans are inherently good, and that we are all on this planet to evolve into something greater, leaving the world a better place than when we came into it. How do we foster this?

- **Volunteer with your children.** It is well documented that a helper's high is associated with greater health outcomes and feelings of overall life satisfaction. When we engage in self-less service to others, we feel like we are a part of something bigger than ourselves, and we have more appreciation for what is in our own lives.

- **Get inspired.** Teach your children to listen to their favorite music, read an uplifting story, or watch an inspirational movie. Learning about other people's stories can show them that there can be positives in the most difficult situations.

- **Explore how your child's gifts can make a difference in the world.** Once we know what is meaningful to our children and we have started exploring purpose, we can ask our children how their gifts can make the lives of others better. Maybe your daughter is good with animals so she volunteers at an animal shelter. She sees the difference she can make in the life of another creature, and this inspires her to study to become a veterinary technician. When she works with animals, she feels like she can impact change in her world—this makes her feel hopeful, like she is in the passenger seat in her own life. She is a part of a global community and works collectively to make the planet a better place to live. Once that seed of hope is planted, even when things seem dark, she will have something powerful to hold on to. A reason to get up each morning, knowing her time on this earth has meaning.

We close this chapter with a reminder that the three pillars—purpose, belonging, and hope—must be firmly in place for a child to be able to face life's challenges head-on.

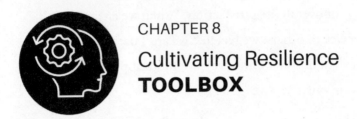

CHAPTER 8

Cultivating Resilience
TOOLBOX

Pillar 1: Purpose

Foster interest: Create opportunities for nondirected play (this allows for a child's natural interests to blossom). Let your child direct the play (they can play alone or with you—as long as they are in the driver's seat).

Creative exploration: Create space in your home for nondirected exploration—a craft table with markers, scissors, paint, and other materials.

Turn down the pressure valve: As a parent stay invested in the pursuits your child is interested in, but don't thwart their innate joy by becoming over-involved.

Let them help: Get your child engaged in REAL household chores. Not only do chores increase feelings of connection and competency, but they also expose your child to activities they may not naturally gravitate toward.

Talk to them: Don't just talk AT your child, talk to them. Be authentically curious. Listen more than you talk.

Ask open-ended questions:

- How did that happen?
- What are you really good at?
- What might you change?
- What is your plan?

- What do you like to do?

- What do you see?

- What scares you?

- Do you have any ideas...

- What is your strength?

- What would you do differently the next time?

It's in the micro-moments: Turn your phone off, tune in, actively listen to your child, tell them how much you love them, hug them, learn from them.

Savoring moments activity: We are more likely to remember special moments when we write them down or tell them to someone else. Make a list in a journal or on your phone of favorite moments with your child.

Fostering a growth mindset

- **Focus on process praise:** We always focus on the effort a child puts in, instead of on an outcome. Examples include: "You are studying so hard," "you are putting a lot of thought into how to balance the blocks."

- **Make praise specific and sincere:** Avoid inauthentic praise. Really think about the intention behind praising a child. Think about the areas of growth and development you are seeing: this is where praise has the most impact.

- **Teach children about the brain:** We can teach this to children from a young age. Our favorite work is: *Big Life Journal: Illustrated & Guided Journals Helping Kids, Tweens & Teens Build Self-Esteem & Resiliency.*

- **Accept mistakes as learning opportunities:** Normalize making mistakes. Talk about your own mistakes. At dinnertime, make it a routine question: "What was your oops today?"

- **Understand the role of emotion:** Talk to kids about "good stress,": stress that helps our body to prepare for new challenges and for growth. Talk to them about how these signals can create a desire to back away from a challenge, but it is often a signal telling us that we are about to discover new strengths.

Pillar 2: Belonging

Focus on security over socialization:
- Instead of rushing your young child to socialize and to be involved in community activities, focus on their sense of security—their family needs to be their safe space.
- Focus on effort versus outcome when talking to your child about their activities.
- Allow them to pursue their unique passions without judgment.
- Make room for all of their feelings (not just the ones you are comfortable with).
- Embrace them fully for who they are, not who you thought they would be or should be.
- Use phrases like:

  "I love you just the way you are"
  "You are important"
  "In our family…"
  "You belong in our family"
  "Nothing you could do would stop me from loving you"

Foster belonging by creating a cooperative family culture:
- Spend quality time together
- Prioritize relationships over things: "Our relationship is

more important than this argument. Let's cool down and come back to this discussion after a walk."

- **Validate emotions:** "You are so frustrated."

- **Paraphrase:** "Ah, so you are nervous about the sleepover because you are worried that you won't know some of the children?"

Pillar 3: Hope

When a child is struggling, we want to explore what stressors there may be in their environment, in their relationships, and what skills may require attention.

Environment stressors:

- Questions could include: Is the environment overwhelming? Underwhelming? Lacking in cultural connection?

- Not developmentally appropriate? Too bright? Too dark? Too cold? Too hot?

Relationship stressors:

- Are the adults in a child's life stressed?

- Is connection lacking?

- Is safety lacking?

- What activities make your child feel loved?

- Where do you find shared moments of joy together?

- What moments are difficult together?

- What is one step that could make those moments a little easier?

Skill building:

- What is my child struggling with?

- What skill do we need to work on?

- Break the skill into components; actively work on nurturing strong feelings of competency with your child experiencing competency as they learn.

Volunteer as a family: Volunteering helps us to connect with our community, to be with others who may be struggling, and to fully engage with a wide array of feelings.

Get inspired: Choose one hero a month as a family—read books, watch a movie, and talk about what it means to inspire others.

Explore how your child's gifts can make a difference: We find meaning when we actively experience making a difference in the world.

CHAPTER NINE

THE POWER OF PLAY

We know you are likely as exhausted as many parents are, and the thought of playing Barbies with your six-year-old might not be at the top of your parenting wish list—you might even dread it. We want to make space for the fact that you may experience some trepidation while reading, and not because the information isn't valuable, but rather because play is often difficult for parents to engage in for a variety of reasons. Parents often feel too busy, too tired, or it feels too awkward for them. We want you to keep an open mind and know that children have a natural proclivity to play on their own, and we're not asking you to play all day long with them. What we are asking is that you make the space for play in your home, in lieu of screens or scheduled activities, and when you do find the time, even if it's just an hour a week, or fifteen minutes a day, play with your child to help them feel seen, heard, and valued. We're here to explain how vitally important this is to your child's development, but luckily, you don't have to do nearly as much as you think to help facilitate this.

Play is fundamental to a child's well-being—arguably to anyone's, regardless of age. Studies across species indicate that: "For humans and other animals, play is a universal training course and language of trust. The belief that one is safe with another being or in any situation is formed over time during regular play. Trust is the basis of intimacy, cooperation, creativity, successful work, and more." Play is a child's language and is often an unconscious expression of a child's inner conflicts and a way to resolve fears, build confidence, and learn self-advocacy skills.

The basic building blocks of play are evident in the early days of a child's life and are comprised of gentle coos, giggles, and spit bubbles. It is in these moments, as the caregiver responds to the infant's cues, that the foundation of trust is developed. The infant is reassured that their caregiver is intimately connected, attuned, and, on a deeper evolutionary level, able to protect them. Our propensity for play tends to dwindle as our children get older. Yet if we stop and reflect on the fact that play is the foundation of trust and that as trust shifts, develops, and deepens over time, so should play. In Kim Payne's work, he cites play deprivation as one of the key factors in the "undeclared war on childhood." Play has become the forgotten instrument of love and connection and one of the keys that unlocks the door to childhood development. When parents engage in or observe child-driven play (play that is chosen by the child without the adult's input), they are honored with being able to see the world through their child's eyes. These deeply relational experiences show the child that the parent is present and invested in their exploration of the world.

Let's examine the benefits of play in terms of cognitive, physical, and psychological growth.

THE BENEFITS OF PLAY

Play lights up the brain

Play is an essential component of healthy brain development. Play helps children prime their brains for an academic setting by nurturing executive functioning skills. Think about the planning, problem-solving, and emotion regulation that goes into building a fort. Play is a natural vehicle for learning.

The connection between play and cognitive development became more evident in 1964 when Marion Diamond conducted research that raised one group of rat pups in a stark, solitary environment and another group of rat pups in a highly stimulating, toy-filled environment. After a while, the researchers examined the brains of the rats from each group. The rats that had been in the stimulating environment had cerebral cortices that were much thicker than the rats who had been in solitary confinement. Research conducted at a later stage confirmed the same results: rats who played more were higher functioning.

Further rat studies have shown that, after a bout of rough-and-tumble play, BDNF (brain-derived neurotrophic factor) increases in their brains. BDNF is a growth factor and long-chain protein, and it is sometimes referred to as brain fertilizer, as it is vital for the growth and maintenance of brain cells. BDNF is essential for learning, memory, and alertness. Low levels of BDNF in humans has been linked to depressive symptoms and to a lower stress tolerance. It is highly likely that the human brain responds in similar ways. The more we play, the more BDNF increases, and the more the brain lights up.

Play nurtures sustained focus

Children have also been shown to focus more after they have had time to engage in free play. Interestingly, research shows that the benefits of sustained focus after play are far greater after unstructured free time to play vs. structured play (like gym class).

Play nurtures receptive and expressive language

A British research study looked at the play of children from age one to six years old and measured symbolic play. The children were asked to engage in imaginative play. Researchers found that the children who scored highest in the symbolic play categories also had better receptive (what a child understands) and expressive language (what a child says) than their counterparts.

Play nurtures problem-solving

Links have been found between a child's ability to engage in pretend play and their ability to solve divergent problems (a divergent problem has multiple solutions). Play has also been shown to help calm the fight-or-flight response. When children engage in play, they receive small bouts of adrenaline. "Will she catch me?" "Will the tower fall over?" "Will my superhero fly?" These tiny bouts of adrenaline help to inoculate children against bigger stressful moments in their life. Play gives a child an arena to practice certain behaviors with minimal risk. This is a beautiful path to resiliency. Each time a child experiences stress, recognizes they can withstand the stress, and emerges on the other side to the stressful situation with new strength, this creates a neural pathway between challenge and competency.

Play nurtures physical strength

Play has been shown to enhance children's understanding of how the body moves and engages with the world. It builds active, healthy bodies in a natural, joyful way. All movement in play nurtures physical strength, but rough-and-tumble play is often overlooked as the star of the show. Physical rough-and-tumble play helps children understand and experiment with their world. It is something that all mammals engage in. In our younger years, we tend to be more body based than cognitive based. Highly physical play helps children work through emotional struggles, and it releases stress hormones and stimulates endorphins and oxytocin (those feel-good hormones that increase bonding). It also stimulates the BDNF in the amygdala (where emotions are processed in the feeling brain) and in the prefrontal cortex (where executive functioning skills live in the thinking brain).

Play nurtures emotional strength and resiliency

Play allows children to conquer their fears, master new challenges, build confidence, and enhance resiliency. "The function of play is to build social brains that know how to interact with one another." When children drive play, they practice decision-making skills, discover interests and passions, learn self-advocacy skills, and master new social and emotional skills. Play led by an adult has been shown to be less effective in these domains. Children's creativity and leadership skills tend to dip when an adult leads the play.

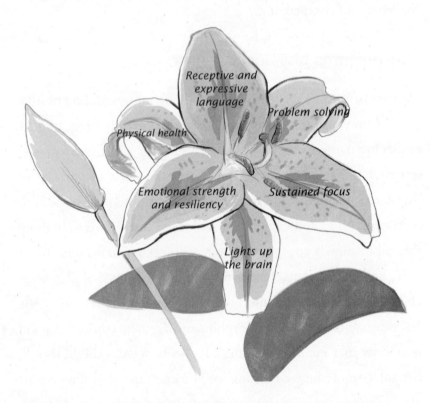

Let's explore a clinical example: Aaron played quietly on the floor of my play therapy room. His mother brought him into therapy because of nightmares and separation anxiety. Aaron was a shy and sensitive boy, but in his play, he created frightful scenes of aggression and death. His mother was very concerned about this play, and she had tried to veer him away from it at home, encouraging him to paint or play with Lego instead. I encouraged this mom to allow the play to happen, and as long as he wasn't hurting himself or others, it was completely appropriate. The truth was this was a little boy who was highly sensitive, and he absorbed everything around him and felt very deeply. His classroom was quite chaotic this year, and he felt overwhelmed by all the emotions and noise—the overwhelm was projected as death and aggression in his play.

We started to see changes in Aaron after about seven weeks of playing out these themes, both in the playroom and outside of it. His sleep improved, he separated more easily from his mother at school drop-off, and the nightmares became less vivid. I worked with his mother on ways to decrease overstimulation at home and gave his teachers some ideas for accommodations in the classroom. Aaron was simply looking for a way to express his overwhelm, and at six, he didn't have the words yet. The play experience gave Aaron the platform to express his deep-seated emotions and develop the internal resources to cope.

Play remains essential as we move through our teens and adulthood, though it changes form—we may hit a hockey puck, bake, collect items, climb mountains, or explore new cultures. "Play is a state of mind." It helps to relieve stress, improve memory and cognition, and foster empathy, compassion, and intimacy.

When we look at the incredible cognitive, physical, and emotional benefits of play, it becomes glaringly obvious that play is a vital ingredient in nurturing resiliency in our children. Play fosters experiences of confidence and competency, primes the prefrontal cortex, inoculates against stress, and it fosters connection, communication, and joy as it provides a safe arena for children to practice and enhance social and emotional skills.

There are many different types of play: structured play, individual play, risky play, and therapeutic play are all examples of what we like to call "joy infusers." Let's take a closer look at these types of play and how you can incorporate them into your home.

STRUCTURED PLAY

Structured games, puzzles, and activities can be highly beneficial for a child. In the therapy room, we usually begin the therapeutic journey with nondirected play. As a child's psychological world becomes more evident, we gradually introduce more structured activities. For example, if a child struggles with impulse issues, we may play Simon Says, or we may create an obstacle course to help nurture problem-solving skills.

As our children's thinking brain comes more online around the age of five years old, we may find that they become more interested in sitting down and playing a board game. Board games are a wonderful way to foster executive functioning skills such as problem-solving, emotion regulation, logical thinking, and creative manipulation of materials in a fun, nonthreatening way. For children who struggle with frustration around structured games, it can be helpful to gradually build skills: start off with easier activities, and then use a laddered approach to increase tolerance.

These activities can also be extremely helpful in enabling children to process feelings that they may not have the words for yet. There are various board games designed for specific therapeutic reasons—anxiety, anger, grief, divorce, and separation. At the Institute, these games are only seen as one of several tools—a tool that some children will resonate with, while others will not.

The most important rule of thumb is to follow your child's lead. When children feel safe to explore and trust their own intuition, they will naturally gravitate and become curious about activities that nurture growth.

INDIVIDUAL PLAY

Our children do not need to have supervised play all day, every day. Creating a mix of parent-child play and individual play is optimal. Often, we rush to fill the "boredom" gaps for our children—yet it is in these moments of boredom that the sparks of creativity are ignited. It is in these quiet moments that a child discovers who they truly are. Don't rescue them; let the space be theirs. So many of us struggle with what to say when our children are bored. Kim Payne suggests "out-boring the boring" and simply replying "something to do is right around the corner!"

If your child really struggles, consider creating a boredom jar with your child where they write down different ideas for free time on popsicle sticks. When your child is bored, they can use the jar for inspiration.

RISKY PLAY

In a world that has become more and more bubble-wrapped, few of our children are given the gift of being able to engage in risky play. Risky play refers to the opportunity to experiment and learn through (primarily) outdoor activities that entail a level of uncertainty and thrill. One of our favorite definitions is: "Risky play is subsumed within physical activity play and has been defined as thrilling and exciting and where there is a risk of physical injury." When children engage in risky play, they typically experience feelings of hesitation, fear, or mastery. Often we will see the same activity being explored repetitively.

Think for a moment about a child who has just learned how to navigate the monkey bars. There is fear, excitement, and eventual mastery as they try the same sequence again and again. The research is clear that risky play is positively correlated with psychological well-being, physical movement, independence, curiosity, self-awareness, and developing perceptual motor capacity. Interestingly too, children who engage in risky play are more likely to be able to assess dangerous situations and mitigate risk. Building this "risk muscle" from an early age is an essential part of helping a child to experiment with risky situations, to test boundaries, and to navigate new psychological terrain.

At the Institute, we firmly believe that if this muscle is developed early, it helps our children make informed decisions when it comes to assessing and dealing with difficult situations in their teen years. This is not a skill that just develops when our teen is in a tricky situation at a party one day. It's a skill that has been built through years of different experiences. Risky play helps to build a solid staircase toward being able to trust one's own judgment calls.

There are six types of identified risky play: play at great heights, play at high speed, play with dangerous tools such as saws and knives, play near dangerous elements such as fire and water, rough-and-tumble play, and play where there's a chance of getting lost or "disappearing." It is really important to note that risky play does not mean unsupervised play.

In risky play, an adult is close by but allows the child to explore and confront risk without rescuing the child. In these instances, it is important to give the child enough space (while still ensuring all safety precautions are being followed) and to only direct when necessary. The motto needs to be "as safe as necessary" instead of "as safe as possible." This is a difficult one, as some parents may jump in quickly with "be careful" or "don't do that." It's really important to reflect on where you land as a parent on the rescuing continuum and to assess if you have some personal work to do.

The next time you feel the urge to yell "be careful," you should stop, assess, and ask yourself if there is a real danger or not. If there is, then help your child to maneuver out of the situation. If there is not, then consider replacing "be careful" with helping your child to really notice his or her environment.

Instead say: "Notice how strong that branch is." "Do you see how quickly the water is moving?" "Can you hear the wind in the trees?" "Do you feel excited?" We can also get them to problem solve. "What is your plan to cross the log or which hand do you want to move next?" In shifting our language, we move from being in control of our children to helping them be in control themselves.

The bottom line is to play. Swing on the monkey bars, become a knight with your child, blow bubbles, and build snowmen. Play is like a protective shield from life's inevitable road bumps, and it connects us to our child, builds resiliency, and fosters well-being. Keep playing. It's one of the simplest and best parenting tips out there.

SOMETIMES PLAY ISN'T WHAT YOU THINK IT IS

Now here is where we want all of you to take a deep breath in: you don't have to "play" with your kids all the time. If we look at studies of child development cross-culturally, the concept of child-centered activities doesn't exist, particularly in nonindustrialized nations. As an example, Suzanne Gaskins, a psychological anthropologist at the University of Chicago, has studied Maya parenting in Central America, and similar to many other nonindustrialized societies, these parents don't engage in "play" with their children. In fact, they don't entertain their children at all. These parents welcome and encourage their children to participate in the family's everyday life. They help cook, clean, fix bikes, and take care of family members. Children are invited to be an active part of the family and subsequently learn the skills to be self-sufficient. That doesn't mean these children don't engage in nonstructured play; it's just that the parents don't encourage it or play with them. While children are allowed and encouraged to help with chores, they will get bored or sidetracked by play. Parents will allow this (because having children help can get in the way of being productive), and that's where you would see games, imaginative play, and gross motor play break out.

Children have an innate desire to help at a young age. Helping you while you fix the car, assisting you while preparing a meal, or helping their sibling get dressed in the morning is part of a child's world. Dr. Stuart Brown, a psychiatrist and founder of the National Institute for Play, suggests that there are seven patterns of play that are present throughout all stages of life. It is purposeless (not goal-driven), voluntary (they do it because they love it, not because they have to), and there is an inherent attraction to it. While doing it, there is freedom from time constraints (i.e., they lose track of time when they are doing it), and they lack a feeling of self-consciousness when engaging in the activity. It has improvisational potential (they can infuse their imagination and personal choices in the activity), and it has a continuation desire that makes you want to do it more. This means that helping around the house—if it comes from an innate, self-driven place— can be considered play!

IS PLAY ONE OF THE SECRETS TO THE HAPPIEST CHILDREN ON THE PLANET?

In the groundbreaking book *The Danish Way of Parenting*, Jessica Joelle Alexander cites that the Danes' proclivity to allow for unstructured free play as a key to unlocking happiness and resilience in children.

In Denmark, dating back to 1871, Niels and Erna Juel-Hansen came up with the first pedagogy based on educational theory, which incorporated play. They discovered that free play is crucial for a child's development. For many years, Danish children weren't even allowed to start school before they were seven. In Denmark, parents try not to intervene in their child's play worlds unless it's absolutely necessary. They trust their children to be able to do and try new things and give them space to build their own trust in themselves. In Danish schools, there are programs in place to promote learning through sports, play, and exercise for all students, and instead of homework, children are let out of school as early as 2 p.m. and encouraged to engage in play.

In her book, Jessica Alexander encourages parents to reduce the use of electronics and to focus instead on creating a sensory-rich environment that sparks exploration and cortical growth in the brain. She has wonderful ideas that include fostering and encouraging the use of art in nonstructured ways. In addition, she recommends letting children explore outside with the suggestion of mixing children of different age groups to enhance and deepen play. Jessica suggests letting children be free to play without adult intervention, letting children guide the play when we do engage with them, and allowing children to play alone.

ANTIDOTE TO ANXIETY

Play is crucial for adapting to stress. When children are engaged in play it actually turns on the sympathetic nervous system, or the gas pedal of the brain, associated with the stress response. In play, the fight-or-flight centers of the brain are activated and chemicals such as cortisol and adrenaline are released in small to moderate amounts, producing eustress. The child will explore through play how to handle their dysregulation through what we call mastery play—this is where risky play, mentioned earlier in this chapter, is crucial. It enables them to test a precarious situation, decide how much anxiety they can handle, and learn ways to manage anxiety, overcome their fears, and develop competency. They also learn how to regulate their emotions, modulate their behavior, and develop an internal locus of control: the belief that they have the power to control their lives and the things that happen to them.

By exposing children's brains to these chemicals in small, consistent amounts, the brain becomes less responsive to stress over time. In other words, the child has practiced handling these neurochemicals in psychologically safe and manageable ways. When the child is faced with a larger stressor—such as being teased at school or having to try a scary new activity—the brain knows how to manage the physiological state associated with anxiety, and the child has the emotion regulation skills and coping skills in place to overcome the stressor.

OUR RECOMMENDATIONS FOR TOYS

We want you to buy less stuff for your children. Children don't need endless piles of toys. In fact, they need very few toys at all. The less they have, the more they will be forced to create and utilize their imagination. Having too many toys isn't more fun—it's more confusing and overwhelming. Imagine if on your desk at work, you have five different laptops, three iPads, and five smartphones to choose from, in addition to all the stationery and stacks of paper and documents on your desk. It's hard to get to the actual "work" when there are too many choices and too many distractions—it creates a choice paralysis. Similarly, the actual "work" of playing can be impeded when children have too many choices; it prevents flow.

We love the recommendations made by Kim John Payne in his book *Simplicity Parenting*, and we recommend you use this as a guide to promoting deep, meaningful connections in play at home.

Based on his recommendations, parents should purge any toys that light up/make obnoxious sounds, that are replicas, broken, or have a strong storyline attached to them that prevents children from creating their own stories. What should we keep: blocks; Lego (without the manuals); natural objects such as rocks, feathers, sand, leaves, pine cones, or shells; dress-up clothes; items that encourage gross motor movement such a skipping ropes, balls, or Hula-Hoops; a variety of art supplies; simple figures or dolls; climbing structures or tents; books; kitchen items such as play food, dishes, pots, and pans; and old household items that no longer work. It's also recommended that you cycle through toys, meaning keep 75% of your toys in bins in a spare room or closet, and every few weeks, you replace the toys in your child's playroom/area with the toys that have been put away. This will make the toys feel new without having to purchase new toys.

CHAPTER 9

The Power of Play
TOOLBOX

Play lights up the brain

Games that target working memory: Storytelling, pretend play, scavenger hunt

Games that target impulse control: Simon Says, musical statues, board games

Games that target flexibility: Pretend play, obstacle courses, games of chance

Play nurtures sustained focus, receptive and expressive language and problem-solving

Child-directed play/imaginative play with puppets, dolls, silk scarves, nature items, movement toys

Play nurtures physical strength

Rough-and-tumble play, catch, tag, playground activities, organized sport

Structured games

Some children respond well to structured games that help them with emotional wellness:

Anxiety

Create a worry monster made from playdough or clay. Once complete, some questions may include:

- What is your monster's name?
- Tell me about the colors you chose.
- When did he first come into your life?
- When is he really big in your life?
- When is he smaller?
- How do you make him smaller?
- What do you want to tell your worry monster?
- What is one thing we want to try to do to shrink him this week?

ADHD

Obstacle courses where you have to stop, pause, think, and then continue

Games on a trampoline, which helps to develop gross motor skills and provides a physical release of energy

Board games that nurture strategic thinking: CATAN Junior, ICE COOL, Mouse Trap, The Magic Labyrinth

Anger

Create a volcano that erupts. Once complete, questions may include:

- What does it feel like in your body when the volcano starts to rumble?
- What does it feel like in your body when the volcano erupts?
- What do you do to keep the rumbling low?
- How does it feel when the rumbling is soft?

Grief and Loss

Create a memory box/memory corner/memory book.

Risky play

Risky play is positively correlated with psychological well-being.
Ideas include: swinging on monkey bars, climbing trees, riding a
bike at high speed down a hill, playing with tools like a hammer,
playing near fire or water, engaging in rough-and-tumble play
(play wrestling), and play where there's a chance of getting lost
(hiding in the park). An adult is close by, but not hovering.
Motto: Safe as necessary NOT safe as possible
Instead of Be Careful, say:

- Notice where your foot is.

- What is your plan?

- What is your body telling you?

- Which direction is the water flowing?

Sometimes play isn't what you think it is

Welcoming children to participate in everyday life:
- Caring for a sibling

- Sweeping

- Helping with yard work

- Cooking

- Washing the car

Is play one of the secrets to the happiest children on the planet?

Key secrets
- Don't intervene in a child's play unless necessary

- Reduce electronic use

- Create a rich sensory environment (objects to smell, touch, see from different angles, listen too, and play with in different ways)
- Let children explore outside
- Mix children of different age groups
- Let children play alone
- Let children direct play

Our recommendations for toys

- Less is better.
- Remove broken toys, noisy toys, and toys that are no longer played with.
- Keep blocks, Lego, natural rocks, feathers, sand, leaves, pine cones, or shells; dress-up clothes; items that encourage gross motor movement such a skipping ropes, balls, or Hula-Hoops; a variety of art supplies; simple figures or dolls; climbing structures or tents; books; kitchen items such as play food, dishes, pots, and pans; and old household items that no longer work.

PART 2: ICP'S THERAPEUTIC PLAY MODEL

Toys are children's words and play is their language.
—GARY LANDRETH

While you now know the importance of play, many parents are unsure of how to play with their child, or they would like the skills to work with their child in a way that's intentional and can help foster positive mental health outcomes. We created this model of therapeutic play based on our work as play therapists, and as moms who play with our own children, and it expands on the work of Gary Landreth—a foundational clinician in both play therapy and Child-Parent Relationship Therapy (CPRT).

Play therapy is to children what counseling is to adults. Play therapy utilizes play, children's natural medium of expression, to help them express their feelings more easily through toys instead of words. As registered play therapists, our work focuses on deepening a child's play so that they can harness their innate resiliency. The beauty of therapeutic play is that it does not have to be isolated to a play therapist's office. There are many skills that can be utilized at home to help your child thrive. The Institute is very proud of its therapeutic play model. At the Institute, all our work is guided by the neurological development of a child. Our model is based on the brain and focuses on priming and integrating the four quadrants of the brain through play: the thinking brain, the lower floor of the brain (feelings and body brain), the right-hand hemisphere of the brain, and the left-hand hemisphere of the brain.

Sample session: If you want to see what this looks like, we have created a sample session for you to see. Please visit: **myparenting-handbook.com/ch9session**

Let's do a quick recap of the brain. If you are unsure, you can always return to our earlier chapter on the brain. The upstairs floor of the brain is our thinking brain (which includes the prefrontal cortex) and is responsible for emotion regulation, language, consequences, understanding problem-solving, and considering different perspectives. The lower floor of the brain, which includes the brain stem (body brain) and limbic system (feelings brain) is responsible for regulating the body, attachment, emotion, the stress response, and autonomic functions.

The brain is further divided into the right-hand side and the left-hand side. The right-hand side is where feelings, passion, creativity, and play live. The right-hand side develops first and is dominant in children. The left-hand side is where logic and language live.

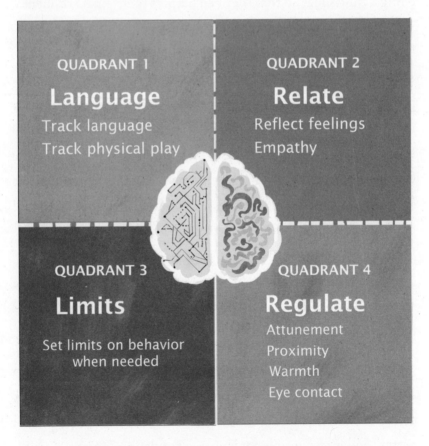

In our therapeutic play model, we work with the quadrants in the following way.

Quadrant 1: Language

We are nurturing the upper, left hemisphere of the brain. This is where we use verbal communication to track a child's language and play sequences.

Quadrant 2: Relate

We are nurturing the upper, right hemisphere of the brain. This is where we reflect a child's feelings during the play and model empathy.

Quadrant 3: Limits

We are nurturing the lower, left hemisphere of the brain. This is where we set limits as needed within the play.

Quadrant 4: Regulate

We are nurturing the lower, right hemisphere of the brain. This is where we focus on attunement, proximity, warmth, and eye contact within the play.

We will go into more elaborate detail on each quadrant shortly.

This model does not offer a formula for playing; instead, it helps you to become more aware of how to utilize play therapeutically. You will become aware of how to utilize nonverbal and verbal communication, as well as the power of relationship and limit setting to deepen the play experience. It is important to note that not all quadrants will be used in every play session, and they may occur in a different order to reflect your child's needs. Your role is to be mindful of the quadrant that your child is in and to assess how you utilize your body and your words in each quadrant.

STEP 1: REFLECT ON YOUR OWN PLAY HISTORY

How we play with our children is shaped by our own childhood experiences of play. Some of us may try to recreate our experiences of joyful play with our parents, while others may mindfully wish to create a different play experience for their children. When we are tired, stressed, or frustrated, we are more likely to sink into our own childhood patterns. There is a chance some of you do not remember playing, and that's okay. If that's the case, you might feel very uncomfortable playing. We just want you to be aware of that discomfort and know that your child has the innate capacity to play, and your role will be to follow their lead.

Take a few minutes to reflect on your play history:

1. What are some of your earliest play-based memories?
2. Who did you play with when you were young?
3. What sort of games did you naturally gravitate toward?
4. What sort of activities did you naturally gravitate away from?
5. What was your mom's role in your play?
6. What was your dad's role in your play?
7. How did you play in your teens and tweens?
8. What rough-and-tumble play was allowed in your home?
9. What would you like to retain from your childhood play experiences for your child?

10. What would you like to change from your childhood experiences with your child?

After examining your history, we hope you are aware of some biases you might have. For instance, maybe you spent a lot of time playing board games with your parents, so you really gravitate toward structured activities like this, but you didn't spend a lot of time in imaginative play. Chances are your discomfort with play that involves dress-up, make-believe, role-playing, etc. might make you feel somewhat self-conscious and uncomfortable. Because of this, you might push your child toward activities that are in your comfort zone instead of following their lead and engaging in the activities that they like. Another example would be rough-and-tumble play. Perhaps you were scolded for this in your childhood; some parents were raised in homes where children were to be seen and not heard. This may cause you to discourage this type of play because it is too noisy or because you fear it may lead to aggression. Awareness of our play history is key to understanding how we play with our children.

STEP 2: BE PRESENT

Bring your whole self to the play experience with your child. Children are incredibly intuitive and will know when you come in with "half a tank." Choose a time to play when you can be attuned and fully present. This might mean you only have fifteen minutes in you to play. That's fine. If that's all you can give, just let them know that's all the time you have in advance.

Switch off the television, turn off the radio, and put your phone away. When we are with clients in the play therapy room, we never have our phones visible anywhere in the room. A phone—even powered off—constantly sends a message to the child that there are people we're waiting to hear from, and their play time can easily be interrupted. With our own children, we will put our phones in a drawer and will set a timer on the stove. We find that when we have a set timer, it allows us to be more present and to know that when the timer does ring, we will then be able to focus on household demands.

When we don't set a timer, we're more likely to try and quickly marinate the beef or sweep the floor while we're playing. We know—and our children know—that they do not have our full presence. We remind our children ten minutes and five minutes before the timer ends. At times, there may be tears, but we gently keep our limits, knowing they have had the fullest version of us for our special playtime.

Name the special playtime (Suzie and Dad's playtime), try to limit external distractions (this may require playing with your child when their siblings are otherwise occupied or have another caregiver supervising them), and set your timer. Consistency in weekly sessions is more important than the amount of time per session, so set a time that is realistic for you and your child. We would recommend anything between fifteen and sixty minutes depending on the child and the family's needs, and the more frequent the better for children who really struggle with behaviors or emotional dysregulation. Once the timer goes off, make sure to end the playtime. This helps to create structure around the playtime and helps a child to understand that limits are important and will be maintained.

STEP 3: PREPARE THE PLAY SPACE

Research shows us that less is better for children. When children have fewer toys, their play experience tends to be deeper, more creative, more sophisticated, and less scattered. In choosing toys that nurture creativity, opt for open-ended toys (like scarves and blocks), nature items, dress-up items, and items that help a child to build mastery (like wooden blocks) or that foster physical activity (like a Hula-Hoop). Stay away from electronic toys.

STEP 4: IMMERSE YOURSELF IN THE PLAY

When we let our child direct the play, we are granted the exquisite gift of seeing the world through our child's eyes. This can be tricky for adults, as we are so prone to direct activities. So take a deep breath, and let play be an exercise of mindfulness. Let your child lead. Do not introduce new characters, new plot shifts, or a new game. This is their time for discovery.

Sample script of what to say:

> "This is our special time together; you get to choose whatever we do together." "You have me all to yourself for thirty minutes. You get to be the boss. What would you like to do?"

During this time with our child, all of our energy is directed toward being playful, accepting (of all the parts of the child), curious, and highly empathetic.

STEP 5: REFLECT

Play is truly magical and provides a window into a child's psychological world. After your play experience with your child, reflect on each quadrant and how you were able to utilize the associated skills.

Let's look at the quadrants in more detail.

QUADRANT 1: LANGUAGE

Let's move over to the left-hand side of the model. In this quadrant, we are using language to track a child's physical play and the language a child uses, as this helps to deepen a child's play. You are connecting to and growing the left side of the brain. You track when you are witnessing a child's play, not when you have joined the play (for example, become a character).

EXAMPLES OF TRACKING

Mirroring

Child: "The boy is going to school."
Parent: "Ahh, he is off to school."

Clarifying

Child: (slams truck repeatedly) "They say, 'It's stuck! Help!'"
Parent: "It's stuck, and the truck needs help?"

Summarizing

Child: (Yawns) "I'm sleepy; that was a crazy day."
Parent: "It was a crazy day, and now you're feeling very sleepy."

SPORTSCASTING

Another thing you can do is track your child's movement; you follow what the child is doing, and you narrate their main movements in the play like a sportscaster does when they narrate a play-by-play of a football game.

Imagine that there is an invisible audience, and you are narrating for the audience. You might say in a fun and exciting voice, "look at that one; it is going up, up, up," or "there goes the green one," or "you are going over there."

WHEN YOU BECOME A CHARACTER, STOP TRACKING

If your child invites you into the play and says, "Daddy, you be the princess," then join in with abundance. Remember to stop tracking the play; you are now a character. Let your inner child free, use different voices, and immerse yourself.

If you are unsure of what your character needs to do, then enter your role as neutrally as possible to begin with. You can also use the whisper technique. With the whisper technique, we can ask the child for direction in a whisper: "Does the princess want to go for a sleepover?" or in a hushed voice "What should I do next?" That being said, don't forget that you are still following the child's lead. They are the director. You want to be attuned to their verbal and nonverbal cues and constantly ask yourself: Is my role deepening the play and enriching the story?

There are some important rules of thumb in tracking:

- **No evaluation:** We want to ensure that we don't use evaluative language or praise like "you are so smart" or "you are a great artist." When we use praise children start to perform for us, and the play becomes more externally driven than internally driven; they do it to please us instead of themselves.

- **Follow their lead:** We also want to refrain from making suggestions. As adults, we often don't realize that we constantly are in control, and we often sabotage a child's play session without realizing it. Let your child lead.

- **Don't label items:** In imaginative play, we don't want to label toys until the child labels the toy. A car may be a carriage, a space shuttle, or a cannon. Until they name it, we call it "that one" or the "blue one" or the "big one." Another important point here is when you are naming things the child is playing with, don't assume what something is unless the child has named that item and its gender. For example, if a child is playing with a doll, don't say "she" and assume it's a girl. Use a gender-neutral pronoun such as "they." This is so important as children are using their imagination to recreate their worlds. We don't know who these characters are or what they are, and if we label them, it becomes about our interpretation of the play instead of our child's unique expression of their inner world. That being said, there are some basic objects that we will label so that it does not get confusing, such as a table, chair, lamp, or door that aren't central to the play itself, but rather background items.

QUADRANT 2: RELATE

Nurturing this quadrant occurs naturally when a child hears your delight in being part of the play and you are connecting to and growing the right side of the brain. It is embedded in the words and actions you use to convey that you are deeply present in the play experience with the child. This may be expressed through mirroring the child's excitement in both your words and your tone: "We are going to have a tea party!" If your child feels frustrated, you might empathize by saying, "You are frustrated that you can't figure that toy out." At the end of playtime, you might say, "You wish you could play a little longer." You mirror what your child says to you, as well as reflect on what you see in the child's body language and expressions.

You may also reflect on the emotions that are evident as the play progresses. "The little one is very sad" or "She is so excited to have a party with her friends." Reflecting feelings often helps a child become aware of the underlying emotional narrative in play. There are times when the child might be engaging in a craft or art activity. In this instance, you would talk about how the child is feeling (instead of the character). It may feel a little strange to reflect at first, but children quickly become used to the rhythm of reflecting. This quadrant is all about connection, feelings, and empathy.

EXAMPLES

- "You are feeling so happy today."
- "Oh, the big one is angry at the little one."
- "You are excited that there are new toys."
- "That one looks really sick and afraid."
- "He feels lonely in that house all by himself."
- "They are all tired and going to sleep."

After the session, try and recall when and how you reflected emotions to your child. Is there a specific feeling that is evident throughout the play? What do you think this may be about? What new ideas would you like to try for this quadrant in your next play session?

QUADRANT 3: LIMITS

In this quadrant, we are using language (left-hand side of the brain) to create safety and structure for a child. This helps to soothe a child's "downstairs" brain when a child is emotionally dysregulated.

In this quadrant, we model compassionate discipline. We only use this if it is absolutely necessary. As much as possible, we want to stay playful and light. We can use the ACT model, as mentioned in an earlier chapter.

EXAMPLES

Acknowledge the feeling: "I can see you are having lots of fun playing with Play-Doh on the carpet."

Communicate a limit: "The carpet is not for Play-Doh."

Target an alternative: "You can use the desk instead."

Another example may be:

Acknowledge the feeling: "I know you want to shoot Mommy's head."

Communicate a limit: "But Mommy's head is not for shooting."

Target an alternative: "You can shoot Mommy below the shoulders."

Set limits only when they are actually needed. Some families may want to agree on a few limits before playtime if a child really struggles with impulsivity or aggression. In this case, limits could include: no hurting Mom with your body and no breaking of toys. Another limit we will discuss with our child is that playtime ends when the timer rings.

QUADRANT 4: REGULATE

This quadrant is integral to creating connection and safety within the play session and nurtures the right hemisphere of the brain. It is within this cocoon of safety that a child can deepen their play experience.

Our focus in this quadrant is all about proximity, presence, warmth, and appropriate eye contact. We use our voice, body, and presence to help a child to feel safe, attuned, and regulated. The message to the child is: I see you, I hear you, I feel you, and I'm with you.

Do a scan of your body, and notice where there might be tension. Find ways to relax this tension so that your body becomes an instrument of safety. Be aware of what your physical presence is conveying to the child. When your body is present, your face and shoulders are relaxed, and your voice is warm and resonant—yet reflecting the intensity of the play—you elicit trust and connection, which are fundamental components to the play experience.

You want to be close enough to create a shared experience but far away enough to give the child as much space as possible to move, play, and explore. You want to be aware of how you position your body. Get down on their level as much as possible (i.e., be on the floor with them). When you stand above your child or sit on a sofa, it tends to distance you from the play and can create a power dynamic. When you are on the floor, it indicates joy and full immersion in the play. My favorite types of therapy rooms don't have any adult-sized sofas or chairs. I know when I'm tired, I'm more likely to settle down into an adult-size sofa, which then impacts the quality of the play with the child.

Eye contact is an intricate part of the dance too. You want to ensure there is some eye contact—specifically when the child addresses you directly. Primarily, though, you want to create a "mutual gaze" in which you focus on the play that unfolds—almost like you are watching a movie with a child. You want to listen with your eyes and your ears.

Once the playtime has ended, reflect on your level of attunement, proximity, warmth, and eye contact within the play.

Is your presence intensifying the play or diminishing the play? What is your child's response to you after the play—does your presence "amp it up," or does your child shut down? Is your child eager to play with you again?

This is all a learning experience. There are times when we will feel as if we entered a whole new world with our child through play, and there are other times when it will feel like it doesn't flow. This is normal and a beautiful reflection of what happens naturally in relationships. The most important part here is that we can reflect, repair (if needed), then jump right back in.

If possible, we suggest that children are not asked to clean up after special playtime. When children are aware of needing to clean up, it can impede the depth of the play, or we end up deconstructing a creation that is an expression of something deep and meaningful to them. That being said, outside of special playtime, we think it is really important that children actively contribute to the household.

After playtime, take a minute to write down and reflect on the limits that were put in place. Think about how they were put in place and how your child responded. What is something you may consider doing differently next time?

As mentioned previously, we do not stay in one quadrant of the play. We move throughout different quadrants in our play experiences with children. ICP's therapeutic play model helps us to become aware of what part of the child's brain we are priming. So for example, when we are tracking movement in a child's play, we know that we are in the upstairs, left hemisphere of the brain. When we set limits, we are using the left hemisphere of the brain and calming the lower floor of the brain. If we use our body to regulate and connect with a child, we nurture the right hemisphere and downstairs part of the brain. If we are using our words to convey empathy and tracking feelings in the play, we are nurturing the right hemisphere of the brain.

This model nurtures greater awareness of how the caregiver can use play to facilitate greater neural integration (connections between parts of the brain), wellness, resiliency, and emotion regulation.

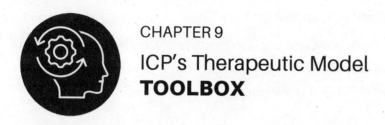

CHAPTER 9

ICP's Therapeutic Model
TOOLBOX

ICP's therapeutic model

This model offers parents a tool to become more aware of how to use play therapeutically. It helps you to utilize nonverbal and verbal communication, limits, and the power of relationship to deepen play. Quadrants may be used in different order in play sessions; some quadrants may not be utilized at all. Your role is to be mindful of how you use your body, your words, and your energy to deepen the play.

Tips to use this model

- **Reflect on your own play history** (this will help you to assess your own comfort level when it comes to play).

- **Be present:** Set a timer for the play session and bring your whole self. Fifteen minutes of quality time is better than sixty minutes of disinterested play. Let your child know how long the play session will be. Share limits with your child if needed (no hurting).

- **Prepare the play space:** Toys that inspire imaginative play are best.

- **Immerse yourself in the play:** Dress up, use different voices, be silly, laugh.

- **Reflect:** Think about what quadrants were utilized, how they were utilized, what quadrants you felt more comfortable with, what quadrants you felt less comfortable with, and what you would like to try in the next play session with your child.

Quadrant 1: Language

We use language to deepen a child's play. Note that this is when we are observing a child's play, not when you have been invited to be a character.

Mirroring
Child: Tada! It's her birthday today!
Parent: Today's her birthday!

Clarifying
Child: She doesn't want to play with anybody. She is going to play right here.
Adult: Oh, she doesn't want to play, she's going to play by herself?

Summarizing
Child: Oh, what a beautiful morning—I have to hurry, I have to brush my teeth, brush my hair, get my school bag ready.
Adult: It is a beautiful day and you've got to hurry and get ready.

Sportscasting
Narrating a child's movement play-by-play.

- You are lying down.

- You're shooting that one over there.

- Your body is getting tired.

Stop mirroring, clarifying, summarizing, and sportscasting when a child asks you to enter their play.

Whisper technique
Use this when your child has invited you to be a character and you are not sure what to do next.

- "What should the frog say?"
- "Should he go to the castle"

Don't evaluate; Don't say "you are so intelligent" or "you are the best at_____." This shifts the play from an internal drive to an external drive.

Follow their lead: Let them direct. Be careful, adults often take over without realizing.

Don't label toys: We don't want to curtail the imaginative process by preemptively labeling a toy. Instead of "the car" use:

- this one
- that one
- the small one
- the big one
- the blue one

Quadrant 2: Relate

In this quadrant, we focus on feelings. We mirror our child's feelings in the words we use and in our tone. We may also reflect on feelings that come up in our child as the play progresses.

- That one is feeling very grumpy.
- She is so happy.
- You wish playtime was longer.
- You are proud that you figured it out!

Quadrant 3: Limits

Limits help a child to feel safe and nurtures deep play (the child does not have to be hyper vigilant as they trust the adult to set the boundaries and so they can engage in the important work of childhood).

- Stay playful

- Minimize rules and limits

- It can be helpful to discuss limits before the play starts: no hurting, no destroying

- Use the ACT model:

  - Acknowledge the feeling: "I know you want to shoot Mommy's head."

  - Communicate a limit: "But Mommy's head is not for shooting."

  - Target an alternative: "You can shoot Mommy below the shoulders."

Quadrant 4: Regulate

In this quadrant, the focus is on connection and safety. Here are some areas to focus on.

- **Proximity:** We want to be close enough to our child when they are playing to convey deep interest, but not so close that it impedes the flow of the play. Do not hover over your child (this creates a stress response in them); get down on the floor and play.

- **Presence:** Turn off your cell phone (preferably don't even have it visible), don't talk to your child about school and chores, be engaged and involved with their play experience.

- **Warmth:** Exude warmth in your voice and your body. When children feel that we are relaxed and warm, they feel safe, and their play experience is deepened.

- **Appropriate eye contact:** When your child talks directly to you, look at them. When they are enacting a play sequence, use a mutual gaze to look at the characters. It's as if you are a watching a show unfold together.

After the session

Warn your child appropriately before the play session is going to end (five minutes, two minutes, there's our timer). Some children may need a transitional activity, like a snack. It is important for these special playtimes that you don't keep playing when the timer goes of; keep the limit. This will help your child to understand that this is a contained, safe experience.

We suggest that children are not asked to clean up after special playtime as this may impeded their willingness to delve deeply into their play process.

CHAPTER TEN

BATTLING OVERWHELM AND CREATING A PEACEFUL HOME

Our lives have become busier than ever, which impacts the well-being of both our children and the adults in the home. Our children spend more time in school, more time completing homework, and more time in extracurricular activities. A childhood imbued with magic and discovery is being swallowed whole by a frenetic society. Ironically, parents are spending more time with their children than any other time in history. Ginsburg has found "even those children who are fortunate enough to have abundant available resources and who live in relative peace may not be receiving the full benefits of play." We need to create a shift and push back on a culture that prides itself on being busy. In doing so, we nurture a space for children to discover who they are.

We help to quieten the anxious, depressed thoughts that emerge when a child has experienced too many accumulative stressors in a world that moves too quickly, that is cluttered by material possessions, and that lacks true connections. When we prioritize cutting back on scheduled activities, decluttering our homes, saying no to excessive play dates, we send a clear message to our children that we prioritize a life of connection and depth.

This chapter was inspired by the groundbreaking work of Kim John Payne, a best-selling author and clinician, and mentor to both Tammy and me throughout the years.

OUR PHYSICAL ENVIRONMENT

Let's start with looking at our homes. Our external environment often reflects our internal environment. Physical environments are living, breathing spaces that impact how we think, feel, and interact with others. We are often completely unaware of the impact that noise, clutter, air quality, space, and light can have on mental well-being. Over time, as James Clear says, "environment is the invisible hand that shapes human behavior. We tend to believe our habits are a product of our motivation, talent, and effort. Certainly, these qualities matter. But the surprising thing is, especially over a long time period, your personal characteristics tend to get overpowered by your environment." This is important when we consider that statistics indicate that in Europe and in the States, we spend about 90% of our time indoors, with 65% of that time being at home. This statistic is probably an underestimate since the onset of COVID-19.

Cluttered homes have been linked to various mental health challenges. In one study, women who reported living in homes full of cluttered spaces were more likely to report feeling fatigued and depressed. Their cortisol levels were also much higher than those who lived in restful homes. The women who lived in restful homes also reported higher rates of psychological well-being.

So many of our children wake up with nervous systems that are already highly activated, and this agitation is often expressed as anxiety, emotion regulation, impulsivity, hyperactivity, or high sensitivity. Do our children really need twenty-five pairs of jeans to choose from and toys and books littering the floor? The "too muchness" of life results in our children never being able to find an anchor, a space to be calm.

TOO MANY DECISIONS

Simplicity reduces decision fatigue. When we are presented with too many choices, our brains work overtime to distinguish between what is a priority and what is not. As the need to make decisions builds throughout the day, we become increasingly fatigued. Interestingly, if you look at research on a judge's likelihood to grant parole, a judge is likely to grant parole 65% of the time immediately after a break. This number drops gradually to close to 0% as the judge gets to the end of a "decision session." Researchers hypothesize that this may be due to decision fatigue in the afternoon. As judges grow more tired, they are more likely to go with the default decision—to keep the accused in jail.

When there is clutter in an environment, our brain tries to simultaneously process multiple streams of information, and we become more likely to act impulsively, experience irritability, and have trouble focusing.

As James Clear suggests in his book *Atomic Habits: Tiny Changes, Remarkable Results*, design an environment that nurtures excellent decisions. When we live in chaos, it's difficult to create a space that feels right for our families.

I often talk to my clients about taking a mental health day to truly look at their homes and to start working on homes that nurture calm, not chaos. As a mama of two under six, I know that there are days when my house is a whirlwind, but my goal is to always try and return it to a space that imbues psychological well-being. Often, we focus on our children keeping their bedroom tidy or picking up their possessions, without taking the time to really think about our homes as a whole.

When we look at the negative impacts of cluttered homes, finding or creating access to natural daylight seems like the perfect antidote. Natural daylight has been shown to work wonders on overloaded sensory systems. Homes that have more natural sunlight pouring in are at an advantage, but for those of us who live in spaces that aren't as light, it is essential to get outside and soak in the rays. Exposure to sunlight has been shown to positively impact mood, alertness, productivity, and sleep. It has also been shown to boost serotonin. Natural light within living spaces has been correlated to higher levels of psychological well-being.

COLOR YOUR WORLD WITH INTENTION

Color within our homes also helps to battle or increase feelings of overwhelm. In environments where there are multiple contrasting colors, there is a higher correlation with overstimulation, leading to increased blood pressure, pulse rate, and muscle tension. On the other hand, homes that are monotone in color may lead to under stimulation, resulting in irritability, frustration, aggression, and a lack of focus. We want rooms that balance color contrasts, just as we may see in natural environments.

Color evokes both a physiological and psychological response in us, which is often governed by implicit memories from our childhood. Think about the spaces within your house that create a feeling of calm. What are the dominant colors in those spaces? Can you think about why those colors may be connected to healing for you?

Research demonstrates that certain colors elicit different responses. For instance, warm lilacs and a blue-green hue are associated with calmness. Orange is connected to making rooms feel smaller and cozier and yellow with feelings of being uplifted. Red can warm rooms and prove welcoming, and warm blues can nurture concentration. It may be an interesting family experiment to move through all your rooms and discuss individual responses to different colors. Helping each other recognize what is calming vs. what is triggering is often insightful and eye-opening.

REDUCE NOISE POLLUTION

I think any parent, no matter what country you live in, that has a house full of rambunctious children will tell you that too much noise poisons calmness. Chronic levels of noise keep the stress response activated and have been linked to anxiety, depression, high blood pressure, heart disease, and stroke. The type of noise that is most harmful is noise that we cannot control: traffic noise or ongoing construction noise. One research study showed that people living in areas with more road traffic noise were 25% more likely, than those living in quieter neighborhoods, to have symptoms of depression even when adjusting for socio-economic factors.

Think about your home and how noisy it is, then take stock of what noise you can control vs. what noise you can't control. For example, turn the TV off, remove any loud clocks, or consider a white noise machine. If possible, see if you can create soothing, tech-free nooks within your home. In implementing quiet spaces, it is essential that parents use these spaces daily and that their children see them using the spaces—read, do a puzzle, create art. When our children see us gravitating to the calm nook, they are more likely to use it themselves.

MAKE OUR BEDROOMS A HAVEN OF CALM

Let's think about our bedrooms. We spend about a third of our life sleeping, and it is important to think about our bedrooms as wellness spaces. Poor sleep has been linked to obesity, high blood pressure, anxiety, depression, shortened life expectancy, compromised immune response, and fertility issues.

Given the information that we have already, we know that to create bedrooms that are optimal wellness spaces, we want to be aware of the following factors: "goodness of fit" in terms of the mattress and pillows, colors in the bedroom, promoting natural light during the day and blackout curtains at night to help set circadian rhythms, an awareness of noise levels (even low-level noise can disrupt sleep), removal of all technology from bedrooms, and less clutter. We also want to be aware of the temperature in bedrooms, as cooler bedrooms generally promote deeper sleep.

Think about what you want from your bedroom. How do you need to organize it to create "flow?" Where does your laundry hamper need to be? How do you need to organize your closets? What needs to be beside your bed to create the optimal sleep experience?

We suggest spending some time sitting in your bedroom and looking at it from every perspective so that you can create a space that works for you. Once again, when we prioritize wellness and sleep, our children are more likely to prioritize wellness and sleep. Studies show that a children's sleep patterns mirror their parents' sleep patterns. Not a big surprise!

TOYS AND BOOKS

Less is more when it comes to toys, books, and clothes. Katja Sylva studied 3,000 children between the ages of three and five and concluded that "when children have a large number of toys there seems to be a distraction element, and when children are distracted, they do not learn or play well."

A second study found similar results. In this study, toddlers were observed in free, supervised play and were given either four or six toys. The study found that the toddlers who had less toys tended to engage with a single toy for longer periods of time, and the play was more creative and focused than toddlers who were given sixteen toys.

When children receive a new toy, they move through two differ-ent stages. The first stage is the exploration stage (what does this toy do), and the second is the play stage (what can I do with this toy). It is in the play stage that the true value of play is nurtured. When we have too many toys, children spend time in the more surface-level stage of exploration and not enough space in the play stage. We want to create an environment that promotes "the flow" of what we want for our family.

As mentioned earlier, we highly recommend that toys are put into rotation (and stored far away when not in rotation), that toys that have broken or missing parts are removed, that there is a lim-ited mix of open-ended toys (silk scarves, Magna-Tiles, objects from nature) and close-ended toys (toys with one outcome, like a puzzle, project kit, tracing) that reflect our child's current interests, and that electronic toys are either removed or highly limited. It is also important to display the toys that are available to play within an accessible, child-friendly manner. So often when we "store" toys that are in rotation, the adult ends up guiding the play by having to pull out and choose the play bins for the child.

Now to tackle all the books in the house: fewer books are better for our young readers. Reading the same book again and again helps with vocabulary acquisition, fluency, comprehension, rhythm, and confidence.

A study conducted by the Center for Early Learning Literacy suggests focusing in on one book at a time, then rereading it at least four times over the next four days so that children can fully grasp the story. Reading the same book to a child is the same as a child repeatedly attempting to master the fireman's pole at the park.

Repeated experiences help to build mastery, nurture confidence, and create stronger neural pathways. This applies to all areas of a child's life—"sameness" is a vital ingredient in nurturing optimal neural health.

SIMPLIFYING SCHEDULES

In 2020, the world slowed down significantly due to the pandemic. Many families experienced a sense of loss, but others began to appreciate a slower rhythm—though this is not necessarily a case of either/or. The over-scheduling hypothesis is the belief that our youth are over-scheduled and that this overscheduling impacts well-being. Research indicates that there are great physical and psychological benefits from being involved in extracurricular activities at a moderate level. Some of these benefits include nurturing positive development, gaining support from positive nonfamilial role models, being part of a community, building skills, participating in meaningful pursuits, and identity formation.

HIGH AND LOW NOTES

The importance of nurturing and developing skills, particularly in the teen years, is evident. At the Institute, we recognize the importance of activities while advocating for gaps between activities. Our children's brains are developing all the way into their late twenties, processing and integrating information, and they desperately need space to rest. It is in the space between activities that we learn about ourselves. Kim Payne describes the need for children to have both "high notes" and "low notes." High notes are soccer practices, big assignments, and trips to the waterpark, and low notes are sitting by the creek, going for a walk, or playing baseball in the backyard.

Unfortunately, many of our children don't have low notes anymore. Gaps are often filled with technology, which has the opposite effect of a low note. It stimulates the sympathetic nervous system instead of nurturing a deep "parasympathetic" sense of self. It's crucial to think about how we role model the importance of downtime. What value do we place on simplified schedules vs. being busy? Research shows us that valuing "being busy" is often a cultural perspective. In North America, busyness is seen as a status symbol, while in Italy, having ample leisure time is considered a higher status symbol.

Let's explore a clinical example: Breanne came to see me for both her children's anxiety. She explained that her fourteen-year-old daughter, Sam, was a "perfectionist" and had chronic low self-esteem where her mind felt berated by negative thoughts, and her six-year-old son, Brayden, struggled with being alone at home and had separation anxiety. He needed both her and her husband to be with him all the time, including during playtime. The only exception was if Brayden was playing Minecraft on the family's iPad. Sam was high achieving and was involved in many extracurriculars such as dance, drama, and piano. Brayden played soccer and baseball, and took swimming lessons. Neither had "behavioral" issues, but both struggled with sleep, racing thoughts, and being alone.

Both parents worked, but if they weren't at work, they were usually driving their children to their activities. When I asked about family dinners, playtime, and screen time, Breanne explained that since the children were in different activities, they typically ate at different times or were on the road eating out of the vehicle. Sometimes they would be able to fit a movie night in, but now that Sam was older, she preferred to be in her room listening to music or using social media on her phone to communicate with her friends when she wasn't at one of her activities. Both Breanne and her husband indicated they felt burned out and exhausted. They felt their house was perpetually a disaster as they were hardly home, work was very demanding, and their marriage wasn't what it was because they weren't getting the time together that they needed, but they felt torn by the demands of parenting. There was no space for downtime, to just be, to connect as a family. The entire family was running on fumes.

Do you slow down? Do you fill the "low notes" with tech? What does your life tell your children about your values? Many of us may need to shoulder very full work schedules, but the gaps, the moments of quiet, communicate family values to our children. How we approach leisure time has been identified as one of the eight parental factors that nurture resilience in children.

I often ask families to really think about the activities that dominate their "nonwork time." Nonwork time is divided into "free" and "bound time." Bound time comprises of essential activities like grocery shopping, home maintenance, and driving to work. Free time comprises activities that we choose to spend our time on. The family creates a list of activities that fall under bound time and then discusses the level of comfort and satisfaction regarding the amount of time spent in this category. The family then creates a list of activities that fall under free time and rates each activity on a scale of one to ten in terms of happiness. This helps to nurture an awareness of activities that the family may want to either continue to engage in or disengage from.

The final step is to actively schedule downtime. Every family is different—it may be daily downtime, it may be weekly, it may be every other week. Downtime is time spent in a manner that nurtures the soul. It may be reading books together, going for a bike ride, or playing a board game. It is in these quiet moments that we build relational credits with our children. Relational credits are built in an accumulation of moments when a child deeply experiences the feeling of being with people who truly value and see them for who they are. Relational credits are essential for when we hit those road bumps with our children. As Dr. Neufeld says, it is easier to parent a child whose heart we have versus a child whose heart we do not have.

WEEKLY FAMILY SCHEDULE

▬▬ Bound Time
▬▬ Free Time

	Monday	Tuesday	Wednesday	Thursday	Friday	Saturday	Sunday
6:00 am							
7:00 am	Get Ready For Work	Get Ready For Work	Get Ready For Work	Get Ready For Work	Get Ready For Work		
8:00 am						Mow Lawn and Fix Fence	Make Family Breakfast Together
9:00 am							
10:00 am							
11:00 am						Grocery Shopping	Family Bike Ride around Park Trails & Picnic Lunch
12:00 pm							
1:00 pm							
2:00 pm							
3:00 pm			Make Dinner		Make Dinner		
4:00 pm	Make Dinner	Make Dinner		Make Dinner		Order Pizza & Have Family Game Night	Clean House
5:00 pm			Hockey Practise		Hockey Practise		
6:00 pm							
7:00 pm	Read Book Together	Watch Movie Together		Take Rex to Dog Park			Read Book Together
8:00 pm							
9:00 pm	Bedtime	Bedtime	Bedtime	Bedtime	Bedtime	Bedtime	Bedtime
10:00 pm							
11:00 pm							
12:00 am							

FAMILY MEALS

In previous generations, family dinner was a staple, but life shifted in the past twenty years or so. Families now rush from activity to activity, cell phones are in everyone's hands, and the TV has become part of the never-ending background noise. We can sit down and create a family vision, but if this is something we do once and then never revisit, it's useless. Family meals, on the other hand, are daily affirmations of who a family is.

When it comes to defining your family, regular family meals (breakfast, lunch, or dinner) may be one of the most important commitments you make. The research on family meals is overwhelmingly positive. Here are just a few of the benefits:

- Young children: Dinner conversation boosts a young child's vocabulary even more than being read to.

- Children who experience regular family dinners are more likely to engage in healthier eating patterns throughout their lives.

- Numerous studies link regular family meals to lower rates of adolescent risk behavior like binge drinking, smoking, sexual activity, school issues, and eating disorders.

- The psychological wellness factors attributed to family meals are huge. Studies show that regular family dinners lower the risk of teen depression and promote higher levels of resiliency in children who are victims of cyberbullying. Family dinners also nurture higher positive emotions in youth.

For most families, sitting down for every meal will be impossible. The National Center on Addiction and Substance Abuse at Columbia University that looked at over 1,000 teens found that five to seven meals a week (breakfast, lunch, or dinner) is the number of meals needed for children and teens to reap the benefits of family dinners (and the benefits continue to increase as the number of family meals increases).

So what is the magic of family dinners? Yes, we tend to eat better when we all sit down together. But at the heart of it, it's about connection. Of course, we need to question whether regular family meals lead to better outcomes for children or if families that are more connected are more likely to have family dinner, leading to better outcomes. A study that explored this question found that the benefits of family dinner held up when parents focused on connection at the table. It also found that family experiences related to connection also influenced the outcome.

Activities that promoted time together between a parent and a child (going to a movie), parental influence and limit setting (setting a curfew), and resources (income level) also played a role. What the researchers did note is that two of our main daily opportunities to connect with our children are either in the car or at a family meal.

Ultimately, it's not about the dinner table per se; it's really about connection and fostering a sense of belonging. The dinner table is a wonderful reminder to connect daily, but we can be creative about how and when we connect.

The focus on family meals is quintessentially about our children having a space to be heard, a space to hear others, a space to identify with, a space where we can slow down the world and focus on what's important without the TV or phones (turning off electronics for all family members cannot be overstated). This is a beautiful opportunity to facilitate conversations. Try to stay away from yes/no questions, and instead think about ways to talk to your children in a meaningful way. We have included a list of questions in the Toolbox.

This is not about creating a daily idyllic experience. It's about the spilled drinks, the squabbling of siblings, and the peas on the floor; it's about role modeling to our children how to work with the peaceful moments and the more challenging moments. How do we really listen to one another? How do we ask questions? What is important to our family? Is everyone given an equal voice? Do we really talk to one another or just talk over each other? What's important to you? What is the culture of our family?

Think about your current family dinner. If I was to observe your family, what would I see? What would I hear? What would it "feel like"?

Remember to start with small shifts. If you eat one dinner together a week, try sitting down for two meals initially. Think about what your family needs, and pick one goal. Is it less tension, greater conversation, or trying more nutritious food together?

Focus more on the experience than an elaborate meal. Get the whole family involved in the prep, the experience, and the cleanup, as a family meal is not just about the time sitting down. Be the alpha and set the tone of the experience.

Consider adding a ritual to the family meal. This may mean blessing the food, having everyone identify something that they are grateful for, or taking turns initiating conversation starters.

Dinners can be challenging, and so you may need to reflect on your own triggers and/or plan ahead with a partner on how to handle mealtime challenges in a manner that aligns with your values. Don't give up—the more we practice, the more likely we are to experience positive outcomes.

DOWNTIME AND DAYDREAMING

Do you ever recall lying on your bed as a child or teen, staring up at the ceiling while listening to music, and just thinking about life? Letting your mind wander? Slowing down and savoring the low notes enables us to daydream.

Daydreaming is not only normal; it's an essential and adaptive part of life that enables us to function successfully and nurtures the brain in a pivotal way. Daydreaming activates the default mode network in the brain. The default mode network (DMN) is a network of interacting brain regions (such as the medial prefrontal cortex, posterior cingulate cortex, and parietal regions) that is active when a person is not focused on the outside world. Activation of this network allows us to become more skilled at switching to autopilot once we are familiar with a task, freeing up our brain to take in new information. Activation of this network is also related to the formation of empathy and moral development. When we daydream, we are more likely to reflect on our behavior and choices and the impact that these choices had on others. By activating this network, we activate both the executive problem-solving network as well as the creativity network in our brain simultaneously.

According to Harvard University's Health blog, daydreaming, similar to meditation or other restful activities, acts as a natural remedy to alleviate stress. Daydreaming also facilitates problem-solving. In one study, researchers concluded that mind-wandering is an important cognitive process that leads to new ideas. When you spend too much time fixated on a certain idea, you can overlook all sorts of information, but when you move away from a task, it frees your subconscious mind to explore memories and information stored from something you read years ago, then integrate this with your imagination and creativity to come up with a new solution. Daydreaming is also associated with increased goal-driven behavior and higher levels of creativity.

The importance of daydreaming is evident, but how can we give our children this gift unless they have time and space to cultivate it?

THE GIFT OF BOREDOM

Boredom is wonderful for your children, and it ultimately gives parents the gift of space to not entertain your children 24/7. It's not your job to be your child's constant source of entertainment. Our job is to encourage, connect, and keep them safe.

In modern times we have forgotten the gift of boredom. Children are born with the innate capacity to play and explore without intervention as long as they feel safe and secure. We are not saying you shouldn't spend time together or play with your children; we already know this is a great way to connect and foster a secure attachment. However, it was not meant to be something you are responsible for all day long; it robs children of their autonomy and creativity and you of your sanity.

Boredom helps cultivate frustration tolerance, perseverance, executive functioning skills (such as problem-solving skills, flexibility,

and organizational skills), creativity, self-esteem, and original thinking. Boredom equals opportunity. Brains that aren't occupied with
phones, iPads, Pinterest art activities, or endless extracurriculars are
more likely to try new things, experiment, and spark creative energy
to entertain themselves. Play and creativity are hardwired into our
children, but we undermine this capacity if we jump in to entertain
them or give them a screen.

The thought of children coming to us, tugging at our sleeves with
a whine in their voice, stating "I'm bored" is often a trigger for parents, so here is a script to get you through those hard moments:

SCRIPT 1

"I can see you feel really frustrated that you (think you) have
nothing to do. But I also know that feeling bored is really good
for your brain. And I know you are smart and capable, and you
can figure out something to do."

Script 2

If your child keeps pestering, try: "I am happy if you would like
to help out around the house instead. You can do the following
tasks, or you can find something to do on your own."

Either your child will balk at the idea of completing extra chores
around the home, or they will agree and get sidetracked from their
assigned chore (remember the chore is not the end game in this
instance) and find something else to do, which is the goal. If they

don't, you are reinforcing the importance of contributing around the home, and you have one less task to complete yourself.

The ability to be still is a gift that many children never acquire in their childhood. This is primarily due to their parents' inability to be fully present with the "low notes." Often the uncomfortable feelings associated with low notes indicate some form of healing that needs to occur in your own journey. Take some time to reflect on who you are and what behavior you model during still times, as well as what you wish for your child and may need to shift in your family.

SCREEN TIME

You will be busy when you're older, so I hope you take time to smell all the flowers and put all the leaves you want in your bucket now. I hope you read your favorite Dr. Seuss books so many times you start inventing your own stories about the Vipper of Vipp.

I hope you ride the carousel with Max until you've tamed every color horse. I hope you run as many laps around our living room and yard as you want. And then I hope you take a lot of naps. I hope you're a great sleeper. And I hope even in your dreams, you can feel how much we love you.

—MARK ZUCKERBERG AND PRISCILLA CHAN

Mark Zuckerberg, founder of Facebook, and his wife wrote this to their unborn child. Isn't this what we want for all of our children? In a rapidly digitized world, these beautiful, slow moments are disappearing for our children—time to play outside, time to read, time to be.

The roller coaster of information never stops. We can declutter, paint our walls harmonious colors, cut back on activities, but if technology seeps into every orifice of our lives, our efforts in simplifying are greatly diminished. "Common Sense Media," our favorite digital health website, conducted a large-scale study of American youth in 2021 and found that tweens spent on average 5:33 hours a day on entertainment screen use. Teens spent 8:39 hours a day on entertainment screen use. In 2021, many countries were in the midst of battling the pandemic, and so screen time skyrocketed, but it's important to note that these numbers do not reflect any time spent toward educational purposes; it is purely entertainment. These numbers are frightening, but if you put a tracker on your phone to track your leisure screen time, many parents report that their minutes per day are surprisingly high.

Tech is here to stay, and research is showing us that there are many incredible benefits. There are also many drawbacks. Let's start with these first. The brain is incredibly sensitive to its environment and as mentioned in previous chapters is developing rapidly throughout our childhood years. In order to build strong neural pathways, our children need to move. They need to touch objects, experience new challenges, and focus on different activities in order for the brain to mature optimally. With technology, children's bodies are often sedentary for long periods of time, and we see many of them struggle to reach optimal sensory and motor milestones.

Preliminary data from the landmark study Adolescent Brain Cognitive Development indicates that children who are on their screens for more than two hours a day score lower on academic and logic-based tests, while children who spend more than seven hours a day on screens exhibit thinning of the cortex. The cortex is critical in terms of problem-solving, perspective, and logical thinking.

Dopamine, our feel-good neurotransmitter, is another issue when it comes to neural health and technology. Every time our children are on a screen and they receive a new notification, kill an opponent, or get a new "like," they experience a burst of dopamine. We experience this same "burst" when we buy something new, have sex, or see a friend after a long time. Dopamine itself is not bad, but too much dopamine is where we become worried.

Over time, a child's dopamine pathways become overused, and they need to spend longer and longer engaging on a screen to receive the same surge. Excess dopamine wreaks havoc on impulse control and the ability to stop an activity that is impairing other areas of our life. High amounts of screen time has been shown to impact the frontal cortex in a very similar way to the effect of cocaine.

If you look at the brain scan of a screen addict, it looks almost identical to that of a cocaine addict. Excessive screen time in childhood can initiate an ongoing pleasure/reward cycle that can negatively impact development. Many kids struggle to concentrate, to self-regulate, and to perform academically in school: "Unless we are intentionally creating opportunities for focus, for delay of gratification, and for boredom, the portions of the brain that regulate these functions have the potential to show less robust, and possibly even diminished function."

Insulin is a hormone that plays a vital role in the metabolism and control of energy storage in the body. Dysfunction in the secretion of insulin can damage the body's ability to absorb glucose to produce energy. Watching television, playing video games, or sitting in front of a computer or other device for more than three hours each day has been linked to insulin resistance. This puts children and teens at greater risk of diabetes, to atherosclerosis, and to metabolic disorder and obesity, both of which contribute to the formation of heart disease.

In addition, studies of children have found that prolonged exposure to screens can lead to sleep disorders and impairment through the disruption of the hormone melatonin, which regulates sleep and plays an important role in strengthening the immune system. This is more prominent with evening and nighttime exposure to bright light and blue light emitted by self-luminous devices, which can cause circadian disruption. Not all technology is created equal. Technology is divided into "digital vegetables" and "digital candy." Digital vegetables refers to screen time activities that help children to think, to problem-solve, and to be creative. These activities are designed to enhance neural functioning and can positively increase working memory, fluid intelligence, visual attention, and global cognition. Digital candy, on the other hand, refers to passive use of screens, like endless scrolling and video watching.

It is important to mention that for children under the age of two, there is no suitable version of "digital veggies." Research shows that the best type of learning always occurs in person and that no app is going to rival the immense amount of social, emotional, and cognitive information that passes from caregiver to child.

Other advantages of a rapidly digitized world include the ability to harness different learning styles, to access up-to-date information, to connect with online communities, and to develop new skills such as coding or creating new content.

As a clinician, I am often asked about screen time per day for a child. The Canadian Paediatric Society has clear guidelines on screen time for different age groups:

- 0 to 2 years: Screens are not recommended, only video chatting

- 2 to 5 years: Limit regular screen time to less than one hour of high-quality screen time

- 6 years and up: Discuss screen time as a family. Don't view screens an hour before bedtime.

While these guidelines can be helpful, the real work lies in ensuring that a child has balance in their lives. As a clinician, I'm more interested in a child's wellness balance over a week than I am in a daily time limit.

Focus on what wellness means to your family instead of engaging in endless battles around technology. When we think about the wellness balance, some of the areas we may need to consider include being fulfilled emotionally (is your child feeling connected to others), spiritually (is your child pursuing their passions, participating in joyful experiences), physically (is your child eating, exercising, sleeping well, and engaging in self-care), socially (is your child connecting with their peers, teachers, and community members), and cognitively (is your child learning, applying new knowledge, and thinking in diverse ways).

Balance refers to shifting your perspective to consider the whole family's media usage. Children are extremely aware of their parents' use of screens, and it is important that we practice what we teach. Create a family media plan that outlines how and when technology can be used in the home. A family media plan is a wonderful way to model leadership, negotiation, and problem-solving. When we remove the focus from our child's tech use to the family's tech use, the process is far more collaborative than punitive in nature. A family media plan can be found here: **instituteofchildpsychology. com/familymediaplan/**

Your children will one day be adults in a world that is even more technologically based. Think of the values that are important to you and your family, then live them. If you go to bed every night with your phone in your hand, it is highly likely that your child will follow suit one day.

What do you want? What is important to you? Now live it. The way you handle technology and help your child navigate technology will become their road map for the future.

3 TYPES OF DIGITAL PARENTS

There are three types of parenting styles when it comes to technology. Which one do you fall under?

1. **Digital mentor:** Mentors are actively involved in their children's tech use and often participate in screen-related activities with their child by co-viewing and co-playing. Digital mentors have ongoing conversations with their children about technology, digital safety, and digital citizenship.

2. **Digital enabler:** Directly or indirectly encourage their child's tech use. No limits are put in place and children guide their own tech consumption.

3. **Digital limiter:** Strictly limit technology use at home. Little to no technology use is permitted.

Research shows that children of digital mentors are most likely to stay safe online because their parents have created an open line of communication around technology. Digital mentors tend to be authoritative parents. Limits are in place, but children are treated with respect, and the parenting style is constantly embracing new developmental periods. If you want to become a digital mentor, here are some ideas to get you started:

- Have a discussion about how technology impacts the brain and why having limits on screen time is important for everyone in the family (not just the children).

- Create family rituals around screen-free time. For instance, in our home, there are no devices at the dinner table, after 6 p.m., and we implement screen-free days or holidays.

- Have family movie nights where you can engage with your children around what they're watching.

- Talk to your children about online predators and what to look for.

- If you have a teen, talk about the impact of apps such as Instagram, Facebook, Snapchat, TikTok, etc. and why these apps can be good but also, their downsides. When it's appropriate for a teen to have their own account is up to each family, but we recommend the longer you can wait the better (in our practice, we recommend waiting until the eighth grade).

- Talk to your child about their media usage. With older children and teens, try asking them what they think is an appropriate amount, and have them cite their reasons for why they think it's an appropriate amount (given they are aware of the wheel of wellness). If a child feels included in the conversation, they're more likely to feel committed to following through and less likely to push back.

- Ensure parental controls are activated on devices. Research shows that the parental controls are only effective up to a certain point; open communication is far more impactful.

- Put all devices away to instill the importance of disconnecting for all family members (i.e., put all devices on top of the fridge or in the office from 7 p.m. till morning, and use alarm clocks in the bedroom) or limit the Wi-Fi to certain times of the day.

- Have your child play an online game with you.

- For YouTube or TV shows, have them show you the videos they like or watch an episode with them. Look for any talking points about what they're seeing. What makes the video interesting? How are people treating each other? If you have a daughter, ask her about the female characters. Are they leads or merely sidekicks or love interests? Are there characters that look like them or other people in their world? Is there a diversity in the landscape of the videos they are watching?

Battling overwhelm and creating a peaceful home means taking inventory of both our external and internal environments. When you simplify, you make room for the people, the values, and the items that mean the most to you. Choose one small goal (i.e., changing your schedule, decluttering the toys, or moving the books). Now tackle that one area of your life first. It always starts with the first step.

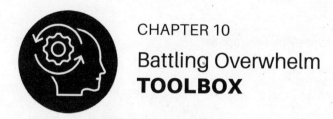

CHAPTER 10

Battling Overwhelm
TOOLBOX

Our physical environment

Factors that enhance well-being in our physical environment

Lighting in homes
Natural daylight

Colors in homes
- Color contrasts that are balanced (as we would see in nature)
- Warm lilacs/blue-green hue: calmest
- Orange: rooms feels smaller and cozier
- Yellow: feelings of being uplifted
- Red: warms rooms
- Warm blues: nurture connection

Reduce noise pollution
- Turn the TV off
- Remove loud clocks
- Implement quiet spaces

Make bedrooms a haven of calm
- Minimize toys in bedrooms
- Use blackout curtains
- Keep electronics out of bedrooms

Declutter
- Rotate toys every few months
- Get rid of broken toys
- Display toys in an accessible, child-friendly manner
- Have a mix of closed-ended toys (puzzles) and open-ended toys (silk scarves)
- Reduce the amount of books you have on display (rotate)

Recommended resources
Simplicity Parenting (K. Payne); *The Life-Changing Magic of Tidying Up* (M. Kondo); *Decluttering at the Speed of Life* (D. White)

High and low notes

Make sure that there are high notes (activities) and low notes (free time)

Actively schedule downtime

Create a list of family activities that fall under "free time" and then a second list of activities that fall under "bound time." As a family discuss your comfort level with the amount of time spent in each.

The gift of boredom
Let your child be bored

Family dinner questions
- What makes you happy?
- What would you do if you could be mom or dad for a day?
- What are three words you would use to describe yourself?

- If you were a parent, what rules would you have?

- If you were a teacher, what rules would you make at school?

- If you were a superhero, what would your name be, and what powers would you have?

- What do you think adults get wrong that kids get right?

- If a man steals a loaf of bread for his starving family, is it wrong? (teens and tweens)

- Name one thing you appreciate about each person at the table.

- What are you most grateful for?

Technology

Examples of Digital Veggies:

- **Code Land – Coding for Kids:** Subscription-based coding game for a range of skills

- **DIY.org – Creative Challenges:** Fun "how to" videos that promote curiosity

- **Swift Playgrounds:** Learning feels like play in sleek, approachable coder

- **PicsArt Photo Editor and Collage:** Photo editor with tons of functionality

Examples of Digital Candy:

- Facebook

- Snapchat

- Instagram

- Candy Crush

Wellness Balance:

Technology use will always be a part of your child's life, but it needs to be within a balanced lifestyle. There may be days where your child has more access to screens, but over a week, ask yourself how much time your child spends engaging in other areas of their life:

- Is your child connected to their family?
- Do they engage in family dinners and other family activities?
- Are they pursuing their passions?
- Are they engaging in joyful activities?
- Are they sleeping well?
- Are they moving their body every day?
- Are they connecting with friends?
- Are they learning and applying new knowledge and thinking in diverse ways?

Family Media Plan:

Complete as a family

Digital Mentor:

- Foster self-awareness when it comes to media
- Intentionally choose to engage in single-tasking (instead of multi-tasking)
- Carve out times and places to disconnect
- Prioritize face-to-face connections

Healthy Media Diet:

Ask yourself:

- What are my kids doing on media?

- How much time do they spend doing it?
- Are choices developmentally appropriate?

Transitioning Out of Screen Time:

Hypnotic screens can create a hypnotic flow with children. This is primarily caused by dopamine, when screens are turned off dopamine levels drop sharply causing emotional/physical outbursts.

- Set limits beforehand with your child
- When time is nearly up, sit beside them, use touch, and ask them about their game. This pulls them back into a state of awareness
- Mention the limit again

Tech Conflict:

- Use a family media agreement
- Communication is better than controls
- Discuss limits and keep warmly to them as a family
- Don't try to teach when feelings are high
- Get help if you are unable to resolve tech issues
- Always reflect on your own tech use

Apps and Programs to Assist with Digital Limits for Children and Adults:

- **Freedom for laptops:** Downloadable program that can deny access to a specific website or to the Internet for an amount of time you designate.
- **kSafe:** A small plastic safe that opens at the top. You put your phone in it, put the lid on, and twist the top, and then you program how long you want to shut your phone away for.

- **Circle:** An app that allows you to monitor websites, and it allows the ability to grant or disallow Wi-Fi access to specific devices.

Parental Controls:
Most smart phones allow you to program how much time is allowed each day

Additional resources:
- Media Smarts
- Common Sense Media

CHAPTER ELEVEN

PUTTING THE OXYGEN MASK ON YOURSELF FIRST

*The most precious inheritance that parents can give
their children is their own happiness.*
—THICH NHAT HANH

The reality is in order for your child to regulate their emotions, they need you to regulate yours. Co-regulation is a prerequisite for self-regulation. However, if everything about our bodies, tone of voice, and emotions is conveying that there is danger looming, how do we adequately communicate to our children that they are safe and send the signals to calm their nervous system?

Whatever is going on with a parent's nervous system is often mirrored in their child's. Imagine you are on a plane, and there is turbulence; the plane starts to vibrate, and the lights flicker. The captain comes on and shakily says: "Folks, this is my first time flying through turbulence this bad, and I'm feeling really nervous about this. Please bear with me as I try to get us through this and land us safely." How would you feel as a passenger? Our guess is terrified, feeling the plane could go down at any moment as you gripped the edge of your seat. When we get stuck in a stress response, this is the message we send to our children.

Being a safe harbor and anchoring our children means we have to ensure we take care of ourselves first. For many people, self-care is laden with guilt, surges of effort, fearmongering, marketing ploys, and little sustainability. Self-care has become a $10-billion industry with millennials spending double the amount of money than their parents, yet many of the praised health and wellness outcomes remain unproven.

Audre Lorde said: "Caring for myself is not self-indulgence. It is self-preservation, and that is an act of political warfare." When we do not care for ourselves, the self disappears. Self-care cannot be a "to-do" item on our list that may or may not happen; it has to be prioritized. When we are able to slow down, tune into ourselves, and take care of ourselves, our children are more likely to model the same behavior.

If we are constantly exhausted, rushing from activity to activity, saying "yes" to everyone, and psychologically struggling, our children become more likely to model the same behavior.

Dr. Bruce Perry's three *R*s of emotion regulation (regulate-relate-reason) is a model that we use consistently at the Institute to explore dysregulation. Although this model is often used to explain how to help children through challenging moments, it is also a wonderful way to explain the importance of self-care, regardless of your age. Let's explore the model, and then we will discuss how the model is related to self-care.

When our stress response has been activated (our nerves are frayed, every additional request from others feels insurmountable, and our tempers flare quickly), we operate with the lower floor of our brain (the body brain and feelings brain), and our fight-flight-freeze-collapse response dominates our ability to connect with others and to live a life that is aligned with our unique value set. It is essential that we learn to regulate our own stress response. Once we are regulated, our ability to connect with others and feel safe (relate) nurtures our ability to think clearly, reflect, and learn (reason).

REGULATE

Regulating is all about soothing our bodies and calming the stress response. The primary building block of self-care is to recognize and regulate stress. Recognizing stress may not be as easy as it sounds. For many people, the physical and emotional signals associated with "stress" are often blanketed with negative connotations. Stress is a normal, adaptive behavior to different triggers in the environment. Stress is what has helped us to survive from an evolutionary perspective, and it is responsible for helping us run from tigers, survive famine and drought, and plan in the midst of disasters. When we come across a stressor in our environment, the sympathetic nervous system (the gas pedal of the brain) is activated, and adrenaline and cortisol course through the body. This then activates the fight-flight-freeze-collapse response in the body.

In moderate doses, stress helps prepare us for new challenges, incites mental focus, and helps propel us in new, creative directions. Studies have shown that when we believe that all stress is "bad," the body follows, and we tend to have worse long-term health outcomes. When we believe that stress can enhance our life, the body follows, and we tend to have better long-term health outcomes. The narrative you have with stress can actually dictate if stress harms the body or not.

For example, excitement, anticipation, and being "revved up" all register in the body in the same way as stress, leading to an elevated

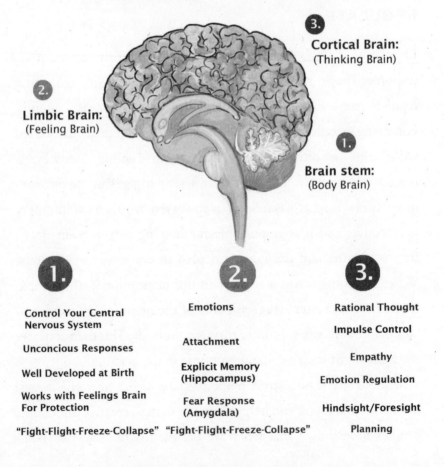

Brain Development

The Brain Develops From the Bottom Up

3.
Cortical Brain:
(Thinking Brain)

2.
Limbic Brain:
(Feeling Brain)

1.
Brain stem:
(Body Brain)

1.

Control Your Central
Nervous System

Unconcious Responses

Well Developed at Birth

Works with Feelings Brain
For Protection

"Fight-Flight-Freeze-Collapse"

2.

Emotions

Attachment

Explicit Memory
(Hippocampus)

Fear Response
(Amygdala)

"Fight-Flight-Freeze-Collapse"

3.

Rational Thought

Impulse Control

Empathy

Emotion Regulation

Hindsight/Foresight

Planning

heart rate, quick breathing, and sweaty palms. But when those bodily sensations are framed in a different manner, such as excitement, we psychologically respond in a more positive way, which impacts how we react to those sensations.

Reflection: How does your family talk about stress at home?

We worry about stress when it is chronic and/or constantly activated unnecessarily. This is often referred to as distress—when the fire alarm is constantly activated even though there is no fire. When we can distinguish between stress and distress, as well as differentiate between healthy signals of stress vs. unhealthy signals, this behavior is likely to be mirrored by our children. A study published in the *Journal of Social Science & Medicine* (Volume 159) revealed how contagious stress actually is. In this study, researchers found elevated cortisol levels in the saliva of students whose teachers reported the highest levels of burnout. The authors suggest: "Stress contagion might be taking place in the classroom among students and their teachers. It is unknown what came first—elevated cortisol or teacher burnout. We consider the connection between student and teacher stress a cyclical problem in the classroom."

We see the cyclical nature of stress in classrooms, homes, and workplaces. Changing these patterns takes hard work and needs to start with the adults first. We are going to do a journaling exercise to explore stress triggers, stress recognition, and possible stress reduction strategies. When you recognize your stress triggers, how they feel in your body, and how to work with the stress, you become empowered, and in control of stress instead of stress being in control of you.

Look at this diagram and circle the symptoms of fight-or-flight that you commonly experience. You can add other experiences in too.

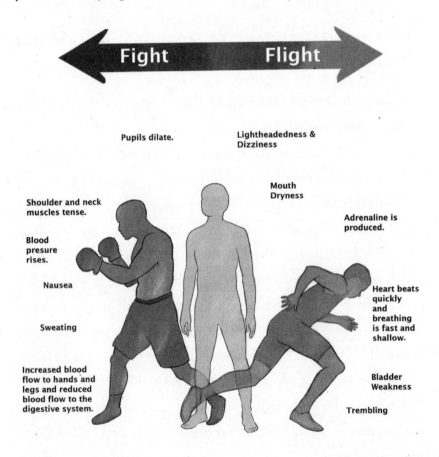

When we recognize stress in the body, it is important to acknowledge the messages that our body sends us, to reframe if necessary, then to work with the cortisol in a healthy way. Early in our evolution when we lived in caves and we were attacked by a tiger, the cortisol in our body would place our body into survival mode. We have evolved over time, and our body still goes into survival mode, but we are no longer running from tigers, and the cortisol in our body is not released. Over time, high levels of cortisol makes us susceptible to extreme fatigue, depression, panic attacks, somatic complaints, and breathing issues. At the Institute, we firmly believe that self-care is about micro-moments; it's about finding activities that "fill your cup daily," so that when the tidal waves of chaos hit, we are more likely to be able to sustain ourselves under the pressure.

Here are some suggestions:

1. **Find a daily mindfulness activity:** This is similar to changing the oil in our car on a regular basis. When maintenance is completed regularly, the car runs better. When we practice mindfulness regularly, we can control our stress levels more effectively. Activities can range from meditation, walks in nature, listening to a guided mediation app, qigong, prayer, or yoga. The benefits of mindfulness are now being widely researched and include greater awareness of one's emotions, decreased rumination, greater emotion regulation, decreased reactivity, increased flexibility, enhanced relationship satisfaction, and a greater sense of well-being. One of our favorite apps for mindfulness is "Calm." Calm is best known for meditation and sleep guides. The app provides concrete tools on how to maximize your meditation experience.

Reflection: Is there a mindfulness activity you enjoy doing? Does this feel like a strategy that would work for you? If so, what is one small step you can take toward incorporating this into a regular practice?

2. **Aerobic exercise:** Low-intensity aerobic exercise is fantastic for lowering cortisol and adrenaline. In addition, it fosters a burst of endorphins—our mood enhancers and natural painkillers. It also helps produce serotonin, which regulates mood and combats depression. In fact, one hour of exercise is more effective than a single dose of antidepressants. Don't overdo it (particularly close to bedtime) as moderate- to high-intensity exercise has been shown to increase cortisol levels. Listen to your body, tune into your stress level after exercise, and be mindful of the aftereffects of movement (the Goldilocks question: Do I feel less stressed, more stressed, or just right?).

   Yoga is an example of an activity in which research overwhelmingly indicates that regular practice decreases cortisol and can potentially mediate stress-related anxiety and depression. Where you exercise may also be a factor contributing to how relaxed you feel afterwards. Walking in a forested environment decreased cortisol levels from 9.70 to 8.37 nmol/L, whereas walking in an urban environment barely changed mean cortisol concentration, from 10.28 to 10.01 nmol/L.

Reflection: Is there an activity that helps you to lower your stress levels? How do you know that it is helping to mediate your stress response?

Dr. Bruce Perry often suggests using rhythmic movement to modulate the brain stem (body brain): "One of the most powerful sets of associations created in utero is the association between patterned repetitive rhythmic activity from maternal heart rate and all the neural patterns of activity associated with not being hungry, not being thirsty, and feeling 'safe.' In other words, patterned, repetitive and rhythmic somatosensory activity becomes an evocative cue that elicits a sensation of safety. Rhythm is regulating." His work focuses specifically on children who have experienced significant developmental trauma and who are at a higher risk of experiencing poor organization in the lower areas of the brain. One of the most well-known side effects of trauma is to alter the brain's stress response system. One way to heal the impact of trauma on the brain is to engage in a patterned, repetitive activity. Even if you or your child has not experienced significant trauma, but your stress response is high, then reorganized, repetitive, patterned activity can shift an easily activated stress response toward greater resilience. This can include walking, skipping, drumming, dance, yoga, massage, grooming or riding a horse, or jumping on a trampoline.

Reflection: What is one way that you could use rhythm to modulate your stress response?

3. **Nature therapy:** Get outside! It's simple—being outside lowers cortisol and raises neurotransmitter levels like dopamine (related to motivation) and serotonin (related

to mood regulation). One research study found that even twenty minutes a day of "nature therapy" significantly lowers stress levels.

The Japanese healing practice of *shinrin-yoku* or "forest bathing" refers to spending time in the forest and mindfully incorporating all five senses (what am I seeing, smelling, hearing, feeling, and tasting). It is about slowing down and being present in the moment. *Shinrin-yoku* has been well documented in terms of its impact to bring down stress levels. We recommend reading *Your Guide to Forest Bathing* by M. Amos Clifford if you want to find out more.

4. **Sleep:** It's important to know that cortisol and sleep both share the same pathway. Both are governed by a complex network called the hypothalamic pituitary adrenal (HPA) axis. That's why when we are stressed, sleep becomes so difficult. Every twenty-four hours, our body follows a sleep-wake cycle that is synchronized with daytime and nighttime. Cortisol follows the same rhythm. Generally, we will see that there will be a peak in cortisol about an hour after you wake up in the morning, and then at night (around midnight), we see the lowest levels of cortisol production. In addition to this, we generally have about fifteen to eighteen small releases of cortisol throughout the day. Cortisol is essential for helping us to wake up and stay energized throughout the day, and then in lowering production at night, it helps us to sleep. "Stress" is anything that spawns the production of more cortisol.

It's when our cortisol levels become too elevated for too long and the HPA axis works overtime that we begin to see our ability to fall asleep, stay asleep, and enter the deep, restful stages of sleep impacted. Sleep deprivation, in turn, can increase in cortisol. Think of the HPA axis as a major highway, with sleep and cortisol trying to drive on the highway. However, if either cortisol or sleep crashes, the entire highway becomes backed up, creating multiple other issues. When sleep is prioritized, cortisol production is lowered, and we are more likely to be able to regulate.

Some of the best sleep hygiene practices include:

- Sleep in a dark, cool, comfortable room.

- Stop using electronic devices an hour before bedtime.

- Avoid alcohol, caffeine, and nicotine in the hours leading up to bedtime, as all three can interrupt the quality of sleep.

- Get into a regular sleep schedule with similar wake/sleep times each day.

- Get plenty of natural daylight and exercise throughout the day. (Don't exercise too close to bedtime as it may wake you up.)

- Avoid occasional napping in the day.

- Don't eat a large meal right before bed, but foods like almonds, kiwi, turkey, crackers, and cheese can help induce a sleep response.

RELATE

The second *R* is relate. To live our best lives, we need to feel connected and safe. As Brené Brown says, "If we want our children to love and accept who they are, our job is to love and accept who we are. We can't use fear, shame, blame, and judgment in our own lives if we want to raise courageous children. Compassion and connection—the very things that give purpose and meaning to our lives—can only be learned if they are experienced. And our families are our first opportunities to experience these things."

The fact is you need healthy, fulfilling relationships outside of your children. This is not selfish; it's a necessity for your emotional well-being. We know loneliness increases cortisol in the body and impacts our bodies in detrimental ways. Feeling lonely is so harmful to our bodies that regularly experiencing this emotion is the equivalent to smoking fifteen cigarettes a day.

Numerous research studies have supported the importance of relationships and emotional well-being. One of the most important studies on lifelong well-being is the Harvard Study of Adult Development, a study that tracked the lives of 724 men over seventy-five years. The study utilized questionnaires, medical reports from doctors, blood samples, brain scans, and interviews to gain a full understanding of the participants' development over a lifetime. The clearest result from this seventy-five-year study is that "good relationships keep us happier and healthier."

The three big takeaways from this study are:

1. People who are more connected to their family, friends, and communities are happier, healthier, and tend to live longer.

2. It is not only about the quantity of friends, but it is about the quality of our relationships. The people who were happiest with their relationships at age fifty were the healthiest at age eighty.

3. Good relationships protect our brains. People who have high-quality relationships tend to have better neurological health.

Throughout this book, we have spoken about the importance of attachment and how our own past often defines how we connect with our children, which in turn shapes how they will eventually attach to their children. Looking after yourself and thinking about the childhood messages that you received and still hold about connection and belonging are so important—not just for your well-being but for your child's well-being too. When you look after yourself, you look after your child.

In our instinctual yearning for relationship, we often confuse connection, belonging, and fitting in. Connection is the experience of being seen, valued, and heard, while belonging is the experience of being an integral part of something bigger. Fitting in is the experience of seeking approval.

Take some time to fill in the exercise below. In the middle circle, fill in the people who bring your soul joy. In the next circle, fill in the people who you enjoy seeing from time to time. In the outer circle, fill in the people who are in your life but who you need to create boundaries with. On the outer edge of the circle, you can put people who need to stay out of all three circles in order for you to be authentic to yourself.

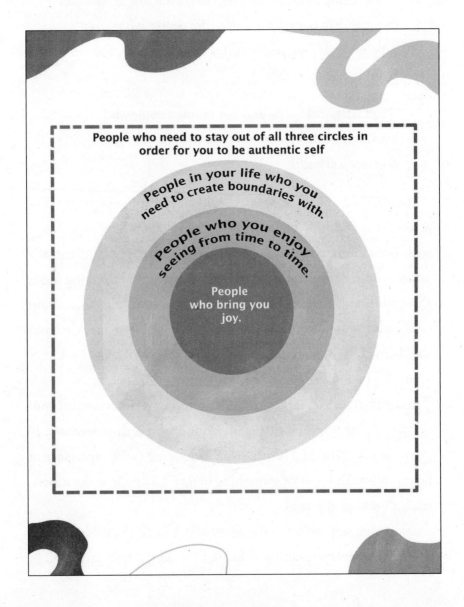

Now have a look at your circles. Are there any changes that need to be made? Is there somebody in your inner circle who you may want to reach out to? Is there someone who you may need to establish boundaries with?

BOUNDARIES IN RELATIONSHIPS

Boundaries are an important part of maintaining healthy relationships. Healthy people set boundaries. Again, what we model in terms of boundary setting is how our children are most likely to understand, incorporate, and live their own boundaries. Boundaries include saying no when there is pressure to oblige but you really don't want to, letting your spouse know his comments about your clothes make you feel self-conscious, or even telling your children you need time to yourself.

Many people struggle with boundaries. This may be due to being a chronic pleaser, due to a lack of self-esteem, or fear of other people's responses. As The Holistic Psychologist says, "how a person reacts to a boundary is for them. How you respond to that reaction is for you." Here are some ideas to help you identify and hold boundaries:

1.   Identify the boundary needed.

2.   Use clear, concise language to convey the boundary.
     Use "I" instead of "you."

     "I need space when I arrive at work in the morning."
     "I feel _____ when _____ because _____.
     What I need is _____."

EXAMPLE

"I feel frustrated when the toys are left all over the floor because I need our home to be a safe and calm space. What I need is for each person to pick up after a toy is finished being played with."

Remember, saying no does not require an explanation. The word "no" is an important part of your mental health toolkit.

Jot down a couple of examples of boundaries that you could use in your own life. Then try using the "I" sentence above. Rehearsal is everything. And just like the other examples in this book, the more we repeat boundary setting, the easier it will become, and the less stressful it will become, and the healthier we will be.

REASON

When our stress response is lowered and we are connected, we can utilize our thinking brains more effectively, and live life more intentionally. When the reasoning brain is fully engaged, we are more likely to be able to consider different perspectives, self-regulate, control impulsive responses, engage creatively, and live a life aligned with our values. The emphasis in this chapter is on navigating the stress response and on connection. When the lower parts of the brain are cared for, we are far more likely to breathe deeply and to be more self-aware. When you are able to cut out the noise of society, the push of prescriptive parenting practices, and the urging of relatives, you open up a new world that helps you to ask yourself: "What do I really want?"

Now think about what you need to live intentionally. Is it seeing a therapist to help you stay on track? Is it practicing mindfulness? Taking reflective walks? Joining a group of like-minded parents? Taking more time to yourself so that you can approach family dynamics from a more anchored perspective? Is it about harnessing the power of boundaries? At the Institute, we would argue that creating space to live the life you want for yourself and for your family is probably the most important thing you will ever do.

We hope that this chapter on self-care has given you some new ideas and has helped you to consider self-care from a different perspective. Self-care happens in a million tiny ways a day, and it sends the implicit message of self-love, self-care, and self-preservation. What more could we possibly hope to convey to our children?

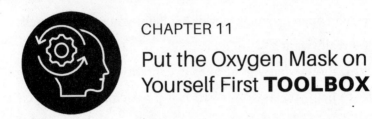

CHAPTER 11

Put the Oxygen Mask on Yourself First **TOOLBOX**

Regulate

As caregivers, it is essential to sooth our stress response and to modulate the brain stem's response to an overwhelming world. Here are some ideas (preferably practiced on a regular basis):

- **Find a daily mindfulness activity:** prayer, qigong, meditation, walking, yoga
- **Aerobic exercise:** Low-intensity aerobic exercise lowers cortisol in the body.
- **Repetitive, patterned activity:** Rhythmic activity calms the stress response—this can include walking, skipping, drumming, jumping on a trampoline, riding a horse.
- **Nature therapy:** Get outside for twenty minutes a day.
- **Sleep:** Ensure that you are prioritizing sleep. When we are sleep-deprived it is almost impossible to modulate our stress response.

Relate

To live our best lives, we need to feel connected. Nurture healthy relationships outside of your partner and your children.

Boundaries

- Identify the boundary needed
- Use clear, concise language to convey the boundary
- Start with tighter boundaries and then loosen them

Reason

Take care of your thinking brain. It is your thinking brain that allows you to consider different perspectives, self-regulate control impulsive responses, engage creatively, and live a life aligned with our values. Here are some ideas:

- Read a book

- Engage in puzzles, sudoku, or crossword puzzles

- Learn a new skill or take up a new hobby

- Play card games, chess, or bridge

- Learn a new language

- Music: singing, choir, learning to play an instrument

Living with intention

When you move from a stress response, you can start to reflect on value-based questions like:

- When your children reflect on their years with you, who do you want to be to them?

- What experiences do you want to be a part of your family story?

- What are your three most important values as a family?

- How do you live these values in a concrete way?

- What is one action/quality that needs to change or shift for you to fully live your family story?

FINAL THOUGHTS

Parenting is messy, beautiful, and consuming. It shifts how we see the world and how we understand ourselves. Make space for the joy, the pain, and the deep vulnerability.

This is about as real as life gets. You don't need this book, or any book for that matter, to be a good parent. You are already good enough. All parents simply need support, and that is what this book is designed to do, to support your growth as a human being. Remember that your children do not need perfection—they need you. But, to give them you, you need to make yourself a priority. Look after yourself, and in turn, your children will learn to look after themselves.

Take the tools and strategies from this book and make them your own; be intentional about how you parent. Start with one small shift and build from there. This is your story—this is your child's story. Together, you will write about how emotions were handled, how challenges were overcome, how resiliency was nurtured, and how hearts were filled. You are incredibly powerful in your child's life—don't doubt how your daily interactions fill the crevices of their soul.

That being said, try to stop ruminating on the past and fretting about the future—all that your children need is for you to BE with them. To be present, attuned, warm, and real. To see them, hear them, and accept them for who they are.

Relax, love deeply, delight in the joyful moments—you've got this.

BIBLIOGRAPHY

Note: Citations are listed in order of appearance within each chapter.

CHAPTER 1

Neufeld, G., Maté G. (2019). *Hold on to your kids: Why parents need to matter more than peers.* Vermilion.

Eagleman, D. (2020). *Livewired.* Doubleday Canada. Edwards, E., & King, J.a. (2009). Stress response: Genetic consequences. *Encyclopedia of Neuroscience*, 495-503.

LeDoux, J. E. (2003). *Synaptic self: How our brains become who we are.* Penguin.

Siegel, D. J. (2020). *The developing mind: How relationships and the brain interact to shape who we are* (3rd ed.). Guilford Press.

Lenroot, R. K., & Giedd, J. N. (2006). Brain development in children and adolescents: *Insights from anatomical magnetic resonance imaging. Neuroscience & Biobehavioral Reviews*, 30(6), 718-729. https://doi.org/10.1016/j.neubiorev.2006.06.001

Ali, M., & Ali, H. Y. (2013). *The soul of a butterfly: Reflections on life's journey.* Simon & Schuster. Anderson, P. (2002). Assessment and development of executive function (EF) during childhood. *Child Neuropsychology*, 8 (2), 71-82.

Siegel, D. J., & Bryson, T. P. (2016). *No-drama discipline: The whole-brain way to calm the chaos and nurture your child's developing mind* (Trade paperback ed.). Bantam Books.

Delahooke, M. (2019). *Beyond behaviors: Using brain science and compassion to solve children's behavioral challenges.* PESI Publishing & Media.

Perry, B. D., & Hambrick, E. P. (2008). The Neurosequential Model of Therapeutics. *Reclaiming Children and Youth*, 17(3), 38-43.

Hughes, D. A., & Baylin, J. F. (2012). *Brain-based parenting: The neuroscience of caregiving for healthy attachment.* W.W. Norton.

Bales, K. L., & Carter, C. (2003). Sex differences and developmental effects of oxytocin on aggression and social behavior in prairie voles (Microtus Ochrogaster). *Hormones and Behavior*, 44(3), 178-184. https://doi.org/10.1016/S0018-506X(03)00154-5

Feldman, R., Gordon, I., Schneiderman, I., Weisman, O., & Zagoory-Sharon, O. (2010). Natural variations in maternal and paternal care are associated with systematic changes in oxytocin following parent–infant contact. *Psychoneuroendocrinology*, 35(8), 1133-1141. https://doi.org/10.1016/j.psyneuen.2010.01.013

Veenma, A., & Neumann, I. (2008). Central vasopressin and oxytocin release: Regulation of complex social behaviours. *Progress in Brain Research*, 261-276. https://doi.org/10.1016/S0079-6123(08)00422-6

Domes, G., Heinrichs, M., Michel, A., Berger, C., & Herpertz, S. C. (2007). Oxytocin improves "mind-reading" in humans. *Biological Psychiatry*, 61(6), 731-733. https://doi.org/10.1016/j.biopsych.2006.07.015

Hughes, D. A., & Baylin, J. F. (2012). *Brain-based parenting: The neuroscience of caregiving for healthy attachment.* W.W. Norton.

Yuan, K., Qin, W., Wang, G., Zeng, F., Zhao, L., Yang, X., Liu, P., Liu, J., Sun, J., von Deneen, K. M., Gong, Q., Liu, Y., & Tian, J.

(2011). Microstructure abnormalities in adolescents with inter- . net addiction disorder. PLOS[266] ONE, 6(6), e20708. https://doi. org/10.1371/journal.pone.0020708

Han, D. H., Bolo, N., Daniels, M. A., Arenella, L., Lyoo, I. K., & Renshaw, P. F. (2011). Brain activity and desire for internet video game play. *Comprehensive Psychiatry*, 52(1), 88-95. https://doi. org/10.1016/j.comppsych.2010.04.004

Sharma, R., Khera, S., Mohan, A., & Gupta, N. (2006). Assessment of computer game as a psychological stressor. *Indian Journal of Physiology and Pharmacology*, 50(4), 367-374.

Kirby, E. D., Muroy, S. E., Sun, W. G., Covarrubias, D., Leong, M. J., Barchas, L. A., & Kaufer, D. (2013). Acute stress enhances adult rat hippocampal neurogenesis and activation of newborn neurons via secreted astrocytic FGF2. *ELife*, 2. https://doi. org/10.7554/eLife.00362

Bucci, M., Marques, S. S., Oh, D., & Harris, N. B. (2016). Toxic stress in children and adolescents. *Advances in Pediatrics*, 63(1), 403-428. https://doi.org/10.1016/j.yapd.2016.04.002

Centers for Disease Control and Prevention (2019). *Preventing Adverse Childhood Experiences: Leveraging the Best Available Evidence*. Atlanta, GA: National Center for Injury Prevention and Control, Centers for Disease Control and Prevention

Jonnakuty, C., & Gragnoli, C. (2008). What do we know about serotonin? *Journal of Cellular Physiology*, 217(2), 301-306. https://doi. org/10.1002/jcp.21533

Stoller-Conrad, J. (2015, April 9). *Microbes help produce serotonin in gut*. Retrieved December 16, 2022, from https://www.caltech.edu/ about/news/microbes-help-produce-serotonin-gut-46495#

CHAPTER 2

Millman, D. (1999). *Everyday enlightenment: The twelve gateways to personal growth*. Warner Books.

Siegel, D. J. (2012). *Pocket guide to interpersonal neurobiology: An integrative handbook of the mind*. W.W. Norton & Company.

Housman, D. K. (2017). The importance of emotional competence and self-regulation from birth: A case for the evidence-based emotional cognitive social early learning approach. *International Journal of Childcare and Education Policy*, 11(1). https://doi.org/10.1186/ s40723-017-0038-6

Cole, P. M., Michel, M. K., & Teti, L. O. (1994). The development of emotion regulation and dysregulation: A clinical perspective. *Monographs of the Society for Research in Child Development*, 59(2/3), 73. https://doi.org/10.2307/1166139

Dvir, Y., Ford, J. D., Hill, M., & Frazier, J. A. (2014). Childhood maltreatment, emotional dysregulation, and psychiatric comorbidities. *Harvard Review of Psychiatry*, 22(3), 149-161. https://doi.org/10.1097/HRP.0000000000000014

Herbers, J. E., Cutuli, J. J., Supkoff, L. M., Narayan, A. J., & Masten, A. S. (2014). Parenting and coregulation: Adaptive systems for competence in children experiencing homelessness. *American Journal of Orthopsychiatry*, 84(4), 420-430. https://doi.org/10.1037/h0099843

Lau, P. S. Y., & Wu, F. K. Y. (2012). Emotional competence as a positive youth development construct: A conceptual review. *The Scientific World Journal*, 2012, 1-8. https://doi.org/10.1100/2012/975189

Gracanin, A., Bylsma, L. M., & Vingerhoets, A. J. J. M. (2014). Is crying a self-soothing behavior? *Frontiers in Psychology*, 5. https://doi.org/10.3389/fpsyg.2014.00502

Porges, S. W. (2003). Social engagement and attachment. *Annals of the New York Academy of Sciences*, 1008(1), 31-47. https://doi.org/10.1196/annals.1301.004

Sharman, L. S., Dingle, G. A., Vingerhoets, A. J. J. M., & Vanman, E. J. (2020). Using crying to cope: Physiological responses to stress following tears of sadness. *Emotion*, 20(7), 1279-1291. https://doi.org/10.1037/emo0000633

Murube, J. (2009). Hypotheses on the development of psychoemotional tearing. *The Ocular Surface*, 7(4), 171-175. https://doi.org/10.1016/s1542-0124(12)70184-2

Golden, J. D. (2019). *Supernatural Healing Exists: Did You Get The Memo?* Lettra Press LLC.

Frey, W. H. (1985). *Crying: The Mystery of Tears* Paperback. Winston Pr.

Murube, J. (2009). Hypotheses on the development of psychoemotional tearing. *The Ocular Surface*, 7(4), 171-175. https://doi.org/10.1016/s1542-0124(12)70184-2

Gross, J. J., Fredrickson, B. L., & Levenson, R. W. (1994). The psychophysiology of crying. *Psychophysiology*, 31(5), 460-468. https://doi.org/10.1111/j.1469-8986.1994. tb01049.x

Gracanin, A., Bylsma, L. M., & Vingerhoets, A. J. J. M. (2014). Is crying a self-soothing behavior? *Frontiers in Psychology*, 5. https://doi.org/10.3389/fpsyg.2014.00502

Pauw, L. S., Sauter, D. A., Van kleef, G. A., & Fischer, A. H. (2019). Stop crying! The impact of situational demands on interpersonal emotion regulation. *Cognition and Emotion*, 33(8), 1587-1598. https://doi.org/10.1080/02699931.2019.1585330

McEwen, B. S. (2008). Central effects of stress hormones in health and disease: Understanding the protective and damaging effects of stress and stress mediators. *European Journal of Pharmacology*, 583 (2-3), 174-185. https://doi. org/10.1016/j.ejphar.2007.11.071

Eagleman, D. (2020). *Livewired*. Doubleday Canada. Edwards, E., & King, J.a. (2009). Stress response: Genetic consequences. *Encyclopedia of Neuroscience*, 495-503. https://doi.org/10.1016/B978-008045046-9.00096-6

Franke, H. (2014). Toxic stress: Effects, prevention and treatment. *Children*, 1(3), 390-402. https://doi.org/10.3390/children1030390

Johnson, S. B., Riley, A. W., Granger, D. A., & Riis, J. (2013). The science of early life toxic stress for pediatric practice and advocacy. *Pediatrics*, 131(2), 319-327. https://doi.org/10.1542/peds.2012-0469

Hart, H., & Rubia, K. (2012). Neuroimaging of child abuse: A critical review. *Frontiers in Human Neuroscience*, 6. https:// doi.org/10.3389/fnhum.2012.00052

Tomoda, A., Navalta, C. P., Polcari, A., Sadato, N., & Teicher, M. H. (2009). Childhood sexual abuse is associated with reduced gray matter volume in visual cortex of young women. *Biological Psychiatry*, 66(7), 642-648. https://doi.org/10.1016/j.biopsych.2009.04.021

Felitti, V. J., Anda, R. F., Nordenberg, D., Williamson, D. F., Spitz, A. M., Edwards, V., Koss, M. P., & Marks, J. S. (1998). Relationship of childhood abuse and household dysfunction to many of the leading causes of death in adults. *American Journal of Preventive Medicine*, 14(4), 245-258. https://doi.org/10.1016/s0749-3797(98)00017-8

Centers for Disease Control and Prevention. (n.d.). *About the CDC-Kaiser ACE study*. Retrieved January 27, 2023, from https://www.cdc.gov/violenceprevention/aces/about.html

CHAPTER 3

Newman, L., Sivaratnam, C., & Komiti, A. (2015). Attachment and early brain development – neuroprotective interventions in infant–caregiver therapy. *Translational Developmental Psychiatry*, 3(1), 28647. https://doi.org/10.3402/tdp.v3.28647

Leblanc, É., Dégeilh, F., Daneault, V., Beauchamp, M. H., & Bernier, A. (2017). Attachment security in infancy: A preliminary study of prospective links to brain morphometry in late childhood. *Frontiers in Psychology*, 8. https://doi.org/10.3389/fpsyg.2017.02141

Nelson, C. A., Fox, N. A., & Zeanah, C. H. (2014). *Romania's abandoned children: Deprivation, brain development, and the struggle for recovery*. Harvard University Press.

Weir, K. (2014, June 1). The lasting impact of neglect. *Monitor on Psychology*, 45(6). https://www.apa.org/monitor/2014/06/neglect

Pollak, S. D., Nelson, C. A., Schlaak, M. F., Roeber, B. J., Wewerka, S. S., Wiik, K. L., Frenn, K. A., Loman, M. M., & Gunnar, M. R. (2010). Neurodevelopmental effects of early deprivation in postinstitutionalized children. *Child Development*, 81(1), 224-236. https://doi.org/10.1111/j.1467-8624.2009.01391.x

Hoffman, K., Cooper, G., Powell, B., Benton, C. M., & Siegel, D. J. (2017). *Raising a secure child: How circle of security parenting can help you nurture your child's attachment, emotional resilience, and freedom to explore.* The Guilford Press.

Rezaei, F., Moghadam, M., Ghaderi, E., & Rostamian, N. (2016). Relationship between attachment styles and happiness in medical students. *Journal of Family Medicine and Primary Care*, 5(3), 593. https://doi.org/10.4103/2249-4863.197314

Rubin, K. H., Dwyer, K. M., Booth-laforce, C., Kim, A. H., Burgess, K. B., & Rosekrasnor, L. (2004). Attachment, friendship, and psychosocial functioning in early adolescence. *The Journal of Early Adolescence*, 24(4), 326-356. https://doi.org/10.1177/0272431604268530

Whiteman, S. D., McHale, S. M., & Soli, A. (2011). Theoretical perspectives on sibling relationships. *Journal of Family Theory & Review*, 3(2), 124-139. https://doi. org/10.1111/j.1756-2589 .2011.00087

Passanisi, A., Gervasi, A. M., Madonia, C., Guzzo, G., & Greco, D. (2015). Attachment, self-esteem and shame in emerging adulthood. *Procedia -Social and Behavioral Sciences*, 191, 342-346. https://doi. org/10.1016/j.sbspro.2015.04.552

Deng, Y., Yan, M., Chen, H., Sun, X., Zhang, P., Zeng, X., Liu, X., & Lye, Y. (2016). Attachment security balances perspectives: Effects of security priming on highly optimistic and pessimistic explanatory styles. *Frontiers in Psychology*, 7. https://doi.org/10.3389/fpsyg.2016.01269

Simmons, B. L., Gooty, J., Nelson, D. L., & Little, L. M. (2009). Secure attachment: Implications for hope, trust, burnout, and performance. *Journal of Organizational Behavior*, 30(2), 233-247. https://doi.org/10.1002 job.585

Thompson, G., Wrath, A., Trinder, K., & Adams, G. C. (2018). The roles of attachment and resilience in perceived stress in medical students. *Canadian Medical Education Journal*, 9(4), e69-77. https://doi.org/10.36834/cmej.43204

Glazebrook, K., Townsend, E., & Sayal, K. (2015). The role of attachment style in predicting repetition of adolescent self- harm: A longitudinal study. *Suicide and Life-Threatening Behavior*, 45(6), 664-678. https://doi.org/10.1111/sltb.12159

Cassidy, J. (1994). Emotion regulation: Influences of attachment relationships. *Monographs of the Society for Research in Child Development*, 59(2-3), 228-249. https://doi.org/10.1111/j.1540-5834.1994.tb01287.x

Bhola, P., & Kharsati, N. (2016). Self-injurious behavior, emotion regulation, and attachment styles among college students in India. *Industrial Psychiatry Journal*, 25(1), 23. https://doi.org/10.4103/0972-6748.196049

Hoffman, K., Cooper, G., Powell, B., Benton, C. M., & Siegel, D. J. (2017). *Raising a secure child: How circle of security parenting can help you nurture your child's attachment, emotional resilience, and freedom to explore*. The Guilford Press.

Siegel, D. J., & Bryson, T. P. (2012). *The whole-brain child: 12 revolutionary strategies to nurture your child's developing mind*. Bantam Books Trade Paperbacks.

Lebowitz, E. R. (2021). *Breaking free of child anxiety and OCD: A scientifically proven program for parents*. Oxford University Press.

Gander, M., & Buchheim, A. (2015). Attachment classification, psychophysiology and frontal EEG asymmetry across the lifespan: A review. *Frontiers in Human Neuroscience*, 9. https://doi.org/10.3389/fnhum.2015.00079

Fong, S. D. (2021). *Parenting from the inside out: A mindful guide to nurture your child's developing mind*. Independently Published.

Hughes, D. A., & Baylin, J. F. (2012). *Brain-based parenting: The neuroscience of caregiving for healthy attachment*. W.W. Norton.

Tronick, E. (2007). *The neurobehavioral and social-emotional development of infants and children*. W.W. Norton.

CHAPTER 4

Fong, S. D. (2021). *Parenting from the inside out: A mindful guide to nurture your child's developing mind*. Independently Published.

Eagleman, D. (2020). Livewired. Doubleday Canada. Edwards, E., & King, J.a. (2009). Stress response: Genetic consequences. *Encyclopedia of Neuroscience*, 495-503. https://doi.org/10.1016/B978-008045046-9.00096-6

Gottman, J. M., & Gottman, J. S. (2008). Gottman method couple therapy. In A. S. Gurman (Ed.), *Clinical handbook of couple therapy* (4th ed., pp. 138-164). The Guilford Press.

Davis, T. (2000). The power of positive parenting. *Challenging Boys*. https://challengingboys.com/the-power-of-positive-parenting-gottmans-magic-ratio/

Shetty, J. (Host). (2020, September 28). John & Julie Gottman on: Dating, finding the perfect partner. In *On Purpose*. https://podcasts.apple.com/us/pod-cast/john-julie-gottman-on-dating-finding-the-perfect/id1450994021?i=1000492786092

Siegel, D. J., & Hartzell, M. (2017). *Parenting from the inside out: How a deeper self-understanding can help you raise children who thrive* (10th ed.). Perigee Books.

Strathearn, L., Fonagy, P., Amico, J., & Montague, P. R. (2009). Adult attachment predicts maternal brain and oxytocin response to infant cues. *Neuropsychopharmacology*, 34(13), 2655-2666. https://doi.org/10.1038/npp.2009.103

Hughes, D. A., & Baylin, J. F. (2012). *Brain-based parenting: The neuroscience of caregiving for healthy attachment*. W.W. Norton.

Admon, R., Lubin, G., Stern, O., Rosenberg, K., Sela, L., Benami, H., & Hendler, T. (2009). Human vulnerability to stress depends on amygdala's predisposition and hippocampal plasticity. *Proceedings of the National Academy of Sciences*, 106(33), 14120-14125. https://doi.org/10.1073/pnas.0903183106

Siegel, D. J., & Bryson, T. P. (2016). *No-drama discipline: The whole-brain way to calm the chaos and nurture your child's developing mind* (Trade paperback ed.). Bantam Books.

Wager, T. D., Davidson, M. L., Hughes, B. L., Lindquist, M. A., & Ochsner, K. N. (2008). Prefrontal-subcortical pathways mediating successful emotion regulation. *Neuron*, 59(6), 1037-1050. https://doi.org/10.1016/j. neuron.2008.09.006

Katie, B., & Mitchell, S. (2021). *Loving what is: Four questions that can change your life* (2nd ed.). Harmony Books, an imprint of Random House.

Oschman, J., Chevalier, G., & Brown, R. (2015). The effects of grounding (earthing) on inflammation, the immune response, wound healing, and prevention and treatment of chronic inflammatory and autoimmune diseases. *Journal of Inflammation Research*, 83. https://doi. org/10.2147%2FJIR.S69656

Payne, K. J. (2019). *Being at your best when your kids are at their worst: Practical compassion in parenting*. Shambhala.

CHAPTER 5

Gershoff, E. T., & Grogan-Kaylor, A. (2016). Spanking and child outcomes: Old controversies and new meta-analysis. *Journal of Family Psychology*, 30(4), 453-469. https://doi.org/10.1037/fam0000191

Tomoda, A., Navalta, C. P., Polcari, A., Sadato, N., & Teicher, M. H. (2009). Childhood sexual abuse is associated with reduced gray matter volume in visual cortex of young women. *Biological Psychiatry*, 66(7), 642-648. https://doi.org/10.1016/j.biopsych.2009.04.021

United Nations. (2006, May 15). *Convention on the rights the child* [Conference session]. Committee on the Rights of the child, Geneva,

Switzerland. https://www.unicef- irc.org/portfolios/general_comments/GC8_en.doc.html

Payne, K. J. (2015). *The soul of discipline: The simplicity parenting approach to warm, firm, and calm guidance—from toddlers to teens.* Ballantine Books.

Donovan, K. L., & Brassard, M. R. (2011). Trajectories of maternal verbal aggression across the middle school years: Associations with negative view of self and social problems. *Child Abuse & Neglect,* 35(10), 814-830. https:// doi.org/10.1016/j.chiabu.2011.06.001

Wang, M.T., & Kenny, S. (2013). Longitudinal links between fathers' and mothers' harsh verbal discipline and adolescents' conduct problems and depressive symptoms. *Child Development,* 85(3), 908-923. https://doi.org/10.1111/cdev.12143

Schore, A. N. (2012). *The science of the art of psychotherapy.* W.W. Norton.

Kazdin, A. E. (2013). *Behavior modification in applied settings* (7th ed.). Waveland Press.

Wipfler, P., & Schore, T. (2016). *Listen: Five simple tools to meet your everyday parenting challenge* (Illustrated ed.). Hand in Hand Parenting.

CHAPTER 6

Landreth, G. L. (2012). *Play therapy: The art of the relationship* (3rd ed.). Routledge.

Cohen, L. J. (2002). *Playful parenting.* Ballantine Books. Cohut, M. (2018, February 2). Searching for purpose? Logotherapy might help. *Medical News Today.* https://www.medicalnewstoday.com/articles/320814

Wipfler, P., & Schore, T. (2016). *Listen: Five simple tools to meet your everyday parenting challenge* (Illustrated ed.). Hand in Hand Parenting.

Berk, L.S., Felten, D.L.,Tan, S.A., Bittman, B.B.,& Westengard, J. (2001). Modulation of neuroimmune parameters during the eustress of humor-associated mirthful laughter. *Alternative Therapies in Health & Medicine*, 7(2), 62-72.

CHAPTER 7

Wahlstrom, D., Collins, P., White, T., & Luciana, M. (2010). Developmental changes in dopamine neurotransmission in adolescence: Behavioral implications and issues in assessment. *Brain and Cognition*, 72(1), 146-159. https://doi.org/10.1016/j.bandc.2009.10.013

Kolari, J. (2011). *You're ruining my life: Surviving the teenage years with connected parenting*. Penguin Canada.

Faber, A., & Mazlish, E. (2006). *How to talk so teens will listen & listen so teens will talk*. William Morrow Paperbacks.

Siegel, D. J. (2015). *Brainstorm: The power and purpose of the teenage brain*. Tarcher Perigee.

CHAPTER 8

Center on the Developing Child. (n.d.). *Resilience*. Harvard University. Retrieved September 19, 2022, from https://developingchild.harvard.edu/science/key-concepts/resilience/

Payne, K. J., & Ross, L. M. (2020). *Simplicity parenting* (Rev. ed.). Ballantine Books.

Center on the Developing Child at Harvard University. (2015, April22). *InBrief: What is resilience?* [Video]. Youtube. https://www.youtube.com/watch?v=cqO7YoMsccU&t=112s

Health Canada. (2015). *First Nations mental wellness continuum framework: Summary report*. Health Canada.

Wallace, C. (2015, November 10). How to help your kids find a purpose. *TIME*. https://time.com/4105664/how-to-help-your -kids-find-a-purpose/

Pinkcast. (n.d.). *Pinkcast 1.20: Discover your purpose (in one minute) with the Napkin Test* [Video]. Daniel H. Pink. https://www.danpink. com/pinkcast/pinkcast-1-20-discover-your-purpose-in-one-minute- with-the-napkin-test

Ericsson, A., & Pool, R. (2016). *Peak: Secrets from the new science of expertise.* Houghton Mifflin Harcourt.

Franke, H. (2014). Toxic stress: Effects, prevention and treatment. *Children*, 1(3), 390-402. https://doi.org/10.3390/children1030390

Gray, P. (2011). The decline of play and the rise of psychopathology in children and adolescents. *American Journal of Play*, 3(4), 443-463.

National Alliance for Youth Sports. (2014, March 14). Playing for the long run: Former college coach shares insights. *NAYS Blog*. https://www.nays.org/blog/playing-for-the-long-run-former-college -coach-shares-insights/

Miner, J. W. (2016, June 1). Why 70 percent of kids quit sports by age 13. *The Washington Post*. https://www.washingtonpost.com/ news/parenting/wp/2016/06/01/why-70-percent-of-kids-quit -sports-by-age-13/

Mahoney, J. L., Harris, A. L., & Eccles, J. S. (2006). Organized activity participation, positive youth development, and the over-sched- uling hypothesis. *Social Policy Report*, 20(4), 1-32. https://doi. org/10.1002/j.2379-3988.2006. tb00049.

Deci, E. L., Koestner, R., & Ryan, R. M. (1999). A meta-analytic review of experiments examining the effects of extrinsic rewards on intrinsic motivation. *Psychological Bulletin*, 125(6), 627-668. https:// doi.org/10.1037/0033-2909.125.6.627

Dweck, C. S. (2016). *Mindset: The new psychology of success* (Updated edition. ed.). Ballantine.

Mindset Works. (n.d.). *Programs that motivate students and teachers.* Retrieved January 3, 2023, from https://www.mindsetworks.com/

Big life journal for teens and tweens (Teen ed.). (2019). Big Life Journal.

Antony, M. M., & Swinson, R. P. (2009). *When perfect isn't good enough: Strategies for coping with perfectionism* (2nd ed.). New Harbinger.

Kross, E., Berman, M. G., Mischel, W., Smith, E. E., & Wager, T. D. (2011). Social rejection shares somatosensory representations with physical pain. *Proceedings of the National Academy of Sciences,* 108(15), 6270-6275. https://doi.org/10.1073/pnas.1102693108

Alexander, J. J., & Sandahl, I. (2016). *The Danish way of parenting: What the happiest people in¬ the world know about raising confident, capable kids.* Tarcher Perigee Book.

Sandahl, I. (2016, August 29). *Reading as the Danes do: Why Denmark's tragic tales are valuable for kids.* Retrieved January 3, 2023, from http://thedanishway.com/reading-as-the-danes-do-why-denmarks-tragic-tales-are-valuable-for-kids/

Neufeld, G., & Maté, G. (2019). *Hold on to your kids: Why parents need to matter more than peers.* Vermilion.

Brown, B. (2015). *Daring greatly: How the courage to be vulnerable transforms the way we live, love, parent, and lead.* Avery.

Neufeld, G., & Maté, G. (2019). *Hold on to your kids: Why parents need to matter more than peers.* Vermilion.

Chamberlain, C., Gee, G., Harfield, S., Campbell, S., Brennan, S., Clark, Y., Mensah, F., Arabena, K., Herrman, H., & Brown, S. (2019). Parenting after a history of childhood maltreatment: A scoping review and map of evidence in the perinatal period. *PLOS ONE,* 14(3), e021346 https://doi.org/10.1371/journal.pone.0213460

Fivush, R., Duke, M., & Bohanek, J. (2010). Do you know...? The power of family history in adolescent identity and well-being. *Journal of Family Life,* 748-769.https://ncph. org/wp-content/uploads /2013/12/The-power-of-family- history-in-adolescent-identity.pdf

Spagnola, M., & Fiese, B. H. (2007). Family routines and rituals. *Infants & Young Children*, 20(4), 284-299. https://doi.org/10.1097/01.IYC.0000290352.32170.5a

Maholmes, V. (2014). *Fostering resilience and well-being in children and families in poverty: Why hope still matters*. Oxford University Press.

Dossey, L. (2018). The helper's high. *Explore*, 14(6), 393-399. https://doi.org/10.1016/j.explore.2018.10.003

CHAPTER 9

National Institute for Play. (2020). *Animals at play*. Retrieved January 25, 2022, from http://www.nifplay.org/vision/animals-play/

Payne, K. J., & Ross, L. M. (2020). *Simplicity parenting* (Rev. ed.). Ballantine Books.

Tamis-LeMonda, C. S., Shannon, J. D., Cabrera, N. J., & Lamb, M. E. (2004). Fathers and mothers at play with their 2-and 3-Year-Olds: Contributions to language and cognitive development. *Child Development*, 75(6), 1806-1820. https://doi.org/10.1111/j.1467-8624.2004.00818.x

Ginsburg, K. R. (2007). The importance of play in promoting healthy child development and maintaining strong parent-child bonds. *Pediatrics*, 119(1), 182-191. https://doi.org/10.1542peds.2006-2697

Bennett, E. L., Diamond, M. C., Krech, D., & Rosenzweig, M. R. (1964). Chemical and anatomical plasticity of brain. *Science*, 146(3644), 610619. https://doi.org/10.1126/science.146.3644.610

Gordon, N. S., Burke, S., Akil, H., Watson, S. J., & Panksepp, J. (2003). Socially-induced brain 'fertilization': Play promotes brain derived neurotrophic factor transcription in the amygdala and dorsolateral frontal cortex in juvenile rats. *Neuroscience Letters*, 341(1), 17-20. https://doi.org/10.1016/s0304-3940(03)00158-7

Pellegrini, A. D., & Holmes, R. M. (2006). The Role of Recess in Primary School. In D. G. Singer, R. M. Golinkoff, & K. Hirsh-Pasek (Eds.), *Play = learning: How play motivates and enhances children's cognitive and social-emotional growth* (pp. 36–53). Oxford University Press. https://doi.org/10.1093/acprof:oso/9780195304381.003.0003

Lewis, J. B., Lupton, L., & Watson, S. (2000). Relationships between symbolic play, functional play, verbal and non-verbal ability in young children. *International Journal of Language & Communication Disorders*, 35(1), 117-127. https://doi.org/10.1080/136828200247287

Wyver, S. R., & Spence, S. H. (1999). Play and divergent problem solving: Evidence supporting a reciprocal relationship. *Early Education & Development*, 10(4), 419-444. https://doi.org/10.1207/s15566935eed1004_1

DeBenedet, A. T., & Cohen, L. J. (2011). *The art of roughhousing: Good old-fashioned horseplay and why every kid needs it*. Quirk Books.

McElwain, N. L., & Volling, B. L. (2005). Preschool children's interactions with friends and older siblings: Relationship specificity and joint contributions to problem behavior. *Journal of Family Psychology*, 19(4), 486-496. https://doi.org/10.1037/0893-3200.19.4.486

MacDonald, K. (Ed.). (1993). *Parent–child play: Descriptions and implications*. State University of New York Press.

Vaughan, C., & Brown, S. (2014). *Play: How it shapes the brain, opens the imagination, and invigorates the soul*. Avery.

Whitebread, D. (2017). Free play and children's mental health. *The Lancet Child & Adolescent Health*, 1(3), 167-169. https://doi.org/10.1016/S23524642(17)30092-5

Dauch, C., Imwalle, M., Ocasio, B., & Metz, A. E. (2018). The influence of the number of toys in the environment on toddlers' play. *Infant Behavior and Development*, 50, 78-87. https://doi.org/10.1016/j.infbeh.2017.11.005

Payne, K. J., & Ross, L. M. (2020). *Simplicity parenting* (Rev. ed.). Ballantine Books.

Brussoni, M., Olsen, L. L., Pike, I., & Sleet, D. A. (2012). Risky play and children's safety: Balancing priorities for optimal child development. *International Journal of Environmental Research and Public Health*, 9(9), 3134-3148. https://doi.org/10.3390/ijerph9093134

Harper, N. J. (2017). Outdoor risky play and healthy child development in the shadow of the "risk society": A forest and nature school perspective. *Child & Youth Services*, 38(4), 318-334. https://doi. org/10.1080/01459 35x.2017.1412825

Siegel, D. J. (2020). *The developing mind: How relationships and the brain interact to shape who we are* (3rd ed.). Guilford Press.

Brown, S., & Vaughan, C. (2010). *Play: How it shapes the brain, opens the imagination, and invigorates the soul.* Avery.

Alexander, J. J., & Sandahl, I. (2016). *The Danish way of parenting: What the happiest people in¬ the world know about raising confident, capable kids.* Tarcher Perigee Book.

Payne, K. J., & Ross, L. M. (2020). *Simplicity parenting* (Rev. ed.). Ballantine Books.

Landreth, G. L. (2019). *Child parent relationship therapy (CPRT): An evidence-based 10-session filial therapy model* (2nd ed.). Routledge.

College of Education: Center for Play Therapy. (n.d.). *What is play therapy?* Retrieved February 11, 2023, from https://cpt.unt.edu/ what-is-play-therapy

Booth, P. B., & Jernberg, A. M. (2010). *Theraplay: Helping parents and children build better relationships through attachment-based play* (3rd ed.). Jossey-Bass.

Golding, K. S., & Hughes, D. A. (2012). *Creating loving attachments: Parenting with PACE to nurture confidence and security in the troubled child.* Jessica Kingsley.

Landreth, G. L. (2019). *Child parent relationship therapy (CPRT): An evidence-based 10-session filial therapy model* (2nd ed.). Routledge.

CHAPTER 10

Ginsburg, K. R. (2007). The importance of play in promoting healthy child development and maintaining strong parent-child bonds. *Pediatrics*, 119(1), 182-191. https://doi. org/10.1542/peds.2006-2697

Clear, J. (2018). Chapter 12 excerpt. *In Atomic habits: An easy & proven way to build good habits & break bad ones: Tiny changes, remarkable results*. Avery.

ASHRAE. (n.d.). *10 tips for home indoor air quality*. https://www. ashrae.org/technical-resources/free-resources/10-tips-for-home -indoor- air-quality

Saxbe, D. E., & Repetti, R. (2009). No place like home: Home tours correlate with daily patterns of mood and cortisol. *Personality and Social Psychology Bulletin*, 36(1), 71-81. https://doi. org/10.1177/0146167209352864

Danziger, S., Levav, J., & Avnaim-pesso, L. (2011). Extraneous factors in judicial decisions. *Proceedings of the National Academy of Sciences*, 108(17), 6889-6892. https://doi.org/10.1073/pnas.1018033108

McMains, S., & Kastner, S. (2011). Interactions of top- down and bottom-up mechanisms in human visual cortex. *Journal of Neuroscience*, 31(2), 587-597. https://doi.org/10.1523/JNEUROSCI .3766-10.2011

Boubekri, M., Cheung, I., Reid, K., Kuo, N., Wang, C., & Zee, P. (2013, June 1). *Impact of workplace daylight exposure on sleep, physical activity, and quality of life* [Paper presentation]. 27th Annual Meeting of the Associated Professional Sleep Societies, Baltimore, MD, United States.

UK Green Building Council. (2016, July). *Health and wellbeing in homes*. https://biid.org.uk/sites/default/files/08453%20 UKGBC%20Healthy%20Home%20FINAL%20WEB.pdf

Orban, E., Mcdonald, K., Sutcliffe, R., Hoffmann, B., Fuks, K. B., Dragano, N., Viehmann, A., Erbel, R., Jöckel, K.-H., Pundt, N., &

Moebus, S. (2016). Residential road traffic noise and high depressive symptoms after five years of follow-up: Results from the heinznixdorf recall study. *Environmental Health Perspectives*, 124(5), 578-585. https://doi.org/10.1289/ehp.1409400

Taylor, D. J., Lichstein, K. L., Durrence, H. H., Reidel, B. W., & Bush, A. J. (2005). Epidemiology of insomnia, depression, and anxiety. *Sleep*, 28(11), 1457-1464. https://doi.org/10.1093/sleep/28.11.1457

Rönnlund, H., Elovainio, M., Virtanen, I., Matomäki, J., & Lapinleimu, H. (2016). Poor parental sleep and the reported sleep quality of their children. *Pediatrics*, 137(4). https://doi.org/10.1542/peds.2015-3425

Leake, J., & Robbins, T. (2001, February 26). *Children play less the more toys they get*. https://rense.com//general8/yots.htm

Dauch, C., Imwalle, M., Ocasio, B., & Metz, A. E. (2018). The influence of the number of toys in the environment on toddlers' play. *Infant Behavior and Development*, 50, 78-87. https://doi.org/10.1016/j.infbeh.2017.11.005

Hollis, L. (2007, January 20). When toys take over. *The Guardian*, Life and style. https://www.theguardian.com/lifeandstyle/2007/jan/20/familyandrelationships.family1

Richer, J. (n.d.). *Attachment: Close observation, clinical application* [PowerPoint slides]. CHOX, DPAG, Oxford. https://slidetodoc.com/attachment-close-observation-clinical-ap- plications-john-richer-chox/

Trivette, C. M., Simkus, A., Dunst, C. J., & Hamby, D. W. (2012). Repeated book reading and preschoolers' early lit- eracy development. *Center for Early Literacy Learning*, 5(5), 1-13. http://www.earlyliteracylearning.org/cellreviews/ cellreviews_v5_n5.pdf

Fredricks, J. A., & Eccles, J. S. (2005). Developmental bene- fits of extracurricular involvement: Do peer characteristics mediate the link between activities and youth outcomes? *Journal of Youth and Adolescence*, 34(6), 507-520. https:// doi.org/10.1007/s10964-005-8933-5

Ginsburg, K. R. (2007). The importance of play in promoting healthy child development and maintaining strong parent-child bonds. *Pediatrics*, 119(1), 182-191. https://doi.org/10.1542/peds.2006-2697

Payne, K. J., & Ross, L. M. (2020). *Simplicity parenting* (Rev. ed.). Ballantine Books.

Bellezza, S., Paharia, N., & Keinan, A. (2016). Conspicuous consumption of time: When busyness and lack of lei- sure time become a status symbol. *Journal of Consumer Research*, ucw076. https://doi.org/10.1093/jcr/ucw076

Hill, M., Stafford, A., Seaman, P., Ross, N., & Daniel, B. (2007). *Parenting and resilience*. Joseph Rowntree Foundation. https://www.jrf.org.uk/sites/default/files/jrf/migrated/files/parenting-resilience-children.pdf

Snow, C. E., & Beals, D. E. (2006). Mealtime talk that sup- ports literacy development. *New Directions for Child and Adolescent Development*, 2006(111), 51-66. https://doi.org/10.1002/cd.155

Gillman, M. W. (2000). Family dinner and diet quality among older children and adolescents. *Archives of Family Medicine*, 9(3), 235-240. https://doi.org/10.1001/archfami.9.3.235

Sen, B. (2009). The relationship between frequency of family dinner and adolescent problem behaviors after adjusting for other family characteristics. *Journal of Adolescence*, 33(1), 187-196. https://doi.org/10.1016/j.adolescence.2009.03.011

Eisenberg, M. E., Olson, R. E., Neumark-Sztainer, D., Story, M., & Bearinger, L. H. (2004). Correlations between family meals and psychosocial well-being among adolescents. *Archives of Pediatrics & Adolescent Medicine*, 158(8), 792. https://doi.org/10.1001/archpedi.158.8.792

Elgar, F. J., Napoletano, A., Saul, G., Dirks, M. A., Craig, W., Poteat, V. P., Holt, M., & Koenig, B. W. (2014). Cyberbullying victimization and mental health in adoles- cents and the moderating role of family dinners. *JAMA Pediatrics*, 168(11), 1015. https://doi.org/10.1001/jamapediatrics.2014.1223

Utter, J., Denny, S., Robinson, E., Fleming, T., Ameratunga, S., & Grant, S. (2013). Family meals and the well-being of adolescents. *Journal of Paediatrics and Child Health*, 49(11), 906-911. https://doi.org/10.1111/jpc.12428

The National Center on Addiction and Substance Abuse at Columbia University. (2012, September). *The importance of family dinners VIII*. CASA Columbia. https://www.fmi.org/docs/default-source/familymeals/2012924familydin- nersviii.pdf?sfvrsn=967c676e_2

Musick, K., & Meier, A. (2012). Assessing causality and persistence in associations between family dinners and adolescent well-being. *Journal of Marriage and Family*, 74(3), 476-493. https://doi.org/10.1111/j.1741-3737.2012.00973.x

Schacter, D., Addis, D., Hassabis, D., Martin, V., Spreng, R., & Szpunar, K. (2012). The future of memory: Remembering, imagining, and the brain. *Neuron*, 76(4), 677-694. https://doi.org/10.1016/j.neuron.2012.11.001

Shrimpton, D., Mcgann, D., & Riby, L. M. (2017). Daydream believer: Rumination, self-reflection and the temporal focus of mind wandering content. *Europe's Journal of Psychology*, 13(4), 794-809. https://doi.org/10.5964/ejop.v13i4.1425

McMillan, R. L., Kaufman, S. B., & Singer, J. L. (2013). Ode to positive constructive daydreaming. *Frontiers in Psychology*, 4. https://doi.org/10.3389/fpsyg.2013.00626

Pillay, S. (2016, November 16). Brain science suggests "mind wandering" can help manage anxiety. *Harvard Health Blog*. https://www.health.harvard.edu/blog/a-differ-ent-way-to-manage-anxiety-evi-dence-from-brain-science-2016111710659

Kam, J. W. Y., Irving, Z. C., Mills, C., Patel, S., Gopnik, A., & Knight, R. T. (2021). Distinct electrophysiological signatures of task-unrelated and dynamic thoughts. *Proceedings of the National Academy of Sciences*, 118(4). https://doi.org/10.1073/pnas.2011796118

Miller, G. (2022, July 20). *The benefits of boredom: What kids can learn from handling more free time*. Child Mind Institute.

Retrieved February 11, 2023, from https:// childmind.org/article/ the-benefits-of-boredom/

Rideout, V., & Robb, M. B. (2019). *The common sense census: Media used by tweens and teens.* Common Sense Media.

Page, A. S., Cooper, A. R., Griew, P., & Jago, R. (2010). Children's screen viewing is related to psychological difficulties irrespective of physical activity. *Pediatrics*, 126(5), e1011-e1017. https://doi. org/10.1542/peds.2010-1154

Paulich, K. N., Ross, J. M., Lessem, J. M., & Hewitt, J. K. (2021). Screen time and early adolescent mental health, academic, and social outcomes in 9- and 10-year old children: Utilizing the adolescent brain cognitive development (ABCD) study. *PLOS One*, 16(9). https://doi.org/10.1371/journal.pone.0256591

Zhao, Y., Paulus, M., Bagot, K. S., Constable, R. T., Yaggi, H. K., Redeker, N. S., & Potenza, M. N. (2022). Brain structural covariation linked to screen media activity and externalizing behaviors in children. *Journal of Behavioral Addictions.* https://doi. org/10.1556/2006.2022.00044

Paulus, M. P., Squeglia, L. M., Bagot, K., Jacobus, J., Kuplicki, R., Breslin, F. J., Bodurka, J., Morris, A. S., Thompson, W. K., Bartsch, H., & Tapert, S. F. (2019). Screen media activity and brain structure in youth: Evidence for diverse structural correlation networks from the ABCD study. *NeuroImage*, 185, 140-153. https://doi. org/10.1016/j. neuroimage.2018.10.040

Kardaras, N. (2016). *Glow kids: How screen addiction is hijacking our kids—and how to break the trance.* St. Martin's Press.

Dodgen-Magee, D. (2018). *Deviced! Balancing life and technology in a digital world.* Rowman & Littlefield.

Nightingale, C. M., Rudnicka, A. R., Donin, A. S., Sattar, N., Cook, D. G., Whincup, P. H., & Owen, C. G. (2017). Screen time is associated with adiposity and insulin resistance in children. *Archives of Disease in Childhood*, 102(7), 612-616. https://doi.org/10.1136/ archdischild-2016-312016

Cheung, C. H. M., Bedford, R., Saez De Urabain, I. R., Karmi-loff-Smith, A., & Smith, T. J. (2017). Daily touch- screen use in infants and toddlers is associated with reduced sleep and delayed sleep onset. *Scientific Reports*, 7(1). https://doi.org/10.1038/srep46104

Figueiro, M., & Overington, D. (2016). Self-luminous devices and melatonin suppression in adolescents. *Lighting Research & Technology*, 48(8), 966-975. https://doi.org/10.1177/1477153515584979

Falbe, J., Davison, K. K., Franckle, R. L., Ganter, C., Gortmaker, S. L., Smith, L., Land, T., & Taveras, E. M. (2015). Sleep duration, restfulness, and screens in the sleep environment. Pediatrics, 135(2), e367-e375. https:// Canadian Pediatrics Society. (2022). *Screentime and young children*. Caring for Kids. Retrieved January 26, 2023, from https://caringforkids

Cassidy, J. (1994). Emotion regulation: Influences of attach- ment relationships. *Monographs of the Society for Research in Child Development*, 59(2-3), 228-249. https://doi.org/10.1111/j.1540-5834.1994.tb01287.xdoi.org/10.1542/peds.2014-2306

Cajochen, C., Frey, S., Anders, D., Späti, J., Bues, M., Pross, A., Mager, R., Wirz-Justice, A., & Stefani, O. (2011). Evening exposure to a light-emitting diodes (LED) -backlit com- puter screen affects circadian physiology and cognitive performance. *Journal of Applied Physiology*, 110(5), 1432-1438 https://doi.org/10.1152/japplphysiol.00165.2011 [Canada's centre for digital and media literacy]. (n.d.). Retrieved January 26, 2023, from https://mediasmarts.ca/

Canadian Pediatrics Society. (2022). *Screentime and young children*. Caring for Kids. Retrieved January 26, 2023, from https://caringforkids

Cassidy, J. (1994). Emotion regulation: Influences of attachment relationships. *Monographs of the Society for Research in Child Development*, 59(2-3), 228-249. https://doi. org/10.1111/j.1540-5834.1994.tb01287.

Fox Johnson, A. (2021, March 16). *New research shows kids' mental health tied to online experiences.* Common Sense Media. https://www.commonsensemedia.org/kids-action/blog/new-research-shows-kids-mental-health-tied-to-online-experiences#

Bjelland, M., Soenens, B., Bere, E., Kovács, É., Lien, N., Maes, L., Manios, Y., Moschonis, G., & Te Velde, S. J. (2015). Associations between parental rules, style of communication and children's screen time. *BMC Public Health*, 15(1). https://doi.org/10.1186/s12889-015-2337-6

Payne, K. J., & Ross, L. M. (2020). *Simplicity parenting* (Rev. ed.). Ballantine Books.

Kondo, M. (2014). *The life-changing magic of tidying up: The Japanese art of decluttering and organizing.* Ten Speed Press.

White, D. K. (2018). *Decluttering at the speed of life: Winning your never-ending battle with stuff.* Thomas Nelson.

CHAPTER 11

Seligson, H. (2020, October 20). What is self care now, anyway? *The New York Times.* https://www.nytimes.com/2020/10/26/us/women-self-care-beauty-leigh-stein.Html

Lorde, A., & Sanchez, S. (1988). *A burst of light: Essays.* Firebrand Books.

Perry, B. D., & Szalavitz, M. (2017). *The boy who was raised as a dog: And other stories from a child psychiatrist's notebook: What traumatized children can teach us about loss, love, and healing* (Rev. paperback ed.). Basic Books.

Keller, A., Litzelman, K., Wisk, L. E., Maddox, T., Cheng, E. R., Creswell, P. D., & Witt, W. P. (2012). Does the perception that stress affects health matter? The association with health and mortality. *Health Psychology*, 31(5), 677-684. https://doi.org/10.1037/a0026743

Oberle, E., & Schonert-Reichl, K. A. (2016). Stress contagion in the classroom? The link between classroom teacher burnout and morning cortisol in elementary school students. *Social Science & Medicine*, 159, 30-37. https://doi.org/10.1016/j.socscimed.2016.04.031

Guendelman, S., Medeiros, S., & Rampes, H. (2017). Mindfulness and emotion regulation: Insights from neurobiological, psychological, and clinical studies. *Frontiers in Psychology*, 8. https://doi.org/10.3389/fpsyg.2017.00220

Harvard Health Publishing. (2021, February 2). Exercise is an all-natural treatment to fight depression. *Mind & Mood*. https://www.health.harvard.edu/mind-and-mood/ exercise-is-an-all-natural-treatment-to-fight-depression

Hill, E. E., Zack, E., Battaglini, C., Viru, M., Viru, A., & Hackney, A. C. (2008). Exercise and circulating cortisol levels: The intensity threshold effect. *Journal of Endocrinological Investigation*, 31(7), 587-591. https:// doi.org/10.1007/BF03345606

Katuri, K., Dasari, A., Kurapati, S., Vinnakota, N., Bollepalli, A., & Dhulipalla, R. (2016). Association of yoga practice and serum cortisol levels in chronic periodontitis patients with stress-related anxiety and depression. *Journal of International Society of Preventive and Community Dentistry*, 6(1), 7. https://doi.org/10.4103/2231-0762.175404

Kobayashi, H., Song, C., Ikei, H., Park, B.-J., Kagawa, T., & Miyazaki, Y. (2019). Combined effect of walking and forest environment on salivary cortisol concentration. *Frontiers in Public Health*, 7. https://doi.org/10.3389/ fpubh.2019.00376

MacKinnon, L. (2012). The neurosequential model of therapeutics: An interview with Bruce Perry. *Australian and New Zealand Journal of Family Therapy*, 33(03), 210-218. https://doi.org/10.1017/ aft.2012.26

Hunter, M. R., Gillespie, B. W., & Chen, S. Y.-P. (2019). Urban nature experiences reduce stress in the context of daily life based on salivary biomarkers. *Frontiers in Psychology*, 10. https://doi.org/10.3389/fpsyg.2019.00722

Hansen, M. M., Jones, R., & Tocchini, K. (2017). Shinrin-Yoku (Forest Bathing) and nature therapy: A state-of-the- art review. *International Journal of Environmental Research and Public Health*, 14(8), 851. https://doi.org/10.3390/ijerph14080851

Stanborough, R. J. (2020, July 20). *How does cortisol affect your sleep?* Healthline. https://www.healthline.com/health/ cortisol-and-sleep

Yazdi, Z., Loukzadeh, Z., Moghaddam, P., & Jalilolghadr, S. (2016). Sleep hygiene practices and their relation to sleep quality in medical students of Qazvin University of Medical Sciences. *Journal of Caring Sciences*, 5(2), 153-160. https://doi.org/10.15171/jcs.2016.016

Jansson-Fröjmark, M., Evander, J., & Alfonsson, S. (2018). Are sleep hygiene practices related to the incidence, persistence and remission of insomnia? Findings from a prospective community study. *Journal of Behavioral Medicine*, 42(1), 128-138. https://doi.org/10.1007/ s10865-018-9949-0

Wang, F., & Boros, S. (2019). The effect of physical activity on sleep quality: A systematic review. *European Journal of Physiotherapy*, 23(1), 11-18. https://doi.org/10.1080/21679169.2019.1623314

Brown, B. (2015). *Daring greatly: How the courage to be vulnerable transforms the way we live, love, parent, and lead.* Avery.

Holt-Lunstad, J., Smith, T. B., Baker, M., Harris, T., & Stephenson, D. (2015). Loneliness and social isolation as risk factors for mortality. *Perspectives on Psychological Science*, 10(2), 227-237. https://doi.org/10.1177/1745691614568352

Mineo, L. (2017, April 11). Good genes are nice, but joy is better. *The Harvard Gazette*. https://news.harvard.edu/gazette/story/2017/04/ over-nearly-80-years-harvard-study-has-been-showing-how-to-live-a-healthy-and-happy-life/

The Holistic Psychologist. (2020, November 13). Boundaries explained. *Facebook*. https://web.facebook.com/the.holistic. psychologist/posts/2168077393315851?_rdc=1&_rdr

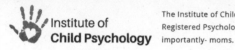